Longman Business English Usage

PETER STRUTT

 LONGMAN

Pearson Education Limited,
Edinburgh Gate, Harlow,
Essex CM20 2JE, England

First published 1992
Fourteenth impression 1999

Set in Linotron 10 on 11pt Garamond Light.

Printed in China
PPLC/14

ISBN 0 582 07153 4

Acknowledgements
We are indebted to The Economist for permission to reproduce an adapted
extract from an article in *The Economist* 14–20 July 1990, p78.

We are grateful to the following for their permission to reproduce copyright
material and photographs:
Extracts from British Standards are reproduced with permission of BSI.
Complete copies can be obtained by post from BSI Sales, Linford Wood,
Milton Keynes, MK14 6LE, for page 161. "Coca–Cola" and "Coke" are
registered trademarks, which identify the same product of The Coca–Cola
Company, for page 135 (left). Digital Equipment Company Limited for page
135 (middle). The Economist for page 103. Financial Times for page 104
(middle & bottom). © 1990 IEEE/Yearbook of Public Telecommunication
Statistics (Geneva, 1990), for page 55. The Image Bank for pages 69 and 70.
International Herald Tribune for page 33 (top). © 1992 Kellog Co, for page
135 (right). Marketing Week/Centaur Communications Limited for page 104
(top). The Wall Street Journal for page 59.

Cartons by Noel Ford.
Illustrated by Taurus Graphics.

To Catherine, Dimitri, Guénaël, Job and Sean

Contents

[1](AmE: catalog)

Introduction

Who is it for?

Longman Business English Usage is designed for all those who have to use (or will have to use) English in their professional career. It is suitable for people who have reached a **broadly intermediate level** of English. It can be used on its own as part of an intensive course, together with a text book to provide back-up material, or on a self-access basis.

What is it for?

The aim is to improve the user's ability to understand and use English grammar and vocabulary in business contexts. Accuracy is essential as errors always create the wrong impression whether they are due to incorrect grammar, inappropriate style, misuse of vocabulary or poor spelling. In business, accuracy is particularly important as misunderstandings lead to inefficiency and can be costly in wasted time, effort and money.

How is it organised?

The entries are organised alphabetically for easy reference. In the majority of cases they oppose two or more language points which commonly cause difficulty e.g. *countable vs uncountable nouns, rise vs raise vs arise, travel vs trip vs journey vs voyage vs tour*. Many entries are cross-referenced when extra information may be found in another section (e.g. *say vs tell* and *reporting information*).

The entries provide straightforward descriptions, with clear examples of meanings and use, of the kind of language most often encountered in professional situations. Care has been taken to provide examples and contexts from a variety of topic areas – imports/exports, banking, management, manufacturing, service industries, information technology, sales and marketing etc. Sometimes a typical error is mentioned and indicated by an asterisk (e.g. NOT * I work here since four years.)

Exercises immediately follow each entry, giving practice in the use of the words, expressions and grammar points previously illustrated. An **Answer Key** is provided for those using the book on a self-access basis.

For further information on vocabulary which is not within the scope of this book readers are advised to consult the *Longman Dictionary of Business English*.

How to use the book

Longman Business English Usage can be used as a reference book on its own, if, for example, you want to look up the difference between *spot prices* and *forward prices*, check the meaning of a word like *barter* or read about *linking words*.

However, most learners will also want to test themselves by doing the practice exercises.

One way of using the book is as follows:

1. Look up the word or point of grammar you are interested in. For points of grammar use the **Contents** list; for individual words it is better to use the ***Index***.
2. Read the explanations and examples carefully.
3. Do the practice exercise(s).
4. Check your answers against the Answer Key.
5. If there are any problems, look at the explanations and examples again.

Glossary

The terminology used to describe the language is deliberately 'non-specialist'. However, it is difficult to avoid using some grammatical labels and for this reason this section explains grammar terms used in this book.

adjective	An adjective is used to describe a noun, e.g. a *high* price.
adverb	An adverb tells us how, when, where, or how often something happens. In the sentence: 'He *occasionally* goes to Senegal', the word *occasionally* is an adverb and tells us how often he goes there. Adverbs can also indicate 'to what extent': e.g. 'I enjoyed his presentation *very much*'.
adverb phrase	A phrase which functions like a single adverb, e.g. 'It'll be ready *by the middle of next week*'.
article	*A/an* and *the* are called articles.
auxiliary verb	*Be/have* and *do* are used as auxiliaries in: 'I *am* waiting'. 'We *have* made a decision'. '*Do* you want to use the phone?' They accompany the main verb and are used to make questions and form certain tenses.
clause	A sentence such as 'She spoke while I listened', can be divided into a main clause (she spoke) and a subordinate clause (while I listened). A subordinate clause cannot stand alone.
collocation	A 'partnership' between words that are found together very frequently and form a fixed expression. For example, in the sentence: 'We *take pains* to get perfect quality every time', the verb *take* and the noun *pains* form a partnership – you cannot use another verb.
consonant	In the word *computer, cmptr* are consonants. The others are **vowels**. Any letter in the English alphabet except *a, e, i, o, u* is a consonant.

countable noun   Nouns which can be used with *a* and in the plural, e.g. *a factory, factories, a policy, policies,* etc.

comparative   *Cheaper* and *more expensive* are the comparative forms of the adjectives *cheap* and *expensive.*

determiner   A word that is used before a noun or an adjective + noun, e.g. *a, the, this, that, some, any,* etc.

formal   Polite conversation and written communication with strangers involve different choices of language than communication with people you know well. You would use formal language with people you have just met or do not know well.

gerund   If one verb follows another and the second verb ends in -ing it is said to be a gerund, e.g. 'I dislike *waiting*'.

infinitive   The base form of the verb e.g. *buy, sell, organise* etc. It is often (but not always) preceded by *to.*

linking word   A linking word connects two parts of a sentence e.g. 'We changed the procedure *because* the old method was inefficient'. We may also use a word to link two sentences e.g. 'Their economy is in difficulty because of the strength of the dollar. *Moreover,* the government is facing increasing pressure from the opposition'.

modal verb   A modal is an auxiliary verb which comes before another verb and usually adds a personal point of view to the main verb e.g. 'She *should* try harder', 'He *might* not come'. The modals include *can, may, might, could, would, should, must, will* and *shall.*

noun   A noun is a word which is used to refer to a person, thing or abstract idea (e.g. *a computer, an executive, expenses, data*).

object   An object can be direct or indirect. In the sentence: 'He made a mistake', the word *mistake* is the direct object. In the sentence 'I sent Mr Wendt a cheque', *Mr Wendt* is the indirect object. In 'Give *me* your phone number', the indirect object is *me.*

particle

A small word like *up, in, off* used in a phrasal verb, e.g. 'She wants to call *off* the meeting'.

passive

The passive is formed with the verb *to be* + *past participle* e.g. 'Tea *is* grown in Sri Lanka'. 'Why *wasn't* I told?' 'Your account has *been* credited'.

past participle

The form of the verb used after *be* or *have*: e.g. 'I was *advised* to wait'. 'Where has she *gone?*'

phrasal verb

A verb which is made up of two parts e.g. *carry on, give up.*

phrase

A phrase is a group of words (often with no verb) forming part of a sentence e.g. *in the office, as a result of, by all means.*

plural

A form of a noun or verb used to refer to more than one e.g. *agents, targets,* the *prices are* low. (→ singular)

possessive

A form used to show that something belongs to someone (*Roger's car, his folder*) or a relationship between two nouns (*executive stress, a level of productivity*).

prefix

In the words *predetermine, predispose, presell, pre* is a prefix.

preposition

Words like *at, by, in, on, through* etc. are prepositions.

quantifier

A word that tells us how many or how much. e.g. *few, little, some, every.*

relative clause

Who, which, that, whose and *whom* introduce relative clauses as in 'She's the person *who* has tripled sales in a year'; 'Tubor plc has a reputation *which* is second to none for quality'.

sentence

A sentence is a sequence of words which, when written, begins with a capital letter and ends with a full stop (.). Do not confuse with *phrase.*

singular

A form of a noun or verb used to refer to one thing only, e.g. *an agent, a target,* and *the price is* low. (→ plural).

stressed
A syllable is stressed if more emphasis is put on it when it is pronounced. You should put the stress on the first syllable of <u>ex</u>port if it is used as a noun and on the second syllable, ex<u>port</u>, if it is a verb.

subject
The subject of an active sentence or clause is the person or thing doing the action expressed by the verb. For example, '*Mrs Walsh* works at Reception', '*He* doesn't want to pay', '*Visitors to London* complain about the high hotel prices.'

suffix
A letter or letters added on to the end of a word to make a new one, e.g. *pay–payment–payee, debt–debtor*, etc. (→ Prefix)

superlative
The cheapest and *the most expensive* are the superlative forms of the adjectives *cheap* and *expensive*.

syllable
A syllable is part of a word that contains a single vowel-sound and is pronounced as a unit. The word *boss* has one syllable, *tar-get* has two and *man-a-ger* three.

synonym
a synonym is a word which means the same (or almost the same) as another, e.g. *dear/expensive, buy/purchase*.

uncountable noun
A noun which cannot have a plural form e.g. *research, training, progress*, etc. Uncountable nouns are not used with the word *a*.

vowel
The letters *a, e, i, o, u* are vowels.
(→ consonant)

1 A vs An

1 We use *a* when the next word starts with a consonant sound:
a bill   *a* price   *a* rate   *a* tax   *a* year

This includes words that begin with a vowel in their written form because the first sound is a 'y' sound.
a university   *a* Eurobond   *a* union

2 We use *an* when the following word begins with a vowel sound (even if there is a consonant in the written form)
an estimate   *an* early reply   *an* hour   *an* import
an offer   *an* MBA   *an* underwriter

3 *A/an* is used before singular countable nouns when they are mentioned for the first time:
If you start *a* business you may need *a* loan.
Can you give me *an* idea of the amount of money you'll need?

4 We also use *a/an* before the names of professions:
Jennifer Baker is *a* systems analyst.
Pat Moss is *an* administrative assistant.
Nigel Adams is *a* switchboard operator.
Susan Bates is *an* engineer.

5 *A/an* is used in expressions of measurement:
The rent for the warehouse is £700 *a* month.
We produce about 3,000 items *an* hour.

In writing *a* can often be replaced by *per*:
We can offer a price of £20 *per* square metre.
Aluminium[1] costs $1530 *per* tonne.

6 Compare these two sentences:
(a) *A* Mr Nguyen phoned and left you a message.
(b) Mr Nguyen phoned and left you a message.

In (a) the speaker is not sure who this person is exactly.
In (b) the speaker knows who the person is.

[1] (AmE **Aluminum**)

Practice

a. Choose *a* or *an* as appropriate:

_____ European	_____ use
_____ uniform	_____ user
_____ unit	_____ utility
_____ offer	_____ yield
_____ undertaking	_____ hundred
_____ one-way street	_____ hourly shuttle
_____ $11m dollar loan	_____ upturn
_____ honour	_____ assistant
_____ holding	_____ inventory
_____ eight-digit phone number	

b. How much does it cost? Look at the pictures and answer the questions below. Follow the example.

Example   QUESTION: How much does the ACE car hire company charge?

        ANSWER: At least £50 *a/per* day.

1. Is there a mileage charge?
2. How much does office space in New York cost?
3. What is the retail price of the new shampoo?
4. How much is a good advertising copywriter paid in the UK?
5. What is the speed limit in the USA?
6. How much is a single room with shower?
7. How much did crude oil cost in 1991?

ACE CAR HIRE

RATES
From £50/day
First 250 miles free
5p/mile thereafter

OFFICE SPACE TO LET
$50 sq. ft.

£1.99

SHAMPOO

ADVERTISING
COPYWRITER
Salary negotiable
in excess of
£50,000 p.a.

SPEED
LIMIT
55
mph

£150/night
Single room
with shower

1991

2 A/An vs One

1 Do not confuse *a* and *one*.
If we say or write:

There has been *a* mistake.

we do not yet know **which** mistake.
The word *one* is used differently:
If we say or write:

There has been *one* mistake which is especially serious.

the use of *one* is linked to the idea of **number** and suggests a contrast – *one* vs a large number.

'How many letters have we received in response to the advertisement?'

'I'm afraid there's only been *one* reply so far.'
(i.e. not two or three or more)

2 In speech *one* is stressed. Compare:

Jill is looking for *a* job. (unstressed)
If there is **one** job Jill particularly likes doing, it's working as a receptionist. (stressed)

3 *One* is often used with *another* when referring to two things that are linked in some way:

The concept of a takeover is simple – *one* company buys up the majority of the share capital of *another*.

4 *One of* is used to refer to a single example in a group:

He is *one of* our top managers.
She is *one of* the most experienced technicians we have.

Practice

a. Choose between *a/an* or *one* to complete these sentences.

1. If there's _____ thing I don't understand it's why _____ intelligent person like you is working in _____ boring job like this.
2. We had only _____ prototype made – it was too expensive to make any more.
3. We should be able to arrange _____ meeting soon.
4. I can't remember when we met but I know it was on _____ Monday.
5. If there is _____ thing I dislike, it's working at the weekend.

6. The XP 300 computer only has _____ disk drive so it is not easy to make backup copies of software.

7. We had many difficulties at the beginning but _____ problem in particular caused us great concern.

8. I can't do more than _____ thing at a time or I get confused.

b. Choose between *a/an/one*.

Our client, [1]_____ subsidiary of [2]_____ US private corporation and [3]_____ leading manufacturer of textile machinery is looking for [4]_____ experienced Works Director to assume responsibility for production at [5]_____ of its British plants. Applicants should have [6]_____ command of at least [7]_____ foreign language, preferably more. Salary according to experience but not less than £60,000 [8]_____ year.

3 Abbreviations

1 This list contains well-known abbreviations commonly used in business contexts. Remember that if you *use* abbreviations the person you write to may not understand the shortened form.

@	at
a/c	account
A.G.M.	annual general meeting
A.O.B.	any other business
approx.	approximately
A.W.B.	air way bill
B/E.	bill of exchange
B/L.	bill of lading
c.a.d.	cash against documents
c	cents
c.c.	copies to
C.E.O.	Chief Executive Officer
cge.	carriage
c/o	care of
Co.	company
C.O.D.	cash on delivery
C.W.O.	cash with order
D/A	documents against acceptance
D/C	documents against cash
dept	department
Div.	Division
E. & OE.	errors and omissions excepted
E.G.M.	extraordinary general meeting
G.D.P.	gross domestic product
G.N.P.	gross national product
H.P.	hire purchase
Inc.	Incorporated
I.O.U.	I owe you
j.i.t.	just in time
Jnr. Jr	junior
K	a thousand (in job advertisements, £25K means £25,000)
lb	pound (weight)
L/C.	letter of credit
Ltd.	limited
mngr.	manager
mo, mth.	month
N/A.	not applicable
N.B.	note
o.n.o., o.b.o.	or nearest offer, or best offer
oz	ounce (weight)
p	pence

P.A.	Personal Assistant
p.a.	per annum
pd	paid
P/E ratio (or P.E.R.)	price earnings ratio
per pro (pp)	for and on behalf of
plc	public limited company
P.R.	public relations
Pte.	private limited company
P.T.O.	please turn over
Pty.	proprietary company
p.w.	per week
qty.	quantity
R & D	research and development
R.O.I.	return on investment
R.S.V.P.	*répondez s'il vous plaît* (French for 'please reply')
s.a.e.	stamped addressed envelope
V.A.T.	value added tax (UK)
VIP	very important person
viz.	namely
w, w/out	with, without

(→ 62   Incoterms)

2 These abbreviations are common in telexes and short messages:

asap	as soon as possible
attn	(for the) attention (of)
cfm	confirm
eta	estimated time of arrival
no.	number
pls	please
qty	quantity
re	with reference to
rgds	regards
tks, thx	thanks

Practice

a. What abbreviations would you use:

1. if you sign a letter on behalf of someone else?
2. if you want someone to turn over the page?
3. if you send copies of a document to other people?
4. if something is calculated on a yearly basis?
5. if you want to shorten 'care of'?

b. What do these messages mean?

```
ATTN:  JOHN PRICE, STOCK MGR
FROM:  GIOVANNI BISIGNANI

PLS CFM ETA FOR MILD STEEL ORDER NO. 6375B

TKS IN ADVANCE
```

```
JULY 1 1991                    TLX MSG NO 6745

TO : MARC GIRARD

FR : MATSUI
   : KARAMA MARU

RE YR TLX 855/634

PLS OPEN L/C THRU OUR BANK:

THE MITSUBISHI BANK LTD
1-5 DOJIMAHAMA 1-CHOME
KITA-KU, OSAKA, JAPAN

AWAIT DETAILS OF L/C ASAP

RGDS
```

4 Adjective formation

1 Many adjectives have no special form:

rich   poor   new   hard   large

2 However, you can recognise many adjectives from their endings. The root word from which the adjective is formed is either a noun or a verb. Here is a list of the most common endings.

-y	wealthy	bulky	risky
-ly	costly	timely	quarterly
-al	professional	continental	promotional
-ial	influential	industrial	secretarial
-ous	famous	dangerous	ambitious
-ary	momentary	voluntary	supplementary

-ic	strategic	economic	dramatic
-less	powerless	useless	cashless
-ful	successful	careful	skilful (AmE: skillful)
-ive	competitive	exclusive	attractive
-ent	confident	convenient	urgent
-ant	important	pleasant	dominant
-ible	negligible	deductible	legible
-able	payable	profitable	adjustable
-ing	leading	growing	promising
-ed	limited	recommended	expected

3 Opposites

There are different ways of saying that something is **not** the case. Very often we use *prefixes* such as *un-, in-, dis-, il-, im-* and *ir-*.

uneconomic	unearned	unsuccessful
indirect	incompetent	inaccurate
dissatisfied	disallowed	dishonest
illegal	illicit	illegible
impossible	imperfect	impatient
irregular	irrevocable	irrecoverable

4 Compound adjectives

Many adjectives are formed by joining two (or more) words together with a hyphen (-).

a *high-class* market
a *top-quality* service
an *up-market* product
a *tax-free* salary
a *price-sensitive* market
an *up-to-date* outlook
a *performance-related* basis

a *large-volume* retailer
a *small-scale* operation
a *down-market* product
a *record-breaking* year
a *long-term* policy
a *problem-solving* approach

Practice

a. Put the word in brackets in its correct form.

1. Cheques should be crossed and made _____ to Red Arrow plc. (*pay*)
2. With the smart card and electronic funds transfer at the point of sale we are becoming a _____ society. (*cash*)
3. Expenditure on training is tax-_____. (*deduct*)
4. We would wish to be your _____ distributor for the Northern region. (*exclude*)
5. All _____ jobs require a knowledge of word processing. (*secretary*)

6. Rents, dividends, capital gains and other forms of
_____ income are liable[1] to tax. (*earn*)

7. We operate a _____ pension scheme[2] for executive
staff. (*supplement*)

8. We see the Japanese market as one of great _____
importance; if we can do well there, we can do well in the Far
East in general. (*strategy*)

9. The figures we've been given are extremely _____;
there are mistakes everywhere. (*accuracy*)

b. Change some of the words in this extract from a letter so
that it makes sense:

...state the assumptions underlying the
forecasts.
I was very satisfy with the poor results in
Germany. As you know this is a key continent
market, the population is young and wealth,
and although you were optimism about the
expect profits we have in fact been very
success in gaining a foothold in this market.
This is all the more disappoint given the
promotion work we put in two years ago.

I know that it is a competition area in which
to do business and that large German industry
concerns are dominate but I nevertheless feel
we should be one of the lead suppliers on
what is a grow market.

This whole matter is urge and I would like
next quarter's results to show a drama
improvement. Therefore, I suggest.....

---

5 Adjective Position

1 Adjectives can be used in two ways.
Before nouns:

an *excessive* price   a *successful* project
an *insurmountable* problem   a *satisfied* customer

After verbs such as:

to be   to seem   to appear

The price seemed *excessive.*   The project was *successful.*
The problem is *insurmountable.*   The customer appeared *satisfied.*

---

[1] (AmE: **subject to tax**)   [2] (AmE: **pension plan**)

2 Most adjectives can be used both ways. However some can be used in one way only.

2.1 Adjectives only used before the noun
These include:

The *former* chairman was called Mr Mathews.
We set up a *joint* venture with a Spanish firm.
The *main* reason for abandoning the scheme was financial.
A good relationship with a trusted supplier is a *major* advantage.
The *previous* meeting was on 5th January.

Nouns are often used as adjectives. They always come before the 'head' noun:

We've received a *bulk* order for 2,000 units.
Have you a *concrete* proposal to make?
Electronics is a *key* industry in Cambridge.

None of the above examples could be transformed to produce sentences such as:
* The meeting which was previous was on 5th January.
* We've received an order which is bulk.

2.2 Adjectives only used after the noun
Past participles which function as adjectives cannot be used before a noun, e.g.

The issues *discussed* at the conference were very pertinent.
(NOT * the discussed issues)

The people *questioned* during the poll thought the new brand name was very appealing.
(NOT * the questioned people)

I'd like to go back to one of the points *raised* during the last meeting.
(NOT * one of the raised points)

The goods *ordered* last month have not yet arrived.
(NOT * the ordered goods last month)

All security cards *issued* from this office must be countersigned.
(NOT * all issued security cards from this office)

The funds *allocated* to the project are insufficient.
(NOT * the allocated funds to the project)

In each case, the words *who* or *which* could be inserted:

The goods (which were) *ordered* last month have not yet arrived.
The people (who were) *questioned* during the poll thought the new brand name was very appealing.

2.3 Adjectives used in both positions but with a change of meaning

The *present* members of the Board. (= those who are members now)
The members of the Board *present*. (= those in attendance)

She holds an extremely *responsible* post. (= it involves making important decisions and carrying out important actions)
He is *responsible* for sales in South East Asia. (= S.E. Asia comes under his authority and control)

We had long, tedious, *involved* discussions on the subject. (= complicated)
There is a lot of documentation *involved* in creating a firm. (= connected)

The President is always *late*. (= not punctual)
We are here to honour the memory of the *late* President. (= dead)

He always has a *ready* answer. (= quick/spontaneous)
Is the report *ready* yet? (= prepared and waiting)

We are *certain* to capture at least 25 per cent of the market. (= sure)
A *certain* person is always trying to leave work 20 minutes early. (= not named but we all know who)
There's a *certain* satisfaction in seeing a project through to completion. (= some).

The customs authorities are most *particular* about the forms required. (= demanding/stringent)
In this *particular* instance I think you're wrong. (= this, but no other)

He is an *outstanding* candidate for the post. (= exceptional)
There are four invoices *outstanding*. (= unpaid)

2.4 Order of two or more adjectives

The table shows the order of adjectives in a sentence.
It is unusual to find more than three adjectives together.

1	2	3	4	5	6	7
fantastic	brand-new				micro-wave	oven
cheap	giant-size				shampoo	bottle
aggressive			American		marketing	strategy
	new	red		plastic		container
attractive			Japanese			model
	tiny			silicon		chips

1 Subjective opinion
2 Qualifier (size, age, shape, etc.)
3 Colour
4 Origin
5 What the noun is made of
6 Purpose/what kind
7 Head noun

Practice

a. Which is correct? Choose the right phrase in *italics*.

1. *The issues raised / The raised issues* at the last meeting are no longer so important.
2. *The main advantage / The advantage which is main* of her idea is that it is so cheap.
3. *The shares issued / The issued shares* by EMEX plc were selling at 360p.
4. *The consumers questioned / The questioned consumers* during the survey found that the product with code number CD-40 had the most flavour.
5. *The ordered articles / The articles ordered* have been sent by air parcel post.
6. *A major feature/A feature which is major* of the new line is its appeal to the youth market.
7. Getting the correct export documentation together can be a time-consuming and *involved process / process involved*.

b. Using a suitable adjective reformulate the part of the sentence in *italics*. The first one has been done for you.

1. *Those who are members of the committee now* all hold senior positions.
The present committee members all hold senior positions.
2. There are five bills *which still require payment*.
3. He has little idea of the planning *that is necessary* when acquiring a foreign firm.
4. *In this case specifically but in no other* I think we can make an exception.
5. As Chairman of the Board he made a *remarkable* contribution to the success of the firm.
6. A certificate of origin, *which can be obtained from* a chamber of commerce, may be needed when exporting goods.

6 Adjectives + Nouns

Some adjectives are frequently found with certain nouns and form a *collocation* (or *word partnership*).
For example:
The result was a **foregone conclusion**; everyone knew in advance.
Having the sales team based in Paris and the marketing department in Dakar doesn't seem to be a very **workable arrangement**.
My wife and I have a **joint account** at the bank.

Practice

You may need a dictionary for this exercise. We suggest you refer to the *Longman Dictionary of Contemporary English*. Put the following adjectives with the correct noun in each sentence.

rough	far-reaching	firm	heated
stumbling	vested	last	stiff
high	common	viable	fruitful

1. We're going round in circles. Let's just see if we can find some _____ ground.
2. She gave a _____ commitment to re-open pay talks.
3. Profit-sharing gives everyone a _____ interest in the success of the firm.
4. The telecommunications revolution will have a _____ effect on all our lives.
5. The only _____ solution would be to design a new engine.
6. After a _____ discussion she stormed out of the meeting.
7. At a _____ guess I'd say we'll need to take on another 20–30 people.
8. The defence of the environment has never been a _____ priority for certain industrialists.
9. We're facing _____ competition from cut-price imports.
10. The biggest _____ block to economic recovery is high interest rates.
11. We look forward to a _____ collaboration between our two firms.
12. We would only sell at cost price as a _____ resort.

7 Adjectives + Prepositions

1 Some adjectives are followed by an infinitive construction (to + verb). These include:

They are **bound to** place an order. (= sure to)
They're quite **content to** continue in their old-fashioned ways. (= happy to)
They are **inclined to** be late in paying. (= tend to)
We are **liable to** make mistakes. (= likely to)
Mr Simpson is very absent-minded and **likely to** forget people's names. (= apt to/he will probably forget them)

I am *pleased to* inform you that your order has been despatched.
(= glad to)
Be careful of what you say – she's very *quick to* take offence.

2 Other adjectives can be followed by a preposition and a noun
phrase, as in these examples:
The Finance Manager[1] is *answerable to* the Finance Director[2].
(= he must justify his decisions to the Finance Director)
Dumping goods on a foreign territory is not *conducive to* good
commercial relations. (= it does not lead to good relations)
We are *confident of* success.
The plan is quite unworkable and *devoid of* any interest. (= it has no
interest at all)
We are *dependent on* our suppliers.
I'm *due for* a rise[3] soon. (= it's nearly time)
She's *expert at* handling difficult customers.
They are *experienced in* logistics.
She is *interested in* fiscal policy.
I am *indebted to* my colleagues without whose help none of this
would have been possible. (= very grateful)
Our country is strongly *opposed to* protectionism.
The British car industry was notoriously *prone to* strikes in the 1960s.
(= strikes happened frequently)
He's *responsible for* logistics.
We're *satisfied with* the quarterly results. (= pleased with)
Personal considerations must be kept *separate from* company policy.
A small container is *sufficient for* our purposes. (= enough)
She's *suitable for* promotion.

Practice

a. Complete these statements as truthfully as possible:

1. In my firm I am answerable _____.
2. I am strongly opposed _____.
3. I have always been interested _____.
4. Personally I am rather inclined _____.
5. I don't think I have many faults but I am liable _____.
6. I am indebted _____.

b. Complete each blank in this extract with a suitable
preposition or infinitive form.

I am pleased [1]_____ you that your order has been
despatched today. I am sorry for the slight delay – as you know
we are dependent [2]_____ suppliers of spare parts, and
strikes in the engineering industry over the past six months

[1] (AmE: **Account Manager**)   [2] (AmE: **Financial Director**)   [3] (AmE: **raise**)

have meant that we are temporarily liable ³_____ delays in delivery of essential components. However, now that the Unions and the Employers' Federation have reached agreement things are bound ⁴_____.

I note that you were satisfied ⁵ _____ the order of the 200 VP vacuum pumps you placed last June. This model is being re-designed at present and if you are interested ⁶_____ a demonstration, please let me know. It is likely ⁷_____ be ready by the end of November.

8 Adjectives vs Adverbs

Learners of English often confuse adjectives and adverbs and make mistakes like these:

*I've been working too hardly this year.
*He drives fastly.

1 Good/well

Good is an adjective: a *good* product
Well is an adverb: The 'Magic Blend' mixer is selling *well*.

The word *well* is also used as an adjective (after verbs such as *to be/look/seem*) when we are talking about someone's health:
Mr Soloviev has gone home – he's not feeling *well*.

2 Words such as *fast/hard* can be used as either an adjective or an adverb:
He's a *fast* talker. (= He talks fast.)
Mrs Nakomo is a *hard* worker. (= She works hard.)

2.1 Note the use of *hardly:*
I can *hardly* read his signature. (= almost not)
We *hardly* ever receive any complaints. (= almost never)
We didn't discuss item 3 on the agenda; there was *hardly* any time and, in any case, *hardly* anyone was present. (= almost no time, almost no one)

3 In some cases two adverbs can be derived from an adjective:
The flight from Geneva was *late*.
The flight arrived *late*.
We haven't seen each other *lately*. (= recently)
We caught a *direct* train.
We drove *direct* from Milan.
The matter doesn't *directly* concern me.

We had *high* hopes for the new model.
Sales were *high* last year.
The MD thinks *highly* of you.

It was a *short* meeting.
Sales fell *short* of target.
I hope to see you *shortly*. (= soon)

Sorry. *Wrong* number.
Don't get me *wrong*. I didn't say we wanted to cancel the contract.
I was *wrongly* informed.

4 Some adjectives end in *-ly*, as do their corresponding adverbs:

There are *hourly* flights.
Flights leave *hourly*.
Very few people come to the *weekly* meeting.
Meetings are held *weekly*.

    4.1 *Daily, fortnightly*[1], *monthly, quarterly* and *yearly* are to
be included in this category. However, note:

Shareholders vote at the *Annual* General Meeting.
The Balance Sheet is audited *annually*.

5 Some adjectives end in *-ly* but have no corresponding adverbs:

A laser printer is a *costly* piece of equipment.
She's a very *friendly* person.
We had a *lively* debate on the subject.
I left because of the *miserly* salary.

Practice

a. Using adverbs and adjectives from **1–5** above, what can you
say about the following?

For example:
How are sales doing?
Sales are doing *well*. (or Sales are *high* at present.)

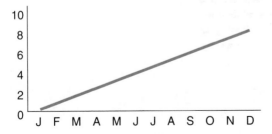

[1] (AmE: **every two weeks**)

1. Extract from a confidential report

> .....Mrs King never leaves the office before
> 7.30 and has never complained when asked to
> replace other members of staff. Over the
> last two months she has worked on two major
> assignments in the Middle East in addition
> to her usual work load.

Mrs King works _____.

2. **Estimated Time of arrival   Flight BA 425
   of flight BA 425: 19.40   arrived at 21.50**

The plane was _____.

3. British Rail Departures: Peterborough – London

Peterborough	Kings Cross
8.12	9.35
9.12	10.35
10.12	11.35

   There are _____ trains from Peterborough to London.

4. **London – Dallas (Concorde) – no stopover**

   It's a _____ flight.

5. **Sales results**

Jan–March	Apr–Jun	July–Sept	Oct–Dec
15,342	14,769	16,638	17,995

   The sales results are published _____.

6.

   > Results for the Group were
   > down by 2.3% over the first
   > nine months to an all time low
   > of £1.6 billion. End year
   > results could be equally
   > disappointing.

   You can _____ read the print.

7. These are the dates of the next few committee meetings:

January 7   January 21   March 4   March 18

Committee meetings are held _____.

6 **Adverb-adjective combinations**

Compound adjectives can be made by joining adverbs and adjectives (or past participles). Examples include:

soundly-based	*widely-held*
tightly-packed	*badly-made*
closely-guarded	*highly-paid*

Practice

b. Below is an advertisement for a burglar alarm.
Combine these adjectives and adverbs and insert them in the blanks.

superbly	*sophisticated*	*guarded*	*closely*
highly	*designed*	*guaranteed*	*fully*

For years the prototype design of the new ¹_____-
²_____ Triple Star burgular alarm was a ³_____-
⁴_____ secret. It still is but now you, the public, can
enjoy the benefits of one of the most ⁵_____-⁶_____
theft-prevention devices on the market. In fact, we are so
confident of its performance that it's ⁷_____-⁸_____
for five years.
FOR FURTHER DETAILS.....

9 Adverbs

1 We use adverbs and adverbial phrases to say:

how			by taxi/on foot.
where	something	They went	to the wrong office/downtown.
when	happens		recently/a year ago.
how often			frequently/from time to time.

2 Some adverbs make the meaning of another part of the sentence stronger or weaker:

She *nearly* forgot to tell you.
They're *terribly* expensive.

His idea is *completely* out of the question.
Prices have gone up *slightly*.
They *thoroughly* disagree with our approach.

3 Do not place an adverb between a verb and a direct object:
She speaks English *very well*.
(NOT *... very well English)

4 Adverbs which tell us *how much* are particularly useful:

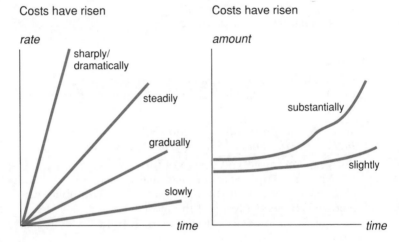

Costs have risen

rate

sharply/
dramatically

steadily

gradually

slowly

time

Costs have risen

amount

substantially

slightly

time

5 An adverb can give a speaker's/writer's opinion.
Examples include:

Actually,
Admittedly,
Frankly,   the results were disappointing.
Surprisingly,
Unfortunately,

6 A major problem is the position of adverbs in a sentence. There
is often some choice of position (e.g. for emphasis) but there
are also restrictions and the rules can be complicated.

The following are the *common* positions according to their
function:

6.1 At the beginning of the sentence

OPINION *Actually,* I think she's wrong.
Hopefully, the situation will improve.

TIME *A year ago,* they employed over 500 people.
To date, we have received 52 enquiries.

6.2 **In the middle of the sentence**

MANNER   Prices could *suddenly* rise.

FREQUENCY   They *never* pay cash.
                 We *seldom* give more than 5% discount.

OPINION   Our performance is *frankly* awful.

TIME   We are *still* waiting for a reply.
          We have *already* sold over 20,000 units.
          I will *soon* have finished.

From these examples we see that the adverb goes:
(i)   before the main verb *or*
(ii)   between a modal (e.g. *could, will*) and the main verb.
(If there are two modals, the adverb goes after the first.)

With *am, is, are,* the adverb comes after:

I am *still* waiting.
She is *obviously* delighted.
We are *always* ready to pay you a visit.

6.3 **At the end of the sentence**

MANNER   I think the negotiations went *very well.*
          He works *fast.*

PLACE   She has never been *there.*
       You'll find him working *downstairs.*

TIME   The Board talked about the merger *yesterday.*
      We're launching a new product *in September.*
      I haven't seen Mr Righetti *lately.*

7 When there are a number of adverbs in the same sentence the *order* is usually:

(1) Manner   (2) Place   (3) Time

We went to Saudi Arabia last month.
(NOT *last month to Saudi Arabia)
They argued violently for a quarter of an hour.
(NOT *for a quarter of an hour violently)

Practice

On the next page you will find the first draft of a letter. The writer has written some words she wants to be incorporated into the body of the letter. Insert them into the correct position in each case.

Thank you very much for your last letter. I am *(terribly* sorry I have not written sooner but I have been very busy. However, I hope to see you at the S.A.A.I. show in Dallas. *(on 5th Oct*

(recently) Further to your request, I have asked a number of companies to quote on making equipment to decorate disposable cigarette lighters. The most favorable price is $25,000 f.o.b. USA with delivery between four and six weeks. However, this is for a basic machine and for anything more sophisticated the price could rise to over $50,000. *(possi*

(already) I have seen the machine in operation and it seems to work. I like the range of designs available and *(very* the quality of the imprints. If you would like a *(in October)* demonstration I suggest we visit *Decotech* together in order to discuss the matter further with their production department.

(→ 55 Frequency)

10 Advertising vs Publicity vs Marketing vs Public Relations

1 *Advertising* means making a product or service known to the public (through the press, television, cinema, etc) in order to sell it.

1.1 *Advertising* is uncountable (* 'an advertising' is incorrect). The countable noun is *advertisement*:

I've placed an *advertisement* in The *Financial Times*.

2 *Publicity* involves attracting the public's attention but not necessary to sell anything specific.

The sponsorship of a boat in the America's Cup gave them a lot of *publicity*.

The scandal of the President's love affair attracted a vast amount of *publicity*.

3 *Marketing* involves all the activities intended to stimulate demand for products and services. e.g. advertising, sales promotion, branding, consumer tests, market surveys and so on.

3.1 The *marketing mix* refers to the combination of promotion, product, price and place needed to ensure a product's success in the market place.

4 *Public relations* has been defined as the 'deliberate, planned and sustained effort to establish and maintain mutual understanding between an organisation and its public'. (Institute of Public Relations). Although it is part of marketing and promotion, PR has no direct involvement in selling. Its function is to build up a good image and reputation, to show that the firm is socially aware and has the public interest at heart.

Practice

Which of these adverts[1] is for: *advertising, marketing* or *public relations?*

a. We are a dynamic young company selling capital equipment to the catering industry. We wish to appoint an energetic and innovative _____ professional to initiate, develop and test out ideas for widening our customer base. The work also involves commissioning and interpreting research together with providing sales support services.

b. We are an independent _____ agency seeking a senior account executive to control a number of consumer and business-to-business accounts. The ideal candidate should have at least three to four years' experience, good communication skills and a sound understanding of the media.

c. As Press and _____ officer you'll be responsible for
• improving our overall corporate image
• developing and maintaining media contacts
• organising and overseeing exhibitions and events

You are likely to be in your mid-30s and have experience in copywriting, media liaison and conference organisation. You are, above all, an excellent communicator and......

[1] (AmE: **ads**)

11 Advise vs Warn

1 *Advise* has two meanings:

1.1 To suggest

I *advise* you to file a patent application immediately.

1.2 To inform:

The Department of Commerce will *advise* you of the new rules and regulations.

1.3 The noun is *advice:*

They're seeking legal *advice*. (= help)

1.4 *Advice* can also mean 'notification':

We've just received *advice* of delivery.

2 To *warn* means to tell someone about a possible danger:

If you knew we were overspending why didn't you *warn* me?

2.1 The noun is *warning:*

Government *warning*. Smoking can seriously damage your health.

2.2 It can also mean 'advance notification':

Before you do anything, give me adequate *warning*.

Practice

Complete the sentences.

1. I _____ you it's going to be expensive!
2. I wouldn't _____ you to buy any junk bonds.
3. She took his _____ and bought the most expensive model.
4. Under our disciplinary procedure you can be dismissed after the third written _____.
5. In a letter of _____ the drawer of a Bill of Exchange notifies the drawee that the bill has been issued.

12 Affect vs Effect

Look at this extract from a letter:

```
Dear Mr Haertig,

I have been asked to consult you on the recent
decline in sales.

Would you please outline the factors you feel
have affected sales over the last 12 months
and make clear, where necessary, the nature of
the effect.
```

1 *To affect* means 'to influence'. An *effect* is a result or consequence of an action:
The political crisis has already had an *effect* on the Stock Market.

2 The word *effect* can have two other meanings:
We tried exporting tea to China, but with little *effect*. (= impact)
In effect, I'm saying that we should make preparations now.
(= in summary)

3 There is also a verb *to effect*, which is fairly formal:
Production was stopped until repairs were *effected*. (= made)

Practice

Which is correct? Choose the right word in *italics*.

1. Do you think a rise in interest rates will *affect/effect* consumer spending?
2. Cultural attitudes can *affect/effect* the success or failure of a merger with an overseas firm.
3. The bad publicity has had an adverse *affect/effect* on our reputation.
4. Payment will be *affected/effected* on receipt of form ATP/219.

13 Agent vs Broker vs Distributor vs Retailer vs Dealer vs Representative

1 An *agent* is a person or organisation who acts on behalf of a principal in order to sell the principal's goods or services to third parties. (→ 96 principal)

2 A *broker* brings together a seller and a client. For this service he/she is paid a commission called brokerage.

3 A *distributor* is someone who has arranged with one or more suppliers to sell a product. He/She is not strictly speaking an agent because he/she buys and sells the goods for himself/ herself and not as the representative of a principal.

4 A *retailer* is someone who buys goods (often in quite small quantities) from a wholesaler and then sells them to consumers in retail outlets (shops, stores, etc.).

5 The word *dealer* implies a one-person operation of buying and selling for individual profit. For example, we may refer to a *dealer* in horses, in antique furniture or in art.
A *dealer* is not likely to buy from a wholesaler though he/she may buy goods in bulk at an auction or clearance sale.
The word *dealer* is also used to describe someone who buys and sells securities on his/her own account.

6 A *representative* or *sales rep* is a member of a sales team and is employed to travel from one place to another in order to encourage potential customers to buy. The synonym *sales engineer* is now seen quite frequently.

Practice

Which of these are incorrect?

car dealer	car retailer	car representative
sole distributor	sole agent	sole retailer
company rep	insurance broker	company dealer
stockbroker	insurance retailer	foreign exchange dealer

14 Agree vs Accept

1 *Agree* can be followed by *that*, an infinitive, or various prepositions. There are a number of possible shades of meaning.

I *agree* with you that we have a problem with our after-sales service. (= share the same opinion)

We *agree* to grant you an extra 1 % discount. (= consent)

Management and unions have *agreed* on a 6 % pay rise. (= decided/settled)

Economists rarely *agree* about the economy. (= share the same opinion on a topic)

Your total does not *agree* with my calculations. (= correspond to/ match)

1.1 Remember that *agree* is a verb and not an adjective, therefore the following sentence is incorrect:
*I am agree with you.

1.2 A passive construction is possible in more formal or legal contexts:

Whereas it is *agreed* as follows: that XYZ plc (hereinafter called 'The Principal')....

The Board of Directors is *agreed* on increased R & D expenditure.

1.3 The noun from *agree* is *agreement:*
We have reached *agreement* on the following points.

2 The verb *accept* is not followed by *to*, but, like *agree*, can be followed by *that*:

I *accept* that the changes could take a long time.

2.1 It is often followed by a noun:
We *accept* the proposed changes.

2.2 *Accept* is commonly used in commercial contexts with the meaning 'take responsibility for':

An importer will *accept* a Bill of Exchange at 60 days.

The warehouse manager *accepts* delivery of goods.

2.3 Common collocations include:

to accept {
an invitation
an offer
a price
a risk
a suggestion
}

2.4 It can also mean 'to take as being true and correct':
The Board *accepted* the findings of the report.

2.5 The noun is *acceptance:*

Please show your *acceptance* by signing on the dotted line.
Please open an *acceptance* credit for Kamala Imports plc.

Practice

Which combinations are possible?

	your conclusion
agree	to go ahead
	her modifications
	to differ
	that quality has suffered
accept	a bill
	with my estimate

15 All vs Whole

1 *All* and *whole* have similar meanings but their position in relation to a determiner (*the, this, his, our,* etc.) is different:

He spent *all **his*** life making money.
He spent ***his** whole* life making money.

*All **our*** branches are in the north.
***This** whole* affair has damaged our reputation.

2 The word *of* can follow *all:*

A sole trader pockets *all (of)* the profits and is liable for *all (of)* the debts.

All (of) his colleagues dislike him.

> **2.1** *All of* is not possible with plural nouns on their own. Compare:
>
> *All* documents have to be sent in duplicate.
>
> *All* of *the* documents have to be sent in duplicate.
>
> (NOT *All of documents)

3 If you want to refer to a limited quantity you can use *not all:*
Not all the pages of the contract have been initialled.

(NOT *All the pages of the contract have not been initialled)

4 With a singular noun we prefer *the whole:*
The whole batch had to be sent back.
They occupy *the whole* building, not just the first floor.

But it is unusual to use *whole* with an uncountable noun:

We spent *all* the money (NOT *the whole money) on a new computer network.

4.1 *The whole* is not followed by a plural noun.

5 The expression *on the whole* means 'in general':

The British, *on the whole*, are in favour of a united Europe.

Practice

Complete the blanks using:

all   *all of*
the whole   *on the whole*

1. Commission will be 10% on _____ sales of up to £600,000 p.a.
2. _____ information is to be treated as confidential.
3. _____ their cheques[1] have bounced.
4. _____ I think we have had a very successful year even if we have had a number of difficult problems.
5. _____ customers have been sent a brochure.
6. He had _____ department against him.
7. _____ visitors must report to Reception.
8. She spent _____ meeting taking notes.
9. We risk changing _____ image of the product if we sell it in supermarkets.

16 Allow vs Permit vs Let vs Enable

1 These verbs are similar but have different shades of meaning and use.

Allow and *permit* can be followed by an object, and optionally, a verb or another object:

Until recently, the club would not *allow* women (to enter).
Until recently, the club would not *permit* women (to enter).
A video link *allows* businesspeople access to specialist legal advice.

2 *Let* needs a different construction; the object is followed by an infinitive without *to:*

Until recently, the club would not *let* women enter.
Please *let* me know urgently.

---

[1] (AmE: **checks**)

2.1 The use of *let* is relatively informal.
(For the difference between *let* and *leave* → 66)

3 Note the use of *allow* to politely introduce something you want to say:

Allow me to point out that...
Allow me to introduce myself. My name is....[1]

4 If you *allow for* problems, extra expenses, etc. you include extra time or money to be able to deal with them:

If you are self-employed, do not forget to *allow for* tax and national insurance.

5 *To enable* means 'to make something possible':
Allow also has this meaning as in:

During the 19th century road and rail transport *allowed/enabled* commerce to expand.

Enable is often preferable if there is no idea of 'permission':

A rights issue *enabled* the company to raise extra capital.
A word processor *enables* a secretary to type faster than on a traditional typewriter.

6 Note that these verbs must be followed by a personal object before an infinitive. We cannot say:

* Our round-the-clock service $\left\{ \begin{array}{l} \text{enables} \\ \text{permits} \\ \text{allows} \end{array} \right\}$ to satisfy demand.

The correct version is:

Our round-the-clock service $\left\{ \begin{array}{l} \textit{enables} \\ \textit{permits} \\ \textit{allows} \end{array} \right\}$ *us* to satisfy demand.

7 A *permit*[2] is an official document which states that the holder may do something:

If you want a job there, you have to have a work *permit*.

---

[1] Very formal usage.   [2] Note the stress: **per**mit

Practice

a. Complete the blanks with either *let*, *allow for*, or *enable*.

ALAN,

PLS ¹_____ ME KNOW ASAP IF YOU FEEL A 5%
PRICE REDUCTION WOULD ²_____ US TO
RECAPTURE THE MARKET SHARE WE HAD TWO YEARS
AGO. MY CALCULATIONS ³_____ AN ESTIMATED
INFLATION RATE OF 6.5% AND I THINK THAT A
UNIT PRICE OF $2.85 WOULD BE ACCEPTABLE.

REGARDS,

PETER

KURT,

IF YOU COULD ⁴_____ AN EXTRA 15% ON THE
BUDGET THIS WOULD ⁵_____ ME TO MAKE THE
NECESSARY MODIFICATIONS. PLEASE ⁶_____ ME
HAVE YOUR THOUGHTS BY FRIDAY AT THE LATEST.

SANDRA

---

b. Complete the following sentences.
If you want the goods to be taken out of bond you'll need a
customs ¹_____.

Gentlemen:

²_____ to introduce ourselves as a
manufacturer of precision engineering
equipment. We are interested is setting up a
factory in Malta in order to . . . .

Dear Derek,

Many thanks for your letter plus samples.
However, I am afraid that this market is not
yet sophisticated enough to ³_____ us to
sell such a product. Nor is it certain that
the customs authorities would ⁴_____ entry
as similar goods have been confiscated in
recent months.

17 Amount

1 It is possible to refer to numbers with greater or lesser degrees
of accuracy.

most accurate	*exactly, precisely*
↓	*almost, nearly, getting on for, well-nigh, not quite, close to/on, not too far off, more or less*
least accurate	*roughly, approximately, around, some, an estimated, or so, thereabouts, somewhere in the* { *region of, order of,*

Examples

Last year we made a profit of *exactly* £535,289.

Nearly 90 per cent of Company Directors say their company is doing
very (24 per cent) or fairly (63 per cent) well.

The firm has a turnover of *getting on for* £10m.

There are *roughly* five million individual shareholders in the UK.

The company employs *some* 500 workers on two sites.

In 1986, the UK business community invested *an estimated* £218m in
sporting events.

2 When the number/amount is not specified at all we can use *a
(certain) number of* (with countable nouns) and *a fair amount
of* (with uncountable nouns):

He has had *a number of* offers of financial assistance.

We do *a fair amount of* advertising in the tabloid press.

Practice

a. The pie chart illustrates the lines of business and sales by area for ISS, a Danish cleaning company.

What do you think the percentages are?

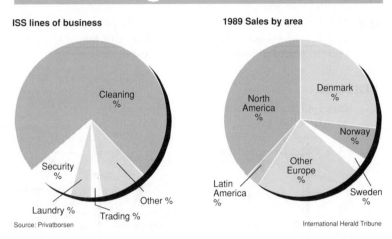

ISS: The Big Cleaner

ISS lines of business

Cleaning %

Security %

Laundry %

Trading %

Other %

Source: Privatborsen

1989 Sales by area

Denmark %

North America %

Norway %

Other Europe %

Latin America %

Sweden %

International Herald Tribune

b. Study the graph. Comment on the figures using a mixture of the expressions on the previous page.

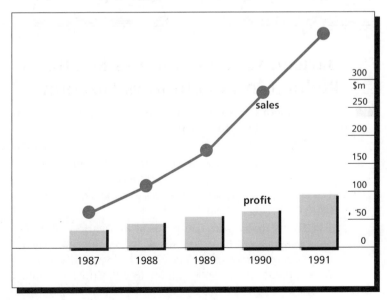

sales

profit

300
$m
250

200

150

100

50

0

1987   1988   1989   1990   1991

18 Balance of Payments vs Balance of Trade

1 The *balance of payments* is a record of all transactions (goods, services and investments) between one country and the rest of the world during a given period. A *balance of payments* deficit implies that a country is spending in excess of its earnings.

2 The *balance of trade* is the difference between a country's *visible* imports and exports (i.e. it does not take *invisibles* (services and investments) into account).

Practice

Label each diagram in the space provided.
a) ADVERSE _____   b) FAVOURABLE _____

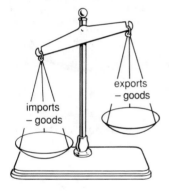

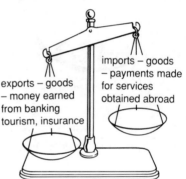

19 Bargain vs Bargaining vs Rebate vs Reduction vs Refund vs Discount

1 We say someone has got a *bargain* if something has been bought at an especially low price:

We got a good second-hand printer for only $200; a real *bargain!*

1.1 We use *bargain* with the verbs *strike* and *drive.*

40 % off list price! You *drive* a hard bargain.
The unions and management *struck a bargain* over pay and productivity late last night.

1.2 The verb *bargain* can be used in a variety of ways:

They *bargained* all day about prices. (= haggled/negotiated)
I didn't *bargain for* her resignation. (= anticipate/expect)
We are *bargaining on* your support. (= counting on/depending on)

2 *Bargaining* means 'negotiation'. *Collective bargaining* consists of talks between unions and employers over pay and conditions.

The unions should try to secure their demands through *collective bargaining* rather than unofficial strikes.

3 *Discount* and *reduction* are very similar and both refer to a cut in cost. For example you could speak of a *quantity discount* or a *quantity reduction*. A *rebate* is a *refund* of money which has already been paid.

We prefer one of these words rather than another with some nouns:

a tax rebate   *a reduction in price*   *a discount rate*

4 The word *rebate* is not used as a verb. However, *refund* is used as both a verb and a noun:

Take it back to the store and they will *refund* your money.
I was overcharged and got a £35 *refund*.

Practice

Insert the appropriate word.

1. Those who are on low incomes are entitled to a tax

_____.

2. I got a second-hand Jaguar in perfect condition for the _____ price of only £10,000.
3. The store manager will _____ the money if you're not entirely satisfied.
4. They're going to drive a hard _____ over import quotas.
5. We came to an agreement on staff representation after some difficult _____ with the management.

20 Barter vs Countertrade

1 *Barter* is trade in which merchandise is exchanged directly for other goods without the use of money. It is a characteristic of quite primitive economies.

2 *Countertrade* transactions are more complex and difficult to arrange. They began in the 1950s and are mainly carried out with developing countries and in Eastern Europe. Their currencies are not freely convertible and they do not possess enough hard currency to make the essential purchases necessary for economic development. They therefore insist on making payment in goods. The transaction may include the exchange of some currency as well as goods. For example, the contract may stipulate that the seller be paid in hard currency provided that the seller agrees to find markets for specified products (often cash crops) from the buyer's country.

Usually only large corporations can set up such deals but they are one way of doing business with countries that have high foreign trade deficits, a large debt problem and small reserves of foreign currencies.

3 Another form of *countertrade* is the *buyback arrangement.* One party supplies the technology or equipment that allows the other to produce goods. The sale of these goods provides the money to repay the supplier.

Practice

Which category, *barter, countertrade* or *buyback arrangement* do these fall into?

1. In the late 1980s Peru arranged to pay its £14bn foreign debt with blue jeans, asparagus, candy, fish, agricultural produce, textiles and gold and silver objects. Creditors who accepted the swap had to agree to buy, with foreign currency, exports valued at twice the amount of the exchange.

2. From 1982 the USSR and Ecuador agreed to exchange LADA and NIVA cars and SKM pickup trucks for bananas.

3. Levi Strauss and Hungary entered into an agreement whereby the firm transferred its knowhow and its trademark to Hungary. A Hungarian firm produced the jeans which were sold locally and marketed in Western Europe by Levi Strauss in compensation for the transfer of technology.

21 Been vs Gone

1 If someone has *been* to a place he/she has travelled there and returned:
'Where have you *been*?'
I've *been* into the city centre.'[1]

2 *Gone* is used when the person is still there, or on the way there:
'Where is Carla?'
'She's *gone* to Birmingham for a couple of days.'

3 We can also use *gone* to indicate that something is missing.
Where's the folder *gone*? It should be in the drawer and isn't.

Practice

You might say these things on the phone. Complete the dialogues with *been* or *gone*.

1. 'Can I speak to Shuko please?'
'I'm afraid she's _____ out for lunch.'
'OK, I'll ring back later.'
2. 'Where have you _____? I haven't seen you for a couple of weeks.'
'I've _____ to Buenos Aires.'
3. 'Sorry to keep you waiting but I've _____ with a customer... No, no, it's all right, he's _____ now.'
4. 'Mr Wang has _____ to Copenhagen so he can't see you until Thursday. Will that be OK?'

[1] (AmE: '**I've** *been* **downtown.**')

22   Borrow vs Lend vs Loan vs Overdraft

Neither a borrower nor a lender be. (Shakespeare)

1 If you *borrow* money, somebody gives you it on a temporary basis:

He's always *borrowing* money but he usually pays it back quite quickly.

2 *Lend* is the opposite of *borrow*. It is an irregular verb:

Could you *lend* me your car?
I *lent* him $100 last week.
The bank has *lent* us £250,000.

3 A *bank loan* is a sum of money which a bank will lend to a person or organisation (the *borrower*) for a fixed period and usually with some kind of approved security. Those who *borrow* money in this way have to pay interest.

The interest payable on a *personal loan* is added to the sum at the start and the repayment is usually by equal monthly instalments.

4 In the UK, if you have an *overdraft* you are allowed to take out more money from your bank account than you have in it. The bank charges interest on a daily basis and is usually less than for a *loan*.

Practice

Write YES or NO in the boxes.

	FIXED SUM	KNOWN PERIOD	REGULAR REPAYMENTS	DAILY CALCULATION OF INTEREST
loan				
overdraft				

23 British English vs American English

The differences between British English and American English are small in terms of grammar. However, there are quite a number of vocabulary and spelling differences (see below).

Grammar
Some of the main differences are as follows:

1 The Americans tend to use a past tense where the British would use a present perfect:

I have finished the report. (BrE)
Have you seen it yet? (BrE)
I finished the report. (AmE)
Did you see it yet? (AmE)

2 In AmE the past participle of *get* is *gotten:*

He's never really *got* over the death of his wife. (BrE)
He's never really *gotten* over the death of his wife. (AmE)

Some Americans say *boughten* instead of *bought.*

3 The verb *dive* is regular in British English (*dive – dived – dived*) but irregular in American (*dive – dove – dived*).

4 The use of prepositions and adverbs changes slightly:

BrE	AmE
check something	check something out
do something again	do something over
meet somebody	meet with somebody
stay at home	stay home
visit someone	visit with someone
at the weekend	on the weekend
Monday to Wednesday	Monday thru Wednesday

5 The adverb *presently* has a different meaning:

The ACC Institute is presently undergoing a reorganisation.
(AmE = right now)
Mr Bennett will be with you presently.
(BrE = soon)

6 On the phone:

Hello, is *that* Mr Waters? (BrE)
Hello, is *this* Mr Waters? (AmE)

7 If a British person received a letter from an American which began: 'I would be *quite* interested to meet you' he/she would be surprised, because the British person would interpret *quite* to mean 'fairly, but not much'. The American meant 'very'.

Vocabulary

1 In business correspondence:

> **1.1** In Britain the day of the month is written first. In AmE the month comes first: 12.5.94 = the twelfth of May (BrE); the fifth of December (AmE).

> **1.2** When writing to a firm, Americans may begin with Gentlemen, although this is becoming less commonly used.

> **1.3** In the United States it is more common to end the letter with *Sincerely* rather than *Yours sincerely/Yours faithfully*.

2 Most of these words would be understood by both American and British speakers but some e.g. *gas, corn* could lead to confusion.

BrE	AmE
anywhere	anyplace
flat	apartment
barrister, solicitor	attorney
car	automobile
(advertising) hoarding	billboard
wallet	billfold
taxi	cab
reverse the charges	call collect
maize	corn
tailor	customize
tailor-made	custom-made
lift	elevator
autumn	fall
ground floor	first floor
puncture	flat
motorway	freeway
petrol	gas
railway	railroad
rise (in salary/prices)	raise
estate agent	realtor
public toilet	rest room
return	round-trip
timetable	schedule
pavement	sidewalk
sleeping partner	silent partner
tube	subway
lorry	truck

toll motorway	turnpike
holiday	vacation
corn	wheat
post code	zip code

3 When acknowledging thanks in AmE say *You're welcome*; in BrE say *Don't mention it* or *That's all right.*

4 When talking about educational background and institutions the vocabulary will be different. For an American *I went to college* could mean *I went to university.* An American *majors* in a subject, an English person *does/reads for a degree.* In Great Britain a *graduate* is a person who has completed a three or four year degree; in AmE the term *graduate* is also used for someone who has completed high school studies. A *graduate student* (AmE) is the equivalent of a *postgraduate.*

5 Note that 10.45 is *a quarter to eleven* in both British and American usage, but Americans also say *a quarter of eleven.* 11.15 is *a quarter past eleven* for both communities but the Americans also say *a quarter after eleven.* 3.30 is *half past three* but the British also say *half three.*

6 If someone says 'John called', an American would interpret this as 'John phoned'. In Great Britain this could be taken as either 'John phoned', or 'John visited'.

7 If you say 'The presentation bombed' in AmE, it means 'the presentation was a disaster'. In Great Britain 'it went like a bomb' means that everyone thought it was fantastic.

Spelling

BrE		AmE	
theat**re**	cent**re**	theat**er**	cent**er**
fav**our**	lab**our**	fav**or**	lab**or**
catal**ogue**	dial**ogue**	catal**og**	dial**og**
real**ise** or real**ize**		real**ize**	
trave**ll**ing, woo**ll**en		trave**l**ing, woo**l**en	
anal**ys**e		anal**yz**e	
ax**e**		ax	
che**que**		che**ck**	
licen**ce**		licen**se** (noun)	
man**oeuvre**		man**euver**	
offen**ce**		offen**se**	

pro**gramme**(BUT computer program)	pro**gram**
specia**lity**	specia**lty**
thr**ough**	thr**u**
ty**re**	ti**re**

Past participle endings:

spelt, burnt, spoilt   spelled, burned, spoiled

Practice

Arnaud Waechter is President of a European consultancy and will be staying in Chicago with a view to interesting American firms in his services.

He has drafted an introductory letter but it is in British English. Make the necessary changes in order to make it fully American.

11/9/91

Dear Sirs,

I plan to visit Chicago next autumn from Monday, October 12th to Wednesday, October 21 in order to meet executives of American companies who have a strong interest in new technology and are seeking to expand or diversify their operations. Based on the information we have got on your company we feel that *Euro Consult* could provide you with a valuable service.

Euro Consult is a service organisation whose speciality is to initiate programmes which assist businesses in taking advantage of investment opportunities overseas through licence, joint venture or acquisition.

Every programme *Euro Consult* offers is highly tailored to meet individual needs and utilises specific proven techniques. We can help you analyse your potential position in Europe, inform you of labour legislation and assist you in gaining a foothold in this market.

I am looking forward to the prospect of meeting you during my visit. A meeting can be set up through your early reply, preferably by telex to 4330986, or FAX 312-491-6274.

Yours sincerely,

Arnaud Waechter

Arnaud Waechter

---

24 Bull vs Bear vs Stag

These terms refer to three kinds of speculators on the Stock Exchange.

1 The *bear* sells shares assuming that the market will continue to fall and that his or her own selling will accelerate the decline. He or she will then be able to buy back at a lower price.

2 The *bull* buys shares on a rising trend and hopes to sell at a higher price and make a profit.

3 The *stag*, in BrE is someone who buys newly issued shares in the expectation of a heavy subscription and a quick rise in price.

4 When describing markets it is possible to say that it is a *bear market* or a *bull market*; the market can also be said to be *bearish* or *bullish*.

Practice

Bull, bear or *stag?*

1. The government is privatising the National Gas Industry. Shares are being offered at the attractive price of 325p each. David Hunt wants to buy 10,000.
2. Ordinary shares in Poseidon plc have increased from 175p to 460p in the last month. Gerald Glynn is buying 5,000 shares.
3. There are rumours of a devaluation following worse than expected trading figures. Amanda Ross is selling most of her portfolio.

25 Business Operations

Using the brief descriptions, match the type of business organisation to each paragraph.

holding
Export Trading Company
subsidiary
partnership
multinational corporation
private limited company

sole trader
licensing agreement
joint venture
franchise
public limited company

1 A _____ is a private individual who runs a one-man business. He/She takes all the profits but also all the risks.

2 There are different kinds of _____ but they are all associations of two or more people sharing the risks and the profits in agreed proportions.

3 A _____ (Ltd. Co.) cannot offer its shares or debentures to the general public. Nor can shares be transferred between members without the consent of the other shareholders.

4 A _____ (plc) must have a minimum nominal share capital of £50,000. Shares can be freely bought and sold by members of the public.

5 A _____ or parent company owns more than half the share capital of another company which is known as a _____.

6 A _____ is an agreement by which a franchisor gives another person or company (the franchisee) the right to sell goods or services using the franchisor's name and/or general business approach in return for a royalty.

7 Under a _____ one firm allows another to exploit its intellectual property (e.g. a patent) in return for a royalty. This agreement provides an opportunity to benefit from R & D already carried out and to test a foreign market without a major capital outlay or management effort.

8 A _____ involves the pooling of resources of two or more companies in a common undertaking in which each party contributes assets and shares risks. It is not necessary for the partners to have an equal stake. The type of contribution varies and many consist of funds, technological skills, plant and machinery or labour.

9 A _____ (MNC) is a firm which owns or controls production or services outside the country in which it is based. Examples include Exxon (USA), IRI (Italy), Unilever (The Netherlands/GB), Nestlé (Switzerland) and Nissan (Japan).

10 An _____ is the American equivalent of the Japanese *Sogoshosha*. It consists of a consortium of firms which enables overseas buyers to purchase US goods without too many complicated procedures. The EximBank guarantees payments to American exporters who trade in this way.

26 Can vs Could vs May vs Might

These are all modal verbs and are used to express a variety of meanings including possibility, deduction and ability. They are also used to make requests, offers, suggestions and express irritation.

Look at each sentence and think about the functions they express.

1 Can

1. *Can* you give me a hand? (= making a request)
2. *Can* I get you something to drink? (= making an offer)
3. Jim *can* play golf like a professional. (= describing ability)
4. He's only 21 so he *can't* be as experienced as he says he is. (= making a deduction)
5. You *can* take the rest of the afternoon off if you like. (= giving permission)
6. The plane *can't have* taken off – there's a snowstorm at the airport. (= making a deduction about the past)

2 Could

1. She *could* speak three languages before she was five years old. (= describing past ability)
2. *Could* you bring another bottle of wine? (= making a polite request)
3. *Could* I come back and see you in a month's time? (= requesting permission)

4. The Eastern European market *could* become very profitable.
(= describing a future possibility)
5. You *could have* got an MBA if you had worked harder.
(= describing a past possibility)

3 May

1. You *may* well be right. (= describing possibility)
2. *May* I sit here? (= requesting permission)
3. Visitors *may* visit the workshops by prior arrangement. (= giving permission)
4. *May* I take your coat? (= making a polite offer)

4 Might

1. She *might* leave the company later this year. (= describing a future possibility)
2. You *might* try giving them a discount if you really want their order. (= making a suggestion)
3. She *might have* told me she would be late. (= expressing irritation)
4. You *might have* got the job if you hadn't insulted the personnel manager. (= describing a past possibility)

Practice

a. Consider the following situations. Using one or more of the modal verbs above, say what you think is a possible outcome in each case:

For example:
One of our executives, Susan Summers has started having an affair with the Vice-President of a firm in direct competition.
She may be asked to stop seeing him.

1. Philip Masters is coming to the end of his probationary period in the firm. He's been late three or four times and tends to spend a lot of the time talking to the secretaries.
2. I have been working over 12 hours a day recently. I seem to be drinking more than usual too. I've been given more responsibility but I don't seem to get on well with my colleagues any more.
3. Although sales of our pharmaceutical products continue to be high and our market share is stable at about 30%, our R & D budget has been cut. The Head of our new product research laboratory has just left to join a competitor.
4. Cheap imports of agricultural products have been undercutting market prices. Farmers have reacted violently, burning lorry loads of foreign vegetables and meat.

b. What *may/might* have happened? What can be done?

For several months Caroline Chu has been building up a database of customer records on her computer system. One day she switches on the system and tries to gain access to a customer's file. She receives the message:
FILENAME NOT FOUND.

c. Read the extract below. Speculate on what *may/might* have happened to produce this change.

Penaldi Robotics was founded by two talented engineers Robin Pender and James Capaldi in 1986.

After five years of operation it was still a relatively small organisation which made its money by solving clients' problems in using automated systems.

A decision was then taken to diversify and build up a group with interests in manufacturing robots and water pollution treatment systems. Over £5m of venture capital was injected into the business. Many different projects were started and additional staff were taken on to cope with the expected increase in orders.

Penaldi Robotics recently went into liquidation with liabilities in excess of £3m.

---

27 Cancel vs Postpone vs Delay vs Extend

1 If you *cancel* an arrangement or an event you prevent it from taking place:
We decided to *cancel* the committee meeting as most of the members were going to be away.

    1.1 If you *cancel* an agreement or a contract it is no longer valid:
They've *cancelled*[1] the order for the pumps because they say they no longer need them.

    1.2 The noun is *cancellation*.

2 If you *postpone* something you put it off until a later time than originally planned, it is rescheduled:
The final decision has been *postponed* until the beginning of next year.
We've had to *postpone* the opening until next month.

    2.1 The noun is *postponement*.

[1] (AmE: **canceled**)

3 A *delay* implies 'waiting':

The flight was *delayed* because of fog.

There may be a *delay* before the spare parts reach you.

4 *To extend* means to prolong for a period of time:

He had to *extend* his visa for another two months.

It also means to increase in space:

We have plans to *extend* the factory which will enable us to step up production.

> **4.1** The noun is *extension*.

Practice

Choose the correct form of the words above.

1. The consignment has been _____ at the customs. We have no idea when it will be released.

2. They've changed their mind and decided to _____ the order. Apparently, they've found a cheaper supplier.

3. The discussion of the new bonus scheme has been _____ until the next meeting of the Works Committee.

4. There has been a _____ so we are able to offer you a seat on the flight to Detroit on 27 May at 09.15.

5. There may be a short _____ while we wait for approval from Head Office.

6. I would like to apply for a(n) _____ to my work permit.

28 Capital

Capital is a large sum of money used as an investment, either in a business or on a Stock Exchange.

There are many technical terms associated with *capital*. These are some of the most common:

> **1.1** *Authorised capital:* the amount of *capital* that a company is allowed to issue, expressed as a number of shares e.g. 3 million shares with a nominal value of 75p each.

> **1.2** *Issued capital:* the amount of *capital* actually issued to shareholders. This may be less than the authorised capital.

> **1.3** *Venture capital:* money used to invest in a high-risk undertaking.

> **1.4** *Working capital:* the money a firm needs to continue trading. It is the difference between the current assets and the current liabilities.

1.5 *Capital equipment:* the machinery, vehicles and equipment owned by a firm.

Practice

The following terms are synonyms for those described above. Which goes with which?

paid-up capital   risk capital   current capital
fixed assets   registered capital

29 Catalogue vs Leaflet vs Booklet vs Brochure vs Insert

1 A *catalogue*[1] is generally quite large, containing at least 50 pages. It contains a list of goods (possibly together with prices and illustrations) that can be bought from a manufacturer or supplier.

2 A *leaflet* is usually one piece of paper, perhaps folded into two or three sections, which gives information on a product, service or event.
We had 5,000 **leaflets** printed to advertise the summer sale.

3 A *booklet* is usually quite thin and probably contains about 20 pages on paper measuring about 21 x 15 cm.

4 A *brochure* is similar to a booklet but is more closely associated with advertising. It is probably printed on glossy paper.
A tour operator's travel **brochure** should quote fixed prices for holidays.

5 An *insert* is an advertisement that is included loose between the pages of a magazine.

Practice

Choose one of the words above to complete the sentences. Be sure to use the correct form.

1. A short 15-page _____ with instructions for use and addresses of authorised distributors is enclosed.
2. The 1,500 page Sears _____ contains about 120,000 articles for sale.

[1] (AmE: **catalog**)

3. I saw the union representative handing out _____
calling for strike action.
4. The _____ was destined for inclusion in *The
Economist, Fortune, Business Week* and *Management Today*.
5. We will need several hundred glossy _____ for the
coming Trade Fair.

30 Change vs Exchange

1 When something *changes* or when you *change* something it
becomes different:

The microchip has *changed* our lives.

1.1 To *change* something also means to replace something
with something else:

The doctor advised her to *change* her job.
I took the jacket back and *changed* it for an overcoat.

1.2 When you *change* money you give someone the same
amount of money in smaller denomination notes or coins:

Can anyone *change* a $20 bill?
I'm sorry, I haven't got *change* for a £50 note. Have you anything
smaller?

1.3 If you *change* buses, trains or planes you get off one
bus, train or plane and continue the journey on another:

You'll have to *change* trains when you get to London.

2 *Exchange* is similar to the meaning of *change* in 1.1 above; if
you *exchange* goods you replace them with something that is
better or more satisfactory:

I took the jacket back and *exchanged* it for a coat.
To *exchange* goods please show proof of purchase.

2.1 However, the word *exchange* generally implies 'giving
and taking'. Compare:

I *changed* my views on monetarism. (I now have a different
opinion.)
We *exchanged* views on monetarism. (We now know each other's
opinion.)

2.2 The *exchange rate* is the amount which one currency
will buy of another:

Today's *exchange rate* is $1 = Y152.

We can also say *rate of exchange*.

31 Check vs Control vs Monitor

1 We *check* something to see if it is correct:

Have you *checked* the figures on the invoice?

or to see whether someone is satisfactory or making progress:

I've *checked* her performance against her performance target and she's doing OK.

1.1 If you do the same operation twice you *double check*:

He's *double checked* the statistics and can't find anything wrong.

1.2 If you *keep* or *hold* something in *check* you try to limit an undesirable effect:

The government has been trying to *keep* inflation in *check* but it is still running at more than 6%.

2 The word *control* refers more to power and domination. It is both a noun and a verb:

After the hostile takeover bid they gained *control* of 95% of the market / *controlled* 95% of the market.

2.1 The adjective is *controlling*[1]:

The Mayer family has a *controlling* interest in the firm.

2.2 A *control* can also be a limitation or regulation designed to prevent someone from doing something:

The Finance Minister has removed foreign exchange *controls*.

As a verb, the meaning here is the same as in 1.2.

The government has been trying to *control* inflation but it is still running at more than 6%.

2.3 *Control* is used in the following expressions:

With high inflation and an increase in the money supply, the Chancellor is not *in control* of the economy.

We thought there was a danger of explosion at the plant but everything is now *under control*.

The consignment has been delayed for reasons *beyond our control*.

He got so angry that he completely lost his *self-control*.

About 5% of the components are sub-standard and rejected by *quality control*.

3 If you *monitor* something you *regularly* check its progress:

We *monitor* our sales results very carefully.
A scanner permanently *monitors* the quality of the surface.

3.1 A *monitor* is also another name for a computer screen or VDU[2].

[1] (AmE: **controling**) [2] (AmE: **VDT**)

Practice

Use one of the above words to complete the sentences.

1. I've _____ the documentation and everything is in order.
2. Inflation has not gone away but it is under _____.
3. We constantly _____ the situation and if anything goes wrong we take action immediately.
4. Despite reducing its stake in ITC by 24%, the Finnish group still has a _____ interest.
5. We apologise for the delay which is due to reasons beyond our _____.
6. Despite pressure from the unions, pay rises have been kept in _____.

32 Claim vs Complain

1 If you *claim* money from an employer, the government, an insurance firm or other organisation, then you:
– make a formal application for it:

Companies may *claim* tax exemption in certain circumstances.

– demand something:

The engineering unions are *claiming* a 12% pay rise.

1.1 If you *claim* something you say it is true, even though others may disagree:

The works manager *claimed* that the factory was not polluting the river.

The opposition party *claimed* an important victory in the local elections.

1.2 If you *claim* credit or responsibility for an action, you say that you deserve the credit or were responsible:

She *claims* much of the credit for her department's success.

1.3 The noun is *claim:*

After the plane crash the airline faced millions of pounds in *claims.*

2 If you *complain* you tell someone about something you think is wrong and should be corrected:

He *complained* to the manager about the terrible service in the hotel.

2.1 The noun is *complaint:*

She made a formal *complaint* to the manufacturer about the safety defect.

33 Comparison

1 Talking about differences (the comparative)

In order to compare people and things it is possible to modify adjectives, adverbs or nouns.

1.1 Adjectives

Look at the table comparing four FAX machines.

NAME	PRICE	SPEED (1 PAGE)	ONE-KEY DIALLING (NO. OF LOCATIONS)	SIZE	WEIGHT	AUTOMATIC DOCUMENT FEEDER
CFT 20	£795	56 secs	50 numbers	300x313x118	4kg	10 sheets
ADM 300	£1,195	24 secs	60 numbers	370x320x158	5kg	30 sheets
SF 250	£1,235	15 secs	40 numbers	424x412x192	8kg	40 sheets
TD 9	£550	60 secs	0	312x312x79	4kg	5 sheets

(The ADM 300 scans documents of three widths; the others except for the TD 9 take two; the TD 9 takes one size of paper only.)

With one-syllable adjectives we use *-er (+ than)*:

The TD 9 is cheap*er than* the CFT20.
The CFT20 is fast*er than* the TD9.

Two-syllable adjectives ending in *y* also take *-er*. The *y* becomes an *i*:

The SF250 is heav*ier than* the CFT20.

1.2 'Long' adjectives (most two-syllable adjectives; all adjectives of three syllables or more) take
$\begin{Bmatrix} more \\ less \end{Bmatrix}$ + *adj (+ than)*:

The SF250 is *more* expensive *than* the ADM300.
The TD9 is *less* expensive *than* the CFT20.

1.3 Quantifiers

More, less and *fewer* can be used with nouns.
Less is used with singular and *fewer* with plural nouns:

The SF250 can take *more* sheets *than* the other three.
You can store *more* numbers in memory with the CFT20 *than* the SF250.
It takes *less* time to send a document with the ADM300 *than* the CFT20.
The TD9 has *fewer* features *than* the other models.

1.4 Adverbs

We use *more* to modify adverbs ending in *-ly*:

The TD9 works *more slowly* than the SF250.

Practice

a. Make comparisons using the words in brackets.

1. Robots / human beings (*fast, cheap, reliable*)
2. Life in Lisbon / life in New York (*cheap, relaxing*)
3. Telephones per inhabitant (*the USA, Mexico*)
4. Your company / its nearest rival (*product range / competitive*)
5. Hours of work (*now, 30 years ago*)
6. Time to make a decision (*the USA, Mexico*)
7. Typewriters / word processors (*slow, complicated, versatile*)
8. Road / rail transport (*flexible, expensive, time-consuming*)

2 Talking about differences (the superlative)

2.1 The superlative is formed in two ways depending on the type of adjective:

the + adjective + –est   (for shorter adjectives)
the + most + adjective   (for longer adjectives)

Our shares fell to *the lowest* level in nine months.
The chemicals division was *the most profitable* last year.
He is *the most innovative* President we've ever had.

2.2 With two-syllable adjectives ending in *y* we use *-est* and the *y* becomes an *i:*

April is *the busiest* month.
29 June is *the earliest* date I can manage.

2.3 Other two-syllable adjectives usually take *the most*:

the most active   the most basic   the most modern
the most tiring   the most senior   the most stable

2.4 Note these important irregular comparatives and superlatives:

good/well	better	the best
bad/badly	worse	the worst
little	less	the least

Practice

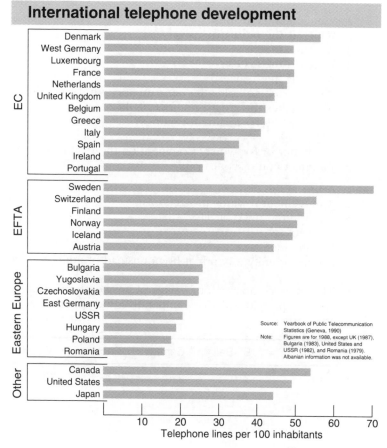

International telephone development

EC:
Denmark, West Germany, Luxembourg, France, Netherlands, United Kingdom, Belgium, Greece, Italy, Spain, Ireland, Portugal

EFTA:
Sweden, Switzerland, Finland, Norway, Iceland, Austria

Eastern Europe:
Bulgaria, Yugoslavia, Czechoslovakia, East Germany, USSR, Hungary, Poland, Romania

Other:
Canada, United States, Japan

Source: Yearbook of Public Telecommunication Statistics (Geneva, 1990)

Note: Figures are for 1988, except UK (1987), Bulgaria (1983), United States and USSR (1982), and Romania (1979). Albanian information was not available.

Telephone lines per 100 inhabitants

b. Look at the chart above and answer the questions.

1. In 1988, which country in EFTA had the most telephone lines per 100 inhabitants?
2. Which EC country had the fewest telephone lines per 100 inhabitants?

True or false?

3. There were fewer telephone lines per 100 inhabitants in Greece than in Italy.
4. There were proportionately more phone lines in Canada than in the USA.
5. Japan had more phone lines per 100 inhabitants than the USA.
6. The United Kingdom had the best telephone network in the whole of Western Europe.

c. Look back at the table on page 53, comparing FAX machines and answer these questions.

1. Which is the cheapest?
2. Which is the most expensive?
3. Which is the bulkiest?
4. Which is the fastest?
5. Which is the heaviest?
6. Which machine holds the most numbers in its memory?
7. Which takes the largest number of sheets?
8. Which is the best value for money?

d. For better or for worse? Comment on these situations as they might affect you or your firm.

1. A rise in the dollar?
2. A movement towards protectionism?
3. A fall in the price of oil?
4. A takeover?
5. Job-sharing?
6. An opportunity to work at home instead of going to work?

e. This table compares four makes of answerphone. Complete the paragraph with suitable comparative and superlative expressions.

	BT Bell	Comtel	Sachiko	AP 300
TARGET PRICE	300	225	235	99
SIZE	>>>>	>>>	>	>>
MAX TIME FOR ANNOUNCEMENT	1'	50''	45''	30''
MAX TIME FOR MESSAGE	3'	3'	2'30''	2'
FAST ERASE	YES	YES	NO	NO
REMOTE CONTROL	YES	NO	YES	NO
SOUND QUALITY	8/10	6/10	7/10	3/10

The BT Bell is [1]_____ expensive of the machines reviewed and the AP 300 [2]_____. Concerning size, the BT Bell is [3]_____ and the Sachiko [4]_____. The Comtel is a little bit [5]_____ than the AP 300. Remember that a small machine may be difficult to operate. The Sachiko is probably acceptable but I personally preferred the other three machines.

Most answering machines limit the time available to make your announcement. The AP 300 gives you [6]_____ time [7]_____ the others but thirty seconds is probably long enough for all except [8]_____ detailed announcements. The time allowed for messages is an important factor in the choice of machine. If the time allowed is [9]_____ a minute it is probably not worth buying the machine. In our survey [10]_____ time allowed was three minutes (the BT Bell and Comtel).

We rated the machines for sound quality out of ten. The Sachiko was slightly [11]_____ the Comtel. [12]_____ was the AP 300 and the messages were often difficult to understand.

It is difficult to say which machine gives [13]_____ value for money. The BT Bell gave [14]_____ performance but is [15]_____ expensive [16]_____ the others. [17]_____ satisfactory was the AP 300 but it was also [18]_____ expensive. Which probably goes to show that you get what you pay for!

3 Talking about similarities
Both *as* and *like* can be used to indicate a resemblance.

3.1 *Like* is followed by a noun:

Like the Bill of Lading, the Bill of Exchange is negotiable and can be transferred to a third party.

The British, *like* the Americans, are attracted to consumer credit.

3.2 *As* is followed by a subject and a verb:

In Japan, do *as* the Japanese do.

or a preposition:

In 1989, *as in* 1988, inflation was relatively low.

3.3 Compare these two statements:

As a Frenchman, he thinks he knows everything about wine. (He is a Frenchman.)

Like a Frenchman, he thinks he knows everything about wine. (He isn't one, but resembles a Frenchman in this respect.)

3.4 When two things are identical, we use *as + adjective/ adverb + as*.

The European market is *as big as* the American one.
He's working on it *as quickly as* possible.

3.5 If two things are different, we can use *not as + adjective/ adverb + as*.

Growth in the 1970s was *not as high as* in the 1960s.
Sales did *not* rise *as rapidly* in the third quarter.

3.6 Note the use of *twice as...(as) / three times as...(as)*, etc.:

Insurance premiums rose *twice as fast* last year *as* in previous years.
Output rose *four times as* much *as* in 1988.

3.7 *The same as:*
On a balance sheet the figures for the assets should be *the same as* for the liabilities.
This expression can be put into the negative:

The Balance of Trade is *not the same as* the Balance of Payments.

Practice

f. Look at the chart on page 59 showing the relative prices of commercial premises in various cities. Are the following statements true or false?

1. Like Brussels, Amsterdam is relatively cheap.
2. Rents in New York are not as expensive as in London.
3. Tokyo is four times as expensive as Los Angeles.
4. Paris is as expensive as Hong Kong.
5. Toronto is about the same as Madrid.
6. Frankfurt is the least expensive of all.

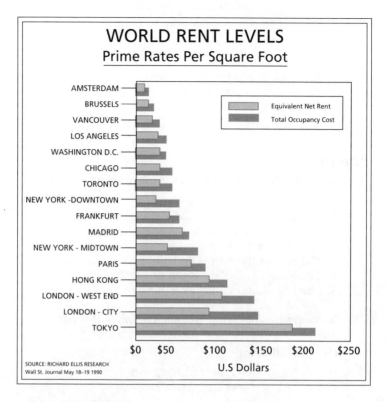

WORLD RENT LEVELS
Prime Rates Per Square Foot

SOURCE: RICHARD ELLIS RESEARCH
Wall St. Journal May 18–19 1990

4 Parallel comparisons

Look at this table.

As this increases/decreases	This also increases/decreases
manufacturing costs	the selling price
size of company	competitiveness
people have to wait	they become impatient
experience	responsibility

The higher the manufacturing costs (are), *the higher* the selling price (is).
The bigger a company (is), *the more competitive* it is likely to be.
The longer people have to wait, *the more impatient* they become.
The more experience you gain, *the more responsibility* you are given

Note that with short adjectives the verb does not have to be mentioned if the meaning is sufficiently clear.

4.1 Sometimes it is possible to omit nouns and verbs.

'How many people shall we invite?'
The more the merrier.

(i.e. The more people we invite, the merrier it will be.)

'When shall we get together again?'
The sooner the better.

(The sooner we get together, the better it will be.)

Practice

g. Complete these sentences using your own words.

For example:
Insurance is like fun; the older you get the more it costs.
1. The more you possess, ⎯⎯⎯⎯⎯⎯.
2. The sooner we leave, ⎯⎯⎯⎯⎯⎯.
3. The higher the rate of inflation, ⎯⎯⎯⎯⎯⎯.
4. The longer someone is out of work, ⎯⎯⎯⎯⎯⎯.
5. The less state interference there is, ⎯⎯⎯⎯⎯⎯.

h. Using parallel comparisons, complete this paragraph.
The first has been done for you.

Use the following:

the higher   *the more*   *the greater*
higher   *lower*   *the smaller*

The chip business is a matter of yields, learning from experience and forward pricing. [1] **The greater** the investment a manufacturer makes in semi-conductor plant, [2]⎯⎯⎯⎯⎯⎯ chips it
can produce. [3]⎯⎯⎯⎯⎯⎯ its output, [4]⎯⎯⎯⎯⎯⎯ its unit
costs and [5]⎯⎯⎯⎯⎯⎯ its operating experience. That trans-
lates, in turn, into [6]⎯⎯⎯⎯⎯⎯ yields and still [7]⎯⎯⎯⎯⎯⎯
unit costs. The secret is to have manufacturing capacity in place
before the competition, then cut prices ahead of the surge in
demand.

34 Cost vs Costing vs Costly

1 There are two verbs *to cost*. They are never used in the progressive form.

1.1 If something *costs* a sum of money it can be bought for that amount:

It **costs** a lot to buy real estate in Manhattan.

The past simple and past participle are both *cost*.

The new equipment **cost** £1.5m to install.
The mistake has **cost** us dearly in both time and money.

1.2 *To cost* also means 'to estimate the price to be charged for an article on the basis of the money spent in producing it'.

The past simple and past participle are *costed:*

We **costed** the initial launch at £5 a packet.
They have **costed** the modifications at $2,000.

2 There are two corresponding nouns, *cost* and *costing*. The *cost* is the amount of money that has to be paid:

We wanted to invest in a new production facility but the **cost** was prohibitive.

A *costing* is an estimation of the price that will have to be paid for a project or business venture:

We did a **costing** and found that the project was feasible.

2.1 These nouns can be used in the plural:

They have had to increase prices in order to cover rising **costs**.
We did several **costings** but none allowed us to make a profit.

2.2 Note too another meaning of *costs* equivalent to 'legal expenses':

He had to pay a £1,000 fine and £150 **costs**.

3 The adjective is *costly* and is a synonym of 'expensive':

It was a **costly** mistake.

Practice

a. Complete the blanks with a suitable word or expression derived from *cost.*

1. The initial _____ shows that the project would involve an expenditure in the region of £200,000.
2. The price of the raw materials was $10,000 and production _____ were $7,000 so the total _____ was $17,000.
3. We've _____ the expense involved in changing to a fully-automated plant and feel the investment is worthwhile.

4. Building a dam is a _____ undertaking, at least $200m.
5. The firm was found guilty of polluting the local river and had to pay a £20,000 fine plus _____.
6. Transport _____ have gone up as a result of the increase in oil prices.

4 There are a number of fixed expressions involving the word *cost*:

We sold the remaining items *at cost price*.
Share prices do not always go up, as I found *to my cost*.
It's a risky affair; have you *counted the cost* of going ahead?
We need to *cut our costs* by half if we are to make a profit.
We must not let our competitors gain an advantage *at any cost*.
We need more *cost-effective* methods of production – there is too much waste.
Salaries in the public sector have not kept up with the *cost of living*,

Practice

b. Complete the blanks with a suitable expression using *cost*.

1. It is not easy to break into a new market, as we learnt _____.

2. You may think it is a good idea but have you _____ of sacking the union representative?
3. They've laid off 100 workers, found cheaper suppliers and introduced more efficient working methods and, as a result, have _____ by over 30%.
4. Even if we sell _____ we may not be able to clear the stock.
5. My salary has not kept pace with the _____.
6. With 1,000% annual inflation and over $100bn foreign debt, the economy must be improved _____.
7. To be really _____ we need to cut overheads and improve working methods.

c. A Financial Quiz
Match the words to the explanations. If in doubt, refer to the *Longman Dictionary of Business English*.

Opportunity cost   *Cost accounting*   *Fixed costs*
Cost-benefit analysis   *Cost, insurance,*   *Variable costs*
                          freight

1. _____ means that the seller's price to an overseas buyer includes all the charges to the port of destination.
2. _____ is a method of putting a price to a planned course of action e.g. building a new airport and seeing whether the advantages are greater than the investment.

3. _____ are those which do not vary with output (e.g. rent, interest on capital).

4. _____ is the price of a product plus the sacrifice of not buying something else. If I buy a computer it costs £X plus the loss of the enjoyment of using the money to buy a stereo. This term is also used to refer to the cost of developing one product, or following one strategy, rather than another.

5. _____ refers to the keeping of records which itemise the expenses of running a business and selling and distributing a product.

6. _____ include items such as materials, labour or energy which fluctuate in proportion to output.

35 Countable vs Uncountable Nouns

Nouns can be considered as belonging to two broad families: *countable nouns* and *uncountable nouns*.

1 *Countable* nouns: can be used in the plural.
                              take determiners such as *many, these, those, several*.
                              are used with *one/ones*

Managers are often over-worked.
Several *people* were absent yesterday.
Mr Silya is a senior *partner*.
We're sending the small *model* back as we need a larger *one*.

Countable nouns include:
many concrete nouns i.e. the names of individual things
(*a factory, a computer*)
units of measurement (*a metre, a kilo, a gallon*)
individual parts of a mass (*a **piece** of advice, a **sheet** of paper*)

2 *Uncountable* nouns:
   – do not take *the* when used in a general sense.
   – have words like *much, little* before them.
   – take the singular form of the verb.
Time is *money*.
We are not making much *progress*.
The consultant gave us good *advice*.

Uncountable nouns include:
many abstract nouns (*hope, importance*)
substances (*gold, uranium, water, petrol*)
verbal nouns (*training, clothing, shopping*)

Some of the more common uncountable nouns are:

advertising	accommodation	advice	behaviour[1]
carriage	commerce	damage	employment
equipment	evidence	freight	information
insurance	legislation	luggage	machinery
merchandise	money	news	produce
progress	research	safety	scope
transport	travel	weather	work

3 The terms *countable* and *uncountable* are grammatical. For example, although it is perfectly possible to count 'money' the word is grammatically uncountable. Therefore it is NOT possible to say *a money or *two monies.

Practice

a. Choose the correct item in *italics*.

1. We've made *a progress / progress* this year.
2. She is *an executive / executive* in a telecommunications firm.
3. We do *a very little advertising / very little advertising*.
4. They have made *an arrangement / arrangement* to meet.
5. She gave me *an advice / advice* on how to invest.
6. We need *a review/review* of our existing product range.
7. We've done *a research / research* into consumer attitudes.
8. She's found *a work / work* in an investment firm.

4 Many nouns have countable (C) and uncountable (U) uses. e.g.
Experience is more important than qualifications. (U)
I had an interesting *experience* when travelling through Tibet. (C)
She told me of her *experiences* in Thailand. (C)
I had to come at short *notice* and so I've had no time to prepare. (U)
The computer can automatically issue invoices and reminder *notices*. (C)
There is a *notice* about the staff committee stuck up in the canteen. (C)
The surveyor estimated the *damage* at £30,000. (U)
The court awarded $50,000 in *damages*. (C)
(NOTE that we cannot say *a damage)

5 Some uncountable nouns *(travel; work)* have a countable equivalent which is a different word entirely *(trip/journey; job/task)*
Travel broadens the mind. (U)
I'm going on a business *trip* to Helsinki. (C)
The *journey* from Rio to Sao Paolo took five hours. (C)

[1] (AmE: **behavior**; this word is countable in AmE.)

I've got too much *work* on my plate. (U)
The *job* I'm doing at the moment is pretty difficult. (C)
Each worker is responsible for a particular *task*. (C)

6 There are a number of nouns which only occur in the plural. Examples include:

They owe me four months' salary in *arrears*.
The talks are being held under the *auspices* of the UNCTAD.
Average *earnings* are higher in the USA than in Britain.
The *goods* will be sent by rail.
We have changed our *premises* to new ones in Lombard Street.
We'll begin *proceedings* with item 1 on the agenda.
You are advised to keep your *valuables* in the safe.

Practice

b. Choose the correct word to complete the sentence.

apartment	*damage*	*course*	*job*	*recommendation*
accommodation	*damages*	*training*	*work*	*advice*
progress	*trip*	*step forward*		*travel*

1. If you're thinking of exporting to the UK you can get a lot of _____ from the Embassy.
2. She's got an interesting _____ in a publishing company.
3. The tribunal awarded $200,000 _____ for unfair dismissal.
4. The creation of a single market was a significant _____ in free trade.
5. She's recently been on a _____ to learn more about human relations.
6. The board made a _____ to increase the share capital.
7. The explosion at the plant caused a great deal of _____.
8. Go away! I've got _____ to do.
9. It's becoming more and more difficult to find suitable _____ in capital cities.
10. If we want a more flexible workforce, we must invest in _____.
11. He's bought an _____ on Fifth Avenue.
12. Did you have a good _____ to Geneva?
13. _____ abroad is a necessary part of an export salesman's job.
14. We've made _____ in the negotiations but still haven't reached agreement on several points.

(→ 79 Noun formation; 80 Noun combinations)

36 Currencies

1 The table below gives the currency used in a number of countries.

Argentina	peso	Mexico	peso
Brazil	cruzeiro	Netherlands	guilder
China	yuan	Poland	zloty
Denmark	krone	Portugal	escudo
Finland	markka	Romania	leu
France	French franc	Russia	rouble
Germany	Deutschmark	Saudi Arabia	riyal
Greece	drachma	Singapore	dollar
India	rupee	South Africa	rand
Iran	rial	Spain	peseta
Italy	lira	Sweden	krona
Japan	yen	Thailand	baht

2 Countries using *dollars* include:

USA　　　　Australia　　Canada　　Hong Kong
New Zealand　Singapore　Taiwan

3 Countries using *pounds* include

UK　　Ireland　　Egypt　　Malta

Countries using *francs* include:

Belgium　　Switzerland　　Luxembourg

Many African countries use *the African financial community franc.*

4 Financial transactions between governments in the EC are in Ecus (pronounced /eɪkjuːz/)
(the Ecu = European currency unit)

5 Problems may arise when using the plural forms of these currencies. Most take the English plural *s*, e.g. *pounds, dollars, francs, Deutschmarks, drachmas (or drachmae), rupees, rials, pesos, guilders, escudos, riyals, pesetas, roubles, dinars.*

However, some are invariable: *yuan, yen, baht, rand.*

Others keep the plural form of the language spoken in the country of origin: *lira – lire, krone – kroner, krona – kronor, markka – markkaa, leu – lei.*

6 *Currencies* are said to be *convertible* (can be exchanged for other currencies at the market rate) or *inconvertible.*

Semi-convertible currencies can only be bought or sold through a country's central bank for documented commercial transactions. The exchange rates are fixed (sometimes with different rates for different commodities). *Semi-convertible currencies* are typical of Third World countries.

7 A *hard* currency is one which is strong and unlikely to fall in value (e.g. the Deutschmark and the yen – at the time of writing). A *soft* currency is one from a country with a weak balance of payments and for which there is little demand.

8 A *basket of currencies* is an agreed range of currencies whose combined value can be used to calculate an average or make comparisons.

Practice

a. Hidden in this puzzle are the names of 20 currencies. See how many you can find. In which countries are these currencies used?

```
S  C  H  I  L  L  I  N  G  Y
P  X  P  M  B  A  H  T  U  U
O  P  E  S  O  R  R  S  I  A
U  F  S  Z  R  I  Y  A  L  N
N  F  E  Y  E  P  R  K  D  M
D  G  T  E  E  Z  O  K  E  A
F  R  A  N  C  L  U  R  R  R
L  H  D  A  L  O  B  O  L  K
R  U  P  E  E  T  L  N  I  K
P  L  C  X  U  Y  E  E  R  A
E  S  C  U  D  O  L  L  A  R
```

b. What do these abbreviations stand for?
Sch   Gld   Esc   Kr   DM   Pts   Dnr   Fr   Rbl

c. A British tour operator has costed a package holiday in Spain at £650. This calculation is based on £1 = 200 pesetas. However, as a result of a recent fluctuation in the exchange rate £1 now equals 190 pesetas.
How much will the tour operator now want to charge?

d. A US firm agrees to purchase pharmaceutical products from a West German supplier for DM 100,000, payment to be made 90 days after delivery. On the day of the agreement the exchange rate was $1 = DM 2.5. Over the next 90 days the dollar falls to $1 = DM 2.25. How much will the American firm now have to pay?

37 **Curriculum Vitae**

1 The *curriculum vitae*[1] or *CV* is an account of an individual's educational background and previous work experience. Prospective employers can judge whether the skills, accomplishments and abilities described match their needs and organisational goals.

> **1.1** The *curriculum vitae* should be clear to read and present an attractive image. It is important to highlight the features which will interest the reader. It should not be too long. Space left blank on the page makes it easy to read quickly.

> **1.2** There are two main formats: the *chronological* and the *functional*. In both types there will be the same basic information (name, address, date of birth and civil status.)

> **1.3** When applying for a post abroad it is helpful to give the names of equivalent qualifications which can be easily understood by the reader. There may not be an equivalent qualification in some cases, so it is a good idea to describe the diploma obtained (e.g. a D.E.U.G.: a University qualification obtained after two years' study).

2 *A chronological CV*
This is the most familiar layout. It is possible to start from the present and work back in time (usual in the US) or begin at the start of one's career and work forward in time. See page 69.

3 *A functional CV*
Here the content is organised into specific categories of abilities. It is useful if you have a short work record or previous jobs unrelated to current goals. It tells a potential employer what you can do. See page 70.

[1] (AmE: *résumé*)

CURRICULUM VITAE

NAME   Pierre Charreau
D.O.B.   1.8.65
ADDRESS   55 Rue des Moines, Strasbourg.
                  67000, France

EDUCATION   1984–7. École Supérieure de Commerce de
                  Reims (one of the leading business schools in
                  France)

                  1988. EDP International: Work experience in
                  market research. Conducted field surveys in
                  the Netherlands and France.

PROFESSIONAL 1989 – 1991. Demont S.A.
ACTIVITY   Financial Controller responsible for:
                  — organising bank credits for civil
                    engineering work
                  — visiting Latin American and Asian
                    subsidiaries
                  — designing data processing, accounting,
                    cost control and reporting systems.
                  — hiring and training local staff for
                    subsidiaries
                  1991 — present. Phoenix Properties.
                  Investment Officer responsible for:
                  — checking feasibility studies and
                    predicting returns on investment
                  — solving legal problems related to
                    investments
                  — negotiating contracts with property
                    developers
                  — setting up joint ventures with foreign
                    partners

RESUME

HEIDI KUNKEL

OBJECTIVE   A sales position leading to higher management where my administrative, technical and interpersonal skills will be used to maximise sales and promote good customer relations.

EDUCATION   B.A. in Communications (1988): Ohio State University

Courses in psychology, sociology and interpersonal communication.

Areas of effectiveness

SALES/ CUSTOMER RELATIONS   During my 4 years at Colelli Enterprises (Columbus, Ohio), I promoted better relations with corporate accounts and recruited new clients over a wider territory. Dealt with customer complaints. Responsible for inventory and follow-up of all orders.

PLANNING/ ORGANISATION   Was responsible for the re-organisation of the sales department's administrative functions. Initiated time and motion studies which led to a $150,000 saving in labor costs.

LANGUAGES   Spanish (fluent), French (average)

REFERENCES   Available on request.

4 When describing activities undertaken the following verbs are useful:

I was responsible for

initiating
planning
negotiating
achieving
implementing
reviewing

5 When stressing abilities, the following words and expressions are useful:

creative	proficient	comprehensive/first-hand knowledge of..
accurate	well-organised	(have) a proven track record in..
efficient	perfectionist	well versed in..
energetic	motivated	perform well under pressure
systematic	methodical	willing to take the initiative

Practice

Write out your own CV in English. If possible, talk about yourself with a partner. Use this language:

I was born in ....
I went to school in ....
After leaving school I went to...and studied at ....
I did a course / degree in ....
Then ....
My first post was in ....
I was responsible for ....
Then ....
At the moment ....
My work involves ....
I think I am ....

38 Damage vs Damages

These words are often confused but have quite separate meanings.

1 *Damage* is both a noun and a verb. It refers to some sort of harmful effect:

Our reputation has been *damaged* as a result of the scandal.

The explosion caused *damage* estimated at $5m.

2 *Damages* are awarded by a court of law in compensation for physical or moral injury:

The cigarette lighter company had to pay £2m *damages* when one of its lighters exploded and burnt the victim.

Practice

Complete the sentences.

1. On receipt of the goods you should declare any _____ to the insurance company.
2. She was awarded _____ of $500,000 for wrongful dismissal.
3. Handle your disks carefully or you may _____ them.

39 Deal in vs Deal with

1 If a company *deals* in a specific kind of goods, its business involves buying and selling those goods:

Ferrinex plc *deals in* construction machinery.

2 To *deal with* means 'to give attention to':

I'm sorry to keep you waiting; the Finance Manager will *deal with* your enquiry when she gets back.

2.1 *Deal with* can also mean 'to have business relations':

We've been *dealing with* our suppliers for seven years.

3 The noun *deal* means 'business transaction':

They can't get the necessary finance so the *deal* is off.

3.1 The expression *clinch the deal* means that an agreement is settled in a definite way:

The offer of cheap financing enabled us to *clinch the deal* and get the contract.

Practice

Complete the sentences.

1. They _____ second-hand cars and lorries.
2. We refuse to _____ firms that don't allow us to trade on open account.
3. I think even a small concession would allow us to _____.
4. I always leave him to _____ the paperwork.

40 Demand vs Enquiry vs Query vs Request

1 If you *demand* something you ask for it very strongly; it is almost an order.

The union is *demanding* both higher wages and a shorter working week. If they don't get them they'll probably go on strike.

1.1 *Demand* can also be a synonym of 'require':

Executive positions *demand* good management skills.

1.2 The noun *demand* can be used countably and uncountably:

The management resisted *demands* for fuller representation.

There is an increase in *demand* for environmentally safe products.

Our new XL45 is in great *demand*. (= is very popular)

1.3 If something is available *on demand* it can be easily obtained:

Our catalogue and price list are available *on demand*.
(= if you ask)

1.4 In economics, *demand* is the opposite of 'supply'; if a commodity is in short supply, the *demand* is likely to be greater.

1.5 If something is *demanding*, it requires a lot of time and energy:

Working in a busy freight forwarding company is a *demanding* occupation.

2 An *enquiry* (also spelt *inquiry*) is a request for information:

We had 750 *enquiries* after we placed an ad in the trade press.

2.1 The verb *make* is used with *enquiry*:

Good afternoon, I'd like to *make an enquiry* about export regulations to Japan.

2.2 An *enquiry* is also a formal investigation:

There will be a full *enquiry* into insider trading on the Stock Exchange.

2.3 The verb is *enquire*:

Hello, I'm phoning to *enquire* about your range of office equipment.

3 A *query* is a question relating to a specific point which needs clarification[1]:

I've a *query* about the National Insurance contributions.

[1] **Query** is not common in AmE; use **question**.

3.1 *Query* can also be used as a verb:

The accountant has *queried* my travel expenses.
(= questioned)

4 *Request* is also both a noun and a verb. If you make a *request* you ask someone to do something:

At my request the Minister agreed to intervene.
They have *requested* our help in the matter.

4.1 *On request* means 'on demand'.

Practice

Complete these sentences with *demand, enquiry, query, request* or words and expressions derived from them.

1. There's very little _____ for ski anoraks in summer.
2. He's put in a _____ for extended leave.
3. After the radiation leakage we set up a full _____.
4. There's a _____ about the date; Mr Wolfeiler may not be able to come that day.
5. They've _____ about whether or not we can supply them with display stands.
6. In a competitive market, prices should vary according to supply and _____.
7. He's in charge of a sales force of over 70 people; it's a very _____ job.
8. I'll _____ and see if it's possible to lease a machine.

41 Director vs Chairperson vs Executive vs Manager

Most firms can be divided into three parts:

capital (shareholders)
management
labour

The management structure can be represented as in the diagram on page 75:

SHAREHOLDERS

Provide the overall BOARD OF DIRECTORS
objectives of the firm (headed by the Chairperson)

CHIEF EXECUTIVE OFFICER (CEO)
(Also known as the Managing Director)

SENIOR EXECUTIVE OFFICERS
(General Manager[1] + senior managers)

MIDDLE / LINE MANAGERS

1 A *director* is a senior manager who sits on the Board under the authority of the *Chairperson* or *President*. The Board is responsible for deciding overall company policy and capital expenditure.

2 The *CEO* or *MD* is the link between the Board and senior management.

3 *Middle managers* (also known as *line managers*) are responsible for running sections or departments within a firm. They are accountable to senior management for their particular area of responsibility as illustrated in the organisation chart.

Senior management

4 In a general manner of speaking, an *executive* is any senior person in the hierarchy of a firm. He/She makes important decisions that are carried out by subordinates.

[1] (AmE: **Executive Vice President/Chief Operating Officer**)

5 Like the *managing director, some directors* are also concerned with the day-to-day running of the firm. In this capacity they are known as *executive directors.*[1] Those who sit on the Board but have no direct interest in the running of the firm are called *non-executive directors.*[2]

6 *Executive* can also be used as an adjective:

Some tour operators specialise in *executive* travel.

Practice

Draw a simple organisation chart for the management structure of the place in which you work.
What are the names of the senior personnel?
What are their titles in English?

42 Draw vs Withdraw

1 *Draw* is an irregular verb (*draw – drew – drawn*) and has several meanings.

1.1 *Draw* is used in the context of bank payments in export transactions when money is transferred from one account to another:

Please find enclosed a copy of the notification received from the Bangkok Bank Ltd., Bangkok to open an irrevocable Letter of Credit in your favour for the sum of $16,200.
You may *draw on* us at 60 days against the credit as soon as we receive proof of shipment.

1.2 If you *draw up* a document you prepare the wording and write it out:

The contract will be *drawn up* and sent to you in due course.

1.3 *Drawn* exists in these combinations:

	attention to
	a blank
	a conclusion
draw	a distinction
	the line
	praise
	a reaction

---

[1] AmE: **inside directors**   [2] AmE: **outside directors**

2 To *withdraw* means 'to take money out of an account'.

You need to prove your identity before **withdrawing** money from the bank.

2.1 It can also mean 'to retract' or 'to remove':

I would like to **withdraw** the rather silly remark I made earlier.

The advertisement breached the Code of Advertising Practice and was **withdrawn.**

2.2 The noun is *withdrawal.*

Practice

Complete the sentences appropriately.

1. Luckily he had time to _____ his life savings before the bank collapsed.
2. Even though the words mean the same in everyday usage, a lawyer will _____ a distinction between a warranty and a guarantee.
3. I will _____ a draft agreement and fax it to you.
4. The safety standards did not conform to EC legislation and the product was _____ from the market.
5. We have opened an irrevocable L/C for £12,685 in your favour which is valid until 15 October. You are authorised to _____ us against this credit once the shipment has been made.

43 Earnings vs Income vs Revenue

1 *Earnings* are the sums of money earned by working. The word *earnings* is always in the plural form:

Women's **earnings** are often less than men's.
You must declare your annual **earnings** to the Inland Revenue.

1.1 *Earnings* is used in the expressions *earnings per share* and *price/earnings ratio.*

2 *Income* is a synonym for *earnings* but may include *unearned income* acquired from other sources e.g. share dividends, property or other investments. It is subject to income tax.

His monthly **income** is well above the national average.
A person's **income** falls dramatically on retirement.

This noun can be used in the plural in the expression *incomes policy*:

The government and Unions have negotiated a *prices and incomes* policy.

3 *Revenue* is similar in meaning to *income* but is more likely to refer to the money that a company or organisation receives through sales. We would not normally refer to a private individual's *income* as *revenue*.

Revenue from advertising keeps the magazine's cost low.

It can be used in the plural:

A decline in oil *revenues* has led to a slowing-down in the programme of modernisation.

> **3.1** In Britain, the government department responsible for tax collection is the *Inland Revenue*. (See example in 1. above)
>
> (→ 102 Salary vs Wages vs Perks)

Practice

Complete the sentences.

1. No one likes paying _____ tax to the Inland _____.

2. The price / _____ ratio is the present market price of a share divided by the company's net _____ per share in the previous accounting year.

44 Economy vs Economics vs Economic vs Economical vs Economise

1 A country's *economy* is the organisation of its wealth-producing commerce and industrty:

Britain's *economy* is increasingly based on services.

The *economies* of many developing countries are based on cash crops.

> **1.1** *Economy* can also mean 'the deliberate saving of money through carefully-controlled spending':
>
> We use recycled paper for reasons of *economy*.
> The budget has been cut so we'll have to make *economies*[1].

[1] (AmE: ...**we'll have to economize**.)

1.2 We can refer to something as a *false economy* when an apparent saving of money in fact results in inefficiency and/or unforeseen extra costs:

Buying second-hand equipment can be a *false economy*.

1.3 We refer to an *economy of scale* when there is a reduction in unit cost owing to an increase in the volume of production:

The doubling of output can lead to *economies of scale* of up to 30%.

2 *Economics* is the scientific study of a society's money, industry and trade:

She studied *economics* at the London Business School.

Note that *economics* is a singular noun (like other subjects, Maths, Physics, Business Studies, etc.) therefore *Economics* **is** ....

3 *Economic* means 'related to the economy':

The 1970s and 1980s were a period of political and *economic* crisis.
Economic growth leads to a per capita improvement in living standards.

3.1 *Economic* can also mean 'cost-effective':

We have to keep wage costs low to make it *economic* for us to continue production.

4 If something is *economical* it does not require a great deal of money to operate:

I have a small car because it's more *economical* to run.

The word can also be used to refer to an efficient way of doing things:

Holding business meetings at an airport can be an *economical* use of time.

5 The verb is *to economise* and means 'to save money':

We need to *economise* in order to keep costs at an acceptable level.
It is unwise in the long run to *economise* on quality.

Practice

Complete the blanks.

1. She majored in _____ at Harvard.
2. What's the _____ situation like in your country?
3. Many countries tried to _____ on fuel in the 1970s.

4. _____ of scale arise when costs do not rise in direct proportion to output.

5. The electric car is more _____ in its use of energy than an ordinary one.

6. Employing too many part-time staff can be a false _____ .

7. Some people think that floating exchange rates can restrict _____ growth.

45 Effective vs Efficient

1 Advertising on commercial TV is the most *effective* method of test-marketing a household product.

2 We have a very *efficient* distribution network.

In **1.** the meaning is that TV advertising has the most 'impact'. In **2.** we learn that the network is highly-organised and functions well.

3 The nouns are *effect, effectiveness* and *efficiency*.

4 If something has become *effective* it has come into force:

The new rate of interest becomes *effective* as from 31 December.

Practice

a. Complete the grid below. Put a tick (✓) if the word on the left can be used with the word in the top column.

	campaign	methods	secretary	solution	speaker
effective					✓
efficient					

b. Complete the sentences.

1. The measures taken to cut unemployment have been _____ as there is now less than 5% of the population out of work.

2. Miss Chen is the most _____ documentalist we've ever had; she's worked out a marvellous classification system.

3. Revised catalogue prices are _____ as from April 1st.

4. Direct mail shots are seldom _____ ; most finish in the wastepaper basket.

46 Ensure vs Insure vs Assure

All these words mean 'make safe or certain'.

1 To *ensure* means 'to make sure that something happens'.

I am doing my best to *ensure* that your order will be dealt with promptly.
In American English *insure* would be used here.

2 To *insure* means 'to provide insurance cover against loss'.

Please *insure* the cargo against all risks.

3 To *assure* means 'to persuade someone that everything is all right'.

We *assure* you that we are doing our best to find the origin of the defect.

> **3.1 The** expression *rest assured* is a useful way of reassuring people about something which is worrying them:
>
> You can *rest assured* that everything is under control.

Practice

Complete this passage.

The Export Credit Guarantee Department enables exporters to
_____ against political risks. In this way the exporter can
rest _____ that there will be no payment problems. Such
a system _____ that firms can open up new markets in
'difficult' countries of high political uncertainty.

47 Equipment vs Material

1 *Equipment* consists of the machines or manufactured goods required for a particular purpose:

They exported FF250,000 worth of stereo *equipment*.
They are starting to import hi-tech telecommunications *equipment*.

2 *Material* is cloth made of cotton, wool or synthetic fibres:

We sell good quality *material* for dressmaking.

3 *Raw materials* are natural substances used in the industrial process:

The Third World is a source of *raw materials* for western industry.

48 **Expect vs Wait**

1 Compare these sentences:

(a) We're *waiting* for the goods to arrive.
(b) We're *expecting* the goods to arrive.

In (a) there is a strong implication that the goods should have arrived earlier. Their late delivery is possibly preventing further action. Sentence (b) looks forward and anticipates their arrival. There is no idea that the goods are late.

In sentences of type (b) both the present simple and the present continuous are possible, with no change of meaning.

I *expect* to be back on Friday.

I'm *expecting* to be back on Friday.

2 *I expect* can be a synonym of 'I think/ I believe'.

'Do you think prices will come down soon?'
'I expect so.'

(NOT *I am expecting so)

Practice

Complete the following.

1. I arrived later than I had _____ because the plane was held up and we had to _____ for two hours before we finally took off.
2. 'A telephone call for me?' I _____ that will be Meike wanting a decision.

49 **Expense vs Expenses vs Expenditure**

1 *Expense* is the money that it costs you to do something. The word occurs in these fixed expressions:

We've modernised our offices *at vast expense*.
We *went to great expense* to improve our social club.
The new machine cost a lot to install but it was *worth the expense* because of the time it has saved.

2 The plural of *expense* is *expenses*; the amounts of money spent can be listed:

Expenses, such as electricity, water, and local taxes come under the heading of overheads.

In some cases, *expenses* will be repaid:

Your interview will be held at 3 p.m. in the Royal Hotel. All reasonable travel and accommodation *expenses* will be reimbursed.

We will pay the technician's return air fare plus *expenses*.

3 If you do something *at someone else's expense* then you do not pay:

I fly first class *at the Company's expense*.

If you do something *at the expense of something* or *someone else*, it is not to their advantage:

Economic progress in the Third World should not be *at the expense of* rural employment.

A devaluation improves the position of exporters *at the expense of* importers.

4 *Expenditure* is a more formal word and is used in the context of the spending of (usually) large sums of money for a particular purpose:

Expenditure on public services has been cut by the government.

Expenditure on TV advertising is huge.

Practice

Complete the blanks using *expense, expenses* or *expenditure*.

1. I enclose a claim form for travel and hotel _____.
2. They went to great _____ to hire the services of a film star to launch the new product.
3. I suggest you have all the documentation translated by a specialist agency; it's well worth the _____.
4. The _____ of millions of pounds on new plant was not accompanied by an increase in production.
5. We increased the pace of work at the _____ of efficiency.
6. The different _____ (rent, heating, cleaning bills, etc.) that a firm must pay for out of trading profit are called overheads.
7. Most agents want 10% commission plus _____ for entertainment, advertising and so on.
8. British Telecom's _____ on telephone exchange modernisation was over £500 million.

50 Few vs A Few; Little vs A Little

1 A *few* means 'a small number of'. It is used before countable nouns. (→ 35 **Countable vs Uncountable nouns**)

Do you mind waiting *a few* minutes?
In *a few* years' time we'll be market leader.

2 *Few* (without *a*) means 'not many'; it is also used before countable nouns:

Few things respond more quickly to exchange rate changes than international travel.

If there are *few* opportunities for promotion, young executives will tend to leave the firm.

3 A *little* means 'a small amount'; it is used with uncountable nouns.

I need *a little* time to think about your offer but I'll phone you first thing tomorrow morning.

> **3.1** It can also mean 'to some extent' when used with an adjective.
>
> The first half-year results were *a little* disappointing.

4 *Little* means 'not much' and is also used with uncountable nouns:

There is *little* time left for discussion so let's come to a decision straight away.

5 Note that *a few* and *a little* tend to have *positive* meaning:

You'll get used to the climate after *a few* weeks.

With *a little* help from the bank manager, the project will get off the ground.

6 *Few* and *little* tend to have *negative* meaning:

He seems to have *little* motivation for the job and should be moved to another section.

Few people like their boss interfering with their work.

Practice

    a. Complete the memo appropriately using *few*, *a few*, *little* and *a little*. (**Note** that this memo contains more examples of these words than you would normally find in a memo of similar length. The idea is to give you practice in using them correctly).

Dear Bill,

Thanks a lot for your letter which I got on
Wednesday. Sorry I haven't got back to you
sooner, but anyway, here are my ideas on the
things you wanted clearing up.

A. You have to fork out about 1/4 of your
pay packet for the taxman.
B. There's no way you can get anything back
on money made abroad.
C. Your best bet is to ask not to pay tax in
the UK and tell the tax people over there
how much you earn.

Hope this is OK.

If there's anything else you want to know
drop me a line.

All the best,

2 A *formal* style is characterised by:
More complex sentences (*You would be well-advised...residence*)
Abstract nouns (*exemption*)
Frequent use of **it-patterns** e.g. *It would not be feasible...*
Use of 'educated' low-frequency vocabulary (*monies, trust,
queries, threshold* etc...)
Avoiding contractions and abbreviations

3 Some indications of *informal* style are:
Short words and sentences (*Thanks a lot.....Wednesday*)
Contractions and abbreviations (*I haven't, there's...*)
Colloquial language (*OK, get back to, your best bet, drop me a
line...*)

Practice

a. Decide which of these sentences are *informal* and which are *formal*. Group together those with a similar meaning.

1. How about looking at Dimitri's idea?
2. Much as I would like to be of assistance, it is beyond my power to intervene.
3. Say 'hello' from me and tell Samira to get better soon.
4. As this matter is entirely beyond our control, we are unable to proceed with a reimbursement.
5. I suggest we consider Mr Bozena's proposal closely.
6. Thanks for your recent note.
7. We can't do anything about it, so we can't give you any money back.
8. I would be grateful if you would convey my best wishes to Mrs El Hazir and I hope she has a speedy recovery.
9. Before we said yes we'd have to work out how much it'd cost.
10. I acknowledge receipt of your letter of 5 January.
11. It's great to know you're backing us all the way.
12. I'd like to help, but I can't do anything.
13. I am pleased to learn that you are giving us every encouragement.
14. Prior to any firm commitment on our part, we would have to assess the financial implications.

FORMAL and INFORMAL STYLES

b. The following is a letter from a firm interested in becoming an agent in the UK for a Swedish manufacturer of garden furniture. Choose the language which is most appropriate for a formal reply.

---

¹*Hi!/Dear Mr Price,*

²*Thanks/Thank you* for your recent letter. We were ³*happy/pleased* to hear that you are interested in marketing our range of garden furniture.

⁴*But/However,* before we ⁵*make any firm decision/ make up our mind,* we would be grateful if you would ⁶*provide us with/give us* further information ⁷*concerning/about* the organisation of your firm, the territory it covers, the number of retail outlets and your market share.

⁸*You would have to get us/We would expect* a minimum turnover of £600,000 before ⁹*being in a position to/we could* offer you a sole agency. ¹⁰*We would want to get/we would wish to achieve* a market share of at least 10% in the first two years.

¹¹*Anyway/This said,* if you feel your firm is able to meet these targets ¹²*it would be nice/it would be useful* to arrange an appointment to ¹³*have a chat about/discuss* the project ¹⁴*in a bit more detail/ further.*

I will be in England from 5 – 12 May and suggest we ¹⁵*meet/get together* then, if this is ¹⁶*convenient/OK.* Please confirm with my secretary if this is ¹⁷*all right/ satisfactory.*

¹⁸*I look forward to hearing from you in the near future/Hope to get a letter from you soon.*

¹⁹*Yours sincerely,/All the best,*

Sven Jorgensen

Sven Jorgensen

---

c. You are Richard Cartwright, the newly-appointed Sales Director of ACG Ltd. You have received the following letter of complaint.

Dear Mr Grant,

Over the last three years we have been placing regular orders for grease-resistant coated paper at the current list price of £1.00.

Our last order for 3,500 rolls, dated 5 March, was invoiced to us with what is referred to as the 'standard 15% discount for bulk orders'.

Although this discount is very welcome it came as a complete surprise, given that in our earlier price negotiations you maintained that you were unable to grant quantity discounts on the grounds that, in order to keep your prices competitive, you worked to extremely tight profit margins.

Had we been informed of discounts for purchases in excess of 3,000 rolls we would have modified the timing of our purchases and placed larger orders at less frequent intervals. In this way we would have made substantial cost savings.

I am disappointed that you appear to have withheld information relative to discounts and look forward to receiving both an apology and a suitable offer of indemnity.

Yours sincerely,

Hugh MacKenzie

Hugh MacKenzie

Your task is to reply to this letter of complaint. You have made these notes. Decide on the tone of the letter you want to write and draft a suitable reply.
- thanks for letter, apologies for misunderstanding
- pricing policy modified in Jan

- customers told about new prices and discounts in previous letter (22 Jan)
- Mr M received this letter – prices referred to are up-to-date
- no compensation
- enclose catalogue and price list
- meeting in London soon? He can choose a date

d. This letter is too formal in tone. Re-write it in a more relaxed and friendly way.

Dear Mr. Evans,

I am writing in response to our recent conversation concerning the three possible choices for the US market. I regret to inform you that I do not consider I am presently in a position to assume responsibility for such a major undertaking. I have a great number of pressing engagements and would not be able to allocate sufficient time.

However, should you make a decision to modify your policy for the Advertising Specialty Market in the USA I would wish to suggest an alternative proposal which we could discuss in Munich at the end of the month.

Sincerely yours,

Raphael Mazzi

Raphael Mazzi

---

54 The Former vs The Latter

1 When two items have been presented in a list, it is possible to refer back to either the first item mentioned or the final one by using the substitution words *the former* (for the first-mentioned) or *the latter* (for the last-mentioned).

For example:

Goods can be paid for either 'carriage forward' or 'carriage paid'. *The former* means that the buyer has to pay for transport costs, *the latter* means that the seller pays for all transport charges up to an agreed delivery point.

Both the Rolls Royce and the Cadillac are luxury cars. *The former* is British while *the latter* is American.

2 Note that *the latter* can be used to refer to the last-mentioned in a list of three but *the former* can only be used if there are two items in the list.

Practice

Complete the passage.

There are two ways for managers to think of workers. One is as a commodity bought for a fixed price which will yield fixed rewards. The other is as a resource that can be developed to a full potential. Many managers of 'human resources' are in the process of changing from _____ view to _____.

55 Frequency

1 The following words tell us *how often* something takes place:

always	most frequent
usually/generally	
often	
sometimes/occasionally	
rarely/seldom	
never	least frequent

1.1 These words are placed after the verb *to be*:

I am *sometimes* late for work.

between the auxiliary and main verb:

They will *never* agree.
I have *always* been in favour of monetary union.

or before the main verb:

We *often* experience problems with our computer network.

2 Note the expressions *once a month, twice a week, three times a year* etc.

We have a job appraisal interview *once a year*.

For emphasis, the expression may be at the beginning of the sentence:

Once a year, we have a job appraisal interview.

But it cannot go before the main verb.

NOT *We twice a year make revised estimates.

3 The word *ever* is used in a question to ask about frequency:

Do you *ever* have to negotiate in English? (= at any time)
Yes, sometimes / often etc.; No, never.)

3.1 *Ever* can also mean 'at any time up to now':

Have you *ever* been to Kyoto?
Profits are higher than *ever*.

Practice

a. Answer these questions truthfully using:

always   usually   often   sometimes   rarely   never

MONEY

1. Do you carry a lot of cash on you when you go out?
2. Do you pay for purchases with a credit card?
3. Do you fill in the counterfoil when you make out a cheque?
4. Do you check your change?
5. Do you ever buy stocks and shares?
6. How often do you read the *Wall St. Journal?*

WORK

7. Do you have trouble completing jobs through frequent interruptions?
8. Do you find it difficult to delegate?
9. Do you feel you have to work excessively long hours?
10. Does your colleagues' lack of organisation put your job at risk?
11. Are you ever frustrated by poor communications?
12. Do you routinely spend weekends working rather than with your family?
13. Have you ever cancelled a holiday because of work?

b. Rewrite the sentences using the word in brackets.

1. I don't have to work at the weekend. (*usually*)
2. She finishes her work on time. (*rarely*)
3. There is an audit. (*once a year*)
4. You should read the small print. (*always*)
5. I have said we should have consulted a lawyer. (*often*)
6. You must turn a customer away. (*never*)

56 The future

There are several ways of referring to future time in English.

1 Prediction

At the present time we expect something to happen.

According to our latest forecasts profits *will* increase by about 15 per cent.

2 Future fact

The company *will* be 50 years old next Monday.
We w*on't* know how well we've done until next month.

2.1 *Will* can be used with a *verb* + *ing* to say that something will be in progress at a future time:

We *will be talking* about sales in Africa during the next planning meeting.

2.2 *Will* + *have* + *past participle* is used to talk about something completed in the future:

By this time next month *we'll have finished* the designs.

3 Promises

I *will* do my best to make sure you get everything by the end of the week.

4 Spontaneous decision for the future

Note that when making statements the contraction *'ll* can usually replace *will*.

'I haven't got time to see her tomorrow.'
'OK, I*'ll* see her myself.'

5 Intentions

We're *going to* open a subsidiary in Cologne.

5.1 *Going to* is also used to refer to a future event for which we have present evidence:

Judging by the number of job applications he's made it looks as if he's *going to* leave the firm very soon.

5.2 *Going to* can suggest great determination:

We're *going to* become the world's leading manufacturer even if it kills all of us.

6 Fixed arrangements and future certainties

The present simple is often used in connection with travel or other activities that involve a schedule.

The plane for Rio *leaves* at 3.30.

An infinitive can also be used to talk about definite arrangements: it makes the arrangement sound official.

We *are to see* Mrs Maarteens on the 21st of this month.
You *are to be* there at 9 a.m. sharp.

7 *Future plans*

I'*m seeing* the advertising manager tomorrow.
When are you *going*? On Tuesday.

These arrangements do not sound as official as those in **6** above.

Practice

a. Which of the headings (**1 – 7**) apply to the following sentences:

1. I will do whatever I can to help.
2. The AGM is to be held in the Kings Arms on 5 April at 3 p.m.
3. I'll give you a lift if you like.
4. The agreement will expire in 18 months' time.
5. Commodity market analysts think that the price of rubber will keep on rising.
6. She says she's going to apply for the new job.
7. The train leaves at 12.04.
8. I'm having lunch with Youcef tomorrow.

8 The choice of the future forms above is not always easy. Sometimes it is possible to use more than one – at other times only one is possible.

The company *will* be 50 years old next Monday. (*future fact*)
The company *is* 50 years old next Monday. (*absolutely definite*)

We're *going* to open a subsidiary in Cologne. (*intention*)
We're *opening* a subsidiary in Cologne. (*plan*)

We're *going to* become the world's leading manufacturer even if it kills all of us. (*intention*)
We *will* become the world's leading manufacturer even if it kills all of us. (*promise* [possibly also a *future fact*])

9 These are some of the restrictions in the choices.
We do **not** use the present continuous to make predictions:
NOT * According to our latest forecasts profit is increasing by about 15 per cent.

nor to make promises:

NOT * Fine, I'm sending you our catalogue and price list straight away.

However this is acceptable in AmE.

It is not possible to announce a spontaneous decision using *going to / the present continuous / the present simple.*

'I haven't got time to see her tomorrow.'

NOT * 'OK, I'm going to see / I'm seeing / I see her myself.'

However, the first two are acceptable in AmE.

Practice

b. Choose the correct form of the verb.

1. *We give you / We'll give you* an extra discount on any repeat order.

2. The Vice-President *is to inaugurate / 'll inaugurate* the new centre on June 5.

3. 'Why have you started packing your suitcase?' *'I'll take / I'm going to take* the first plane back, that's why.'

4. 'I've just realised I can't be free any other day except Tuesday. And as you've got another appointment then we can't see each other until next month.'

'No, Tuesday is OK, *I'll cancel / I'm going to cancel it.'*

c. Economic Indicators

Make predictions for the next six months under these headings:

– the inflation rate in your country
– the rate of interest on personal loans
– the balance of payments
– the value of your currency against the US dollar
– your company's performance
– your own career prospects

d. This is Mr Schroder's schedule for next week.

22 Monday	26 Friday *Night club*
23 Tuesday *10.30 Flight leaves*	27 Saturday *Return home*
24 Wednesday *a.m. Visit to new offices* *p.m. Presentation of prototype*	28 Sunday
25 Thursday *Meeting with patent attorney*	29 Monday

1. Where will he be early Tuesday morning?
2. What time does his plane leave?
3. What's he doing on Wednesday?
4. What will he be doing on Thursday afternoon?
5. What will he be doing on Friday evening?
6. When is he coming back?

c. Look at the table of repayments for a loan. The last four instalments are shown.
At the end of the loan period how much interest will the borrower have paid?

DATE	MONTHLY REPAYMENT	CAPITAL REIMBURSED	INTEREST	CUMULATED INTEREST	CAPITAL OWING
10/04	3087.30	2938.45	118.28	8181.98	8990.65
10/05	3087.30	2967.59	89.14	8271.12	6023.06
10/06	3087.30	2997.01	59.72	8330.84	3026.03
10/07	3087.30	3026.05	30.68	8361.52	0.00

57 Graphs, Tables, Charts and Diagrams

1 A *graph* is useful for showing movements. It has good visual impact and can show how one thing varies relative to changes in another.

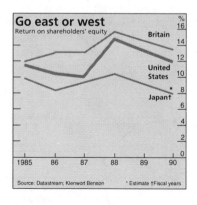

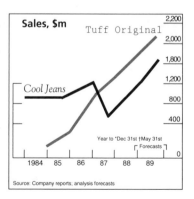

2 A *table* should be understood without any text. It gives information very accurately but has poor visual impact.

% share of top five grocery retailers by country, of total European food sales

Country	1980	1986	1989/90
UK	6.1	6.9	8.0
Germany	8.6	8.8	13.1
France	4.4	9.1	10.8

Source: Management Horizons

3 A *bar chart* is particularly useful when making comparisons. However, it is not as accurate as a table.

GEC ALSTHOM: 1989–90 sales breakdown by activity

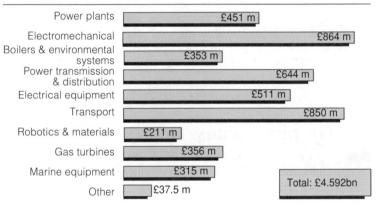

Power plants	£451 m
Electromechanical	£864 m
Boilers & environmental systems	£353 m
Power transmission & distribution	£644 m
Electrical equipment	£511 m
Transport	£850 m
Robotics & materials	£211 m
Gas turbines	£356 m
Marine equipment	£315 m
Other	£37.5 m

Total: £4.592bn

4 A *pie chart* has great visual impact. However, it cannot show movement and may not be effective if there are too many segments. You can work out the angles by multiplying each percentage by 3.6.

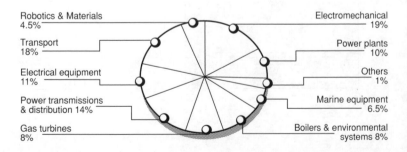

Robotics & Materials 4.5%
Transport 18%
Electrical equipment 11%
Power transmissions & distribution 14%
Gas turbines 8%
Electromechanical 19%
Power plants 10%
Others 1%
Marine equipment 6.5%
Boilers & environmental systems 8%

5 A *flow chart* is useful when showing a number of steps in a sequence. At each stage there may be a decision to be made.

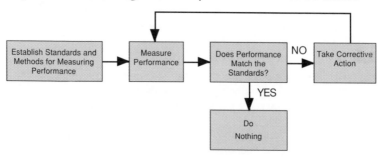

6 A *pictogram* is the least accurate of all presentations but has the greatest visual impact.

Where the oil is
Years of oil reserves remaining, 1990

	0	20	40	60	80	100

Middle East
Latin America
World
Africa
Asia and
Australasia
USSR and
Central Europe
North America
Western Europe

58 Have something done vs Have someone do something

1 Look at this example:

A consignment of goods was shipped from London to Hong Kong. During transportation some of the goods were damaged. When the importer collected the goods he noticed the damage and *had* the consignment *inspected* by an insurance agent in order to claim compensation.

In other words, he *arranged for* the goods to be *inspected* by an insurance agent.
Notice the word order:

He *had* the consignment *inspected*.

       (DIRECT OBJECT)   (PAST PARTICIPLE)

The verb *have* can change tense:

We always *have* our goods shipped by ATLAS transport.
He *had* the report sent to the overseas subsidiaries.
I *am having* a feasibility study prepared.

2 Compare these pairs of sentences:

(a) We have *our debts collected* by a factoring agency.
(b) We have a factoring agency *collect our debts*.
(a) Could you have *the samples tested* by the Technical
    Department?
(b) Could you have the Technical Department *test the samples*?
(a) He had *the documents copied* by Mr Peterson.
(b) He had Mr Peterson *copy the documents*.

Note the different word order and the form of the verb in each
case.
In (b) the emphasis is more on the person or organisation that
does the work.

3 *Have something done* does not always mean that there is a
deliberate arrangement. For example:

He *had his briefcase stolen* at the airport.

This does NOT mean that he organised the theft of his briefcase.
All it means is that his briefcase was taken by someone else.

4 In slightly more informal contexts, *get* is an alternative to *have*.

Will you *get* a few extra copies made please, Susan?
She *got* Mr Unwin to do it.
We *get* our mail delivered by special courier.

Practice

a. Put the words into the correct order:

1. a production the had by done the manager job
sub-contractor.
2. they campaign by an the had organised agency whole.
3. she clean the machine technician a had.
4. are we investigated the a matter having by lawyer.
5. damage had I assessed independent by an surveyor the.
6. the she Mr at had Messud look problem.
7. give I number have of a had a quotation companies me.

b. Study the hotel brochure and then complete the list of all the things a guest can *have done* e.g. *When you stay at the Astor you can have breakfast served in your room.*

ASTOR HOTEL

ROOM SERVICE	For everything you may need, just use the telephone in your room. We will be happy to serve you breakfast in your room.
SHOE CLEANING	Leave your shoes on the landing overnight. We'll clean them for the morning.
LAUNDRY	Just give your clothing to be washed before 9.30 a.m. for same-day service.
RESTAURANTS	Simply phone reception to book a table.
NIGHT PORTER	The Night Porter can arrange for drinks to be brought to your room after the bar has closed.
BUSINESS SERVICE	Arrange for a telex to be sent, documents copied and even translated.

---

1. You can _____ your shoes _____.
2. You can _____ your clothes _____.
3. When you stay at the Astor you can _____ reception _____.
4. If you like you may _____ the Night Porter _____.
5. If you are in business you may like to _____.

c. Two production engineers, Mr Roberts and Mr Brown are talking about their work.

Complete the blanks in the dialogue. Use these verbs:
build   type   install   do (2)   deliver   take

MR ROBERTS Got a busy day?
MR BROWN   Yes! First thing this morning , I've got to
            ¹_____ last month's production figures
            ²_____ by Sally. She's the temp we've got to
            replace Tracy. Tracy's off because she's ³_____
            an extension ⁴_____ onto her house, so she's
            taken unpaid leave.

MR ROBERTS Couldn't she have done them on Friday? She wasn't doing very much when I saw her. In fact I ⁵_____ Bill Preston ⁶_____ her on a guided visit of the factory because she seemed to have nothing to do.

MR BROWN Well, in fact her word processor was being repaired and there wasn't another one available. We're ⁷_____ a new one ⁸_____ tomorrow. What about you? Have you got a busy week?

MR ROBERTS Terrible! I'm ⁹_____ a new piece of equipment ¹⁰_____ on the night shift and I've got to supervise the whole operation.

MR BROWN Can't you delegate? Why don't you ¹¹_____ it ¹²_____ by someone else? Why don't you ¹³_____ Fred Tomkins ¹⁴_____ it?

MR ROBERTS No! The last time I gave him something to do it was a disaster! I'd rather do it myself.

59 Hire vs Rent vs Let vs Lease vs Charter

1 If you *hire* something you pay the owner to be able to use it for a (usually short) length of time:

We *hired* a Mercedes for the weekend.
We *hired* a sales training film for a couple of weeks.
We decided to *hire* a projector rather than buy one.

2 You can use *rent* in much the same way as *hire* for a vehicle or a piece of equipment. You can also *rent* (= pay for the use of) property[1]:

They've *rented* some office space in New York.

3 If you own property and allow others to use it in return for payment then you *let* it[2]:

Mrs Welsh has decided to *let* her chalet to a Dutch couple.
(= The Dutch couple is renting the chalet from Mrs Welsh.)

4 It is possible to *lease* equipment for long periods of time; maintenance is included in the price:

Our firm has *leased* an off-set printer.

It is also possible to *lease* property:

He persuaded the local council to *lease* him the first and second floors of a tower block.

[1] In American usage, **hire** is generally used when referring to a person, while **rent** refers to property: He was **hired** for the job. We **rented** the car.   [2] (AmE: **sublet, let out**)

5 We use *charter* in the context of paying for the private use of a vessel, train or plane:

We plan to *charter* a special train to London.

6 The corresponding nouns are:

rent (for property), *a rental, a lease, a charter* (plane/boat/train)
We do NOT say *a hire or (except rarely) *a let.
Note the expressions: *For Hire, To Let, Hire Purchase, Hiring and Firing*.

Practice

Put a tick (✓) in the grid if the verb can be used with the noun in the top column.

	business premises	a video	a villa	office equipment	a car	a ship	a plane	a stand at an exhibition
hire		✓						
rent								
let								
lease								
charter								

60 Idioms

An idiom is an expression which means something different from the individual meanings of the words which make up the expression.

For example:

They made us *pay through the nose*.

has nothing to do with noses. It simply means that we had to pay a very high price, far in excess of the real value.
If we say:

The European steel industry used to be a *lame duck*.

this has nothing to do with ducks that are paralysed. It means that this industry was unsuccessful and needed constant support.

Practice

a. Use the following idioms to complete the sentences. In one sentence there are two possible answers. Which one?
(If you do not know any of these idioms consult a good dictionary such as the *Longman Dictionary of Contemporary English*.)

in the red	*hard up*	*make ends meet*
like hot cakes	*at a price*	*money for old rope*
a hard bargain	*under par*	*an arm and a leg*
on stream	*foot the bill*	*on a shoestring*

1. He's risen to CEO but _____; his marriage and health are in ruins.
2. It's the third month in a row my bank account has been _____ and the bank manager is getting rather impatient.
3. He's been _____ recently – another victim of stress and the mid-life crisis!
4. Three hours a day in the office, hardly anything to do and a salary twice the national average – it's _____.
5. Many people say that it is up to industry and not the taxpayer to _____ when the environment is damaged by pollution.
6. I'm _____ this month – you couldn't lend me £200, could you?
7. It's difficult to _____ in a high cost capital city if you only have one salary.
8. The power station should come _____ by the end of the decade.
9. She drives _____ – she wants discount and payment at 180 days.
10. We have to run our department _____ – all the other departments get twice as much money for their budget.
11. We launched the new line two weeks ago and it's already selling _____.
12. The tunnel finally opened but it cost _____ to built it.

b. What do you understand by the following:

1. I don't think Richard is *pulling his weight*.
2. Exporting to a certain number of countries is made difficult by the quantity of *red tape*.
3. The strike was called off *at the eleventh hour*.
4. Manurfrance *went bust* in the 1970s.
5. Stop *splitting hairs*; you're looking for differences where there aren't any!
6. The job was *a piece of cake*.
7. *I wasn't born yesterday.*

8. The *dummy run* is scheduled for next week.

9. We're meeting again next week to *tie up loose ends*.

10. Whenever James and I go out in the evening we end up *talking shop*.

61 If

If introduces a condition – something may or may not happen depending on the circumstances.

■1■ If + present simple tense

1.1 *If* can be used to state a general rule:

If your documentation *is* incomplete the goods *are* held up.

1.2 *If* can also be used to speculate about the future consequences of a specific event. In this case, the verb in the second part of the sentence is preceded by *will*.

If our competitor *goes* bankrupt, we *'ll increase* our market share.

If they *offer* us a unit price of £3.50 we *'ll accept*.

In the above examples, the use of the present tense in the first part of the sentence indicates that the situation is *possible*; breaking into the Chinese market is seen as quite likely, the competitor could become bankrupt, and it's also fairly probable that they will offer a unit price of £3.50.

1.3 Note that it is incorrect to use *will* with the first verb; NOT * If they will offer us a unit price....

However, for invitations, it *is* possible to use *will* in the if-clause (the style is formal):

If you *will* come this way, Mr Evans *will* see you now.

■2■ If + past simple tense

This can be used to refer to less probable or impossible situations. The verb in the second part of the sentence is preceded by *would / should / could / might*:

If I *had* $10m I *could* invest in the telecommunications industry. (= but I don't have $10m)

If we *hired* a factoring agency we *would* recover our debts more easily. (This is an idea but it hasn't been tested in practice)

2.1 Note the difference between these two statements:

(a) If you *give* us 5 per cent discount we *'ll* make a firm order of 500 units. (This is almost a promise)

(b) If you *gave* us 5 per cent discount we *'d* make a firm order of 500 units. (This is still only a hypothesis)

3 If + past perfect tense

The above examples refer to present or future time. When talking about things which did not happen in the past (and the consequences if they had happened) we use *If + past perfect tense* together with *would / could / should / might* (+ *have* + *past participle*):

If we *had anticipated* the crash, we *wouldn't have lost* so much money.

If he *had had* more experience, we *might have offered* him the job.

If the tender *had been* lower we *could have won* the contract.

3.1 Note the use of *should* which can replace *if* in sentences like these:

Should you wish to revise your offer, we will give it our best attention.

I would very much like to see you again, *should* the occasion arise.

This is a variant of the structure:

If you wish to revise your offer, we will give it our best attention.

I would very much like to see you again, *if* the occasion *arises*.

3.2 If you want to be very formal you can even write:

If you should wish to revise your offer, we will give it our best attention.

Practice

a. The following dialogue is a discussion between two people about pricing. For 1–10 use the correct form of the verb in brackets. For 11–15 use words of your own choice.

A: ...... Yes I see, but if we cut our prices then they[1](*be*) cheaper than the competition and if our prices are cheaper, we [2](*sell*) more and we'll have a greater share of the market.

B: Perhaps, but if you [3](*reduce*) your prices, your competitors will do the same and you [4](*not have*) a greater market share at all. If all the companies making computer software like yours cut their prices, everybody's profit margins [5](*go down*). There's another thing. If you work to lower profit margins, then your shareholders [6](*not be*) pleased because if you [7](*make*) less profit, you'll have to reduce the final dividend. And if shareholders don't get a return on their capital, they [8](*not invest*). And if they don't invest you [9](*not have*) a company at all!

A: OK, we can raise prices.

B: Possibly, but if you put your prices up, you [10](*price*) yourselves out of the market. And if your competitors' prices are lower than yours, then you [11]_____ anything. And if you don't sell anything, you [12]_____ out of a job!

A: So we have got to make a decision. If we wait to see how the market reacts it [13]_____ too late. We have to lead the market.

B: Why don't you see Antonio tomorrow! Ask him if he thinks you can keep prices at their present levels. If he [14]_____ 'No' then I [15]_____ him myself.

b. Here are some unlikely situations. What would you do if any of them happened to you?

1. Your firm said you had to take a cut in pay.
2. You received an unsolicited order from Patagonia.
3. A letter announcing your dismissal unexpectedly landed on your desk.
4. You were invited to speak at a conference in London on 'Commercial Farming in Space in the twenty-first century: Risks and rewards'.
5. A competitor offered you a bribe to give away company secrets.

c. Last February a company bought a three-month option on the financial futures exchange to borrow at 10% for three months, based on the principal sum of £1 million. At the time the option was sold, interest rates were 10% and the option seller charged a premium of 1 per cent (£2,500). At the end of the three-month period (i.e. in May) interest rates were 12%. How much more interest would they have had to pay if they had not bought the option?

d. What would you have done if.......?
Think of some important turning points in your life e.g. a change of career, marriage, etc. In what way would things have been different if you hadn't done what you did?

62 Incoterms

1 *INCOTERMS* are a set of international rules published by the International Chamber of Commerce, Paris, for the interpretation of the most commonly used terms in foreign trade.
The aim is to avoid disagreements resulting from differences in trading practices in various countries by describing clearly the duties of the seller and the buyer.

2 The terms are grouped in four separate categories:

an E term: the seller makes the goods available to the buyer at the seller's premises and that is all

F terms: the seller has to deliver the goods to a carrier appointed by the buyer

C terms: the seller pays for carriage, but does not accept liability for loss or damage after shipment and dispatch

D terms: the seller bears all costs and risks in shipping goods to the country of destination

Group E Departure	EXW	Ex Works
Group F: Main carriage paid by the buyer	FCA	Free Carrier
	FAS	Free Alongside Ship *
	FOB	Free On Board *
Group C: Main carriage paid by the seller	CFR	Cost and Freight *
	CIF	Cost, Insurance and Freight *
	CPT	Carriage Paid To
	CIP	Carriage and Insurance Paid To
Group D: Arrival	DAF	Delivered at Frontier
	DES	Delivered Ex Ship *
	DEQ	Delivered Ex Quay *
	DDU	Delivered Duty Unpaid
	DDP	Delivered Duty Paid

* = reserved for Sea and Inland Waterway transport.

Practice

Read the descriptions of these INCOTERMS[1] and complete them with the correct name in each case:

1. _____ means that the seller's only responsibility is to make the goods available at his or her premises. The buyer bears the full cost and risk involved in transporting the goods to their destination.

[1] These descriptions provide the most important information about each term. They are not full definitions.

2. _____ means that the seller's obligations cease when the goods are made available to the buyer at a named place in the country of destination. The seller pays for customs formalities but not for customs duty. The term can be used for any mode of transport.

3. _____ (named place of destination) is the same as *CPT* but the seller also pays for insurance during carriage.

4. _____ (named port of shipment) means that the seller's obligations are fulfilled when the goods have been placed alongside the ship on the quay. The buyer is liable for all costs and risks of damage from that moment. Unlike *Free on Board* this term requires the buyer to clear the goods for export. The buyer is responsible for obtaining any export or import licence.

5. _____ (named port of destination). This term can only be used for sea and inland waterway transport. The seller must pay for the transport used to bring the goods to the named port but is not liable for risks from the moment the goods pass the ship's rail in the port of shipment.

In the case of roll-on/roll-off or container traffic, when the ship's rail is irrelevant, it is better to use the *CPT* term.

6. _____ (named place) means that the seller fulfils his or her obligation when the goods (cleared for export) are handed over to the carrier named by the purchaser. In the case of *rail* and *road* transport, delivery is completed when the goods have been loaded. For *sea* transport, delivery is complete when the seller has taken the goods to the transport terminal.

7. _____ is the same as *CFR* except that the seller has to arrange and pay for marine insurance for any risks during transit to the named port of destination.

In the case of roll-on/roll-off or container traffic, when the ship's rail is irrelevant, it is better to use the *CIP* terms.

8. _____ (named place of destination) means that the seller pays for transport to the destination. The risks and costs are then transferred to the buyer when the goods have been given to the carrier. This term is suitable for any kind of transport including multimodal transport.

9. _____ is the same as *DES* but the seller is also responsible for unloading the cleared goods onto the quay or wharf. The contract should make it clear whether or not the seller pays duty, VAT, etc.

10. _____ (named port of shipment). The goods are loaded on board by the seller at a port named in the contract. The risk of loss or damage passes to the buyer when the goods pass the ship's rail. The buyer is responsible for the transport costs from this port to the destination. However, it is the seller who has to obtain any export licence or documentation necessary for the goods to leave the country. In the case of

roll-on/roll-off or container traffic, when the ship's rail is irrelevant, it is better to use the *FCA* term.

11. _____ means that the seller's obligations are fulfilled when the goods have arrived at the frontier. It is recommended that contracts should specify which frontier, e.g. 'Delivered at Franco-Italian frontier (Modane)'. This term is most often used for rail or road transport but can apply to any mode.

12. The term _____ represents the seller's maximum obligation. All expenses are incurred by the seller until they arrive at destination. The term may be used for any mode of transport but is unsuitable if the seller cannot obtain an import licence.

13. _____ (named port of destination) can only be used for sea or inland waterway transport. The seller makes the goods (uncleared for importation) available to the buyer on board ship and bears all the costs and risks involved in bringing the goods to the port of destination.

63 Inversion

1 In a formal style, or for emphasis, words with a negative or restrictive force are placed at the beginning of a sentence. These include:

hardly	scarcely	seldom
little	only	never
not until	no sooner	rarely
under no circumstances		on no account

When these expressions begin a sentence, the normal order of subject and the auxiliary is reversed:

We have never before commissioned such an extensive survey.

→ *Never before* **have we** commissioned such an extensive survey.

Hardly **had the** guarantee expired when the machine broke down.

No sooner **had the** guarantee expired than the machine broke down.

Never **will we** allow our firm to be taken over.

Under no circumstances **can the deposit** be returned.

On no account **should goods** be sent without the correct accompanying documentation.

2 When there is no auxiliary, *do, does* or *did* is inserted. There is still inversion:

We seldom/rarely receive enquiries of this kind.

→ *Seldom/Rarely* **do we** receive enquiries of this kind.

Not until last year **did we** begin to show a profit.

Little **does she** realise that we were prepared to pay a higher price.

Only after three days of negotiations **did we** reach an agreement.

Practice

Re-write each of these sentences so that the meaning stays the same but the emphasis changes.

1. We did not suspect that they had filed a patent.
Little _____

2. It wasn't until two years ago that we decided to change our image.
Not _____

3. Bywater Inc. will not, under any circumstances, be liable for any incidental or consequential damages.
Under _____

4. I never imagined, on joining the firm, that I would one day become its president.
Never _____

5. I have seldom had the opportunity to speak to such a distinguished audience.
Seldom _____

6. You should, on no account, keep your code number and your credit card together.
On no account _____

7. The new drug was launched only after ten years of extensive testing.
Only _____

8. They started complaining as soon as we walked into the room.
No sooner _____

64 Last vs Latest vs Least

These words are used in a variety of ways and are commonly confused. These are the most common meanings.

This is the *last* time we do business with them – they are always late in paying. (= final)

She is *at last* beginning to understand that we need to up-date our image – but it's taken her 18 months. (= finally, and this is a relief)

You can see all our *latest* equipment at the trade exhibition next month in Frankfurt. (= most recent)

Please submit your tender by 30 April *at the latest*. (= not after)

We plan to sell *at least* 50,000 units by the end of the year – if not more. (= a minimum)

'Do you mind if I use your phone?' 'Not *in the least*.' (=not at all)

You may want to discuss the *least* important item on the agenda first.

(→ 33 Comparison)

How can managers encourage creativity in their staff? First, they should develop an acceptance of change. Employees must believe that changes will benefit them and the organisation. Secondly, managers should encourage new ideas and approaches. They should avoid the initial reaction of 'It won't work'. Thirdly, they should encourage employees to work together and exchange ideas. And *last but not least,* a good manager must be prepared to tolerate failure – not all ideas can be expected to work out. (= mentioned at the end but still important)

..... I would be grateful if you would tell me the price of 40 square metres of floor space. My firm would also like to know if it would be possible for you to provide the necessary stands and furniture. *Lastly*, we would need to know whether you can provide video equipment, slide projectors and so on. (= finally)

Practice

Complete these sentences.

1. Rexel was _____ profitable of our operations and we shut it down.
2. Come to the National Exhibition Centre and see all _____ state-of-the-art equipment.
3. They have _____ begun to realise that you cannot go on making cuts in expenditure forever.
4. There are a number of factors that have contributed to our good results. Firstly, we have benefited from a certain stability in the price of raw materials. Secondly, our investment in new plant has begun to pay off. Third, the fall in interest rates has boosted consumer spending. And _____, we must thank the loyalty and dedication of our workforce without whose efforts our firm could never be so successful.
5. 'Would you mind me using your office?' 'No, _____.'
6. The photographs will have to be ready for the end of the month _____, if we are to remain on schedule.
7. I can think of _____ three good reasons why we should encourage greater employee participation in decision-making.

65 Legal Language

In many firms, a knowledge of legal or semi-legal language is necessary as, inevitably, trading relations are confirmed through contractual arrangements.

1 Legal language contains its own jargon which has to be 'translated'.

Upon receipt of any order by the agent for goods the said agent shall immediately transmit the above-mentioned order to the principal who (if such order is accepted by the principal) shall execute the same by supplying the goods direct to the customer.

Upon receipt of any order:	when any order is received
the said agent:	the agent just referred to
shall:	must
transmit:	send, communicate
the above-mentioned order:	the order just referred to
if such order:	if this order
execute:	deal with, carry out
the same:	the order referred to

The essential message is therefore:
When the agent gets an order for goods he/she must send it off to the principal who will then supply the goods if he/she wants to.

2 Contracts often contain words formed of an adverb + preposition:

hereafter   herein   hereto   hereunder   thereof   thereby

These are useful for the kind of precise references which people in the legal profession have to make.

3 Many of the terms used are archaic or, if in current use, are very formal in their effect. This is a small selection:

as *deemed* appropriate by the court	(= judged, considered)
duly completed in triplicate	(= as expected, in the correct way)
in *compliance with* the regulations	(= in agreement with)
notwithstanding any amendments	(= despite)
null and void	(= invalid)
The committee *set forth* its findings.	(= described)
The agreement *terminates* on 30 June.	(= finishes)

Practice

a. 'Translate' these extracts into 'everyday' English.

1. Any dispute whatsoever which may at any time arise hereafter between the parties hereto or their respective representatives concerning the present contract and the interpretation thereof shall be referred to the International Chamber of Commerce in accordance with the provisions of Section G of the present contract or any subsequent legally valid amendment thereof.

2. I hereby declare and agree that if the goods described hereunder are not collected by me or any other person authorised by me in writing to collect the said goods on my behalf within a period of 30 days from this date it shall be construed that I have thereby renounced all further claim of ownership of the said goods on behalf of myself or any other person and consent to the goods being destroyed, or otherwise disposed of, as soon as practicable after the expiration of the aforementioned 30 day period.

4 Legal English can be difficult to read because the sentences are very long and contain many pieces of information. However, it is possible to separate the main idea from the others:

It shall be the duty of each person who has, to any extent, *control of premises* to which this section applies, or of the means of access thereto or egress[1] therefrom, or of any plant or substance in such premises, *to take* such *measures* as it is reasonable for a person in his position to take *to ensure,* so far as it is reasonably practical, *that the premises,* all means of access thereto or egress therefrom available for use by persons using the premises or, as the case may be, provided for the use there, is or *are safe, and without risk to health.*

The information not in italics is, of course, important but serves to expand or restrict the validity of the main ideas.

5 Many of the statements in legal English involve a 'condition':

If x then y ....

If the customer's representative should fail within 2 (two) weeks from the said notification by Duranor Pty to carry out an inspection as aforesaid or to formulate an objection if any in writing *then* the customer shall be considered to have taken over the plant and Duranor Pty shall be entitled to sign the Certificate of Acceptance on the customer's behalf.

[1] egress = exit

From a legal point of view, every action depends on one or more conditions which must be fulfilled before anything can happen.

Practice

b. Underline what seems to you to be the main idea in this paragraph.

If any person, in the course of any trade or business, gives, by whatever means, any false indication, direct or indirect, that any goods or services supplied by him or any methods adopted by him are or are of a kind supplied to or approved by Her Majesty or any member of the Royal Family, he shall, subject to the provisions of this Act, be guilty of an offence.
Trade Descriptions Act 1968 – 12 (1)

c. What condition must be fulfilled in the following paragraph? What will happen if it is/is not?

In case the said letter of credit is not accepted by Glanola plc within 3 (three) weeks after the date of this present contract, because the letter of credit is opened in conditions which are not in compliance with this present contract, then Glanola plc shall be under no obligation to perform their obligations under this contract and shall be entitled to consider this contract as null and void by simple notice in writing.

66 Let vs Leave

1 *Let* introduces the idea of permission; it is followed by a verb without *to*:

He *let* me go home early.

1.1 The past verb form and the past participle are both *let*.

1.2 *Let* is used in the very common expression *let* someone *know*:

I can't say just now, but I'll *let* you *know* at the end of the week.

1.3 *Let's* is used to make a suggestion:

Let's take a taxi. It'll be quicker.
Let's try an alternative approach.

1.4 People often say *Let's say* (= *Let us say*) when they want to introduce an assumption they are making:

So *let's say* we make £750,000 on the initial launch. That will give us enough capital to re-invest in a second promotion.

Let us suppose that inflation will continue to decline and that unemployment will rise.

2 If you *leave* a place or an organisation then you go away from it permanently:
She told me she had resigned and was about to *leave* the firm.

2.1 *Leave* means *depart*:
My flight *leaves* at 4 o'clock.

2.2 If you *leave* something somewhere it means you forget to take it with you:
I'm always afraid I'll *leave* my briefcase on the plane.

2.3 It can also mean 'postpone'.
Why do you always *leave* things until the last minute?

2.4 Note these common expressions:
He never *leaves* anything to chance.
Their organisation *leaves* a lot to be desired.
They *left* me to take charge of the arrangements.

3 The uncountable noun *leave* is a period of absence from work:
He's on sick *leave* until the end of April.

(→ 16, Allow vs Permit vs Let vs Enable, 59 Hire vs Rent vs Let vs Lease vs Charter)

Practice

Complete these sentences.
1. _____ it to me, I can get it done by Wednesday.
2. She's decided to _____; she says she can get twice the salary in the US.
3. I can't give you the figures now because I've _____ them in my office.
4. Don't _____ him take on too much work otherwise nothing will be done properly.
5. We do not want to _____ our competitors steal our market share.
6. _____ assume, for the sake of argument, that net profits increase by 5%.

67 Letter Writing

Look at the layout of this letter.

rhead {

CHARLES P. STEVENSON
Chairman of the Board

WADE STEVENSON II
President

ROBERT L. STEVENSON
Treasurer

Westman Export Corporation
EXPORTERS OF
Cloth Cutting Machines

General office & Factory
187 Washington Street
Buffalo, N.Y. 14203 U.S.A.

Telex 91-9141 EMCO BUF
Cable Address: EMCO
Telephone: 716-856 2200

ences {

Your ref : MV/rj 80
Our ref   : DL/sk 80/190-09

ver's
e and {
ess

Mr Michel Vega
Diffumatex S.A.
18 Rue St. Denis
75011 Paris
France

date { September 7 1991

ing
tation {

Dear Mr Vega,

y of {
er

We are pleased to advise you of our air parcel
post shipment of your order no. 80/190-09 for
Westman spare parts.

We are enclosing for your reference copies of our
commercial invoices as well as a copy of the
certificate of mailing.

We trust this shipment will reach you promptly
and in good order.

ng
ation {

Very truly yours,

ature {

Doreen Stevens

name {

Doreen Stevens (Ms)

tion {

Sales Manager

sure {

Enc: 3 Commercial invoices,
     1 certificate of mailing

1 Addresses

If the letter is written on paper without a letterhead, the sender's address is on the right-hand side.
It is not usual to write the sender's name above the address.
The name and address of the person receiving the letter are on the left.

2 Date

The date can be written in a number of ways:

September 7th   7th September
September 7   7 September

We do not usually write * the 7th of September or * September the 7th (although this is what we say).
In Great Britain 7/9/91 = 7 September: in the USA it means 9 July. Be careful!

3 Opening

There are several ways of starting a letter:

Dear Sir (to a man if the name is unknown)
Dear Madam (to a woman whose name is unknown)
Dear Sir/Madam (to cover both sexes)
Dear Mr Welsh (for a man)
Dear Mrs Todd (for a married woman)
Dear Miss Jones (for a single woman)
Dear Ms Smith (Ms does not reveal the marital status of a woman)

Note that we never write *Mister.

When writing to a firm begin: *Dear Sirs*. However, it is preferable to personalise your mail by writing to someone by name.
If you know the person well, you can of course use the first name (Dear James, Dear Sarah, etc.) but not both first name and surname. We would not write *Dear Sarah Jones.
Note also that we do NOT write *Dear Friend.

4 Closing a letter

There are a number of choices:
Yours faithfully (if the letter opens *Dear Sir, Dear Madam, Dear Sir/Madam*)

Yours sincerely (if you write *Dear + surname*)

Yours truly
Sincerely (yours) } are common (especially in AmE)
Very truly yours

Practice

a. Rearrange these items so that the letter is correctly laid out. Add anything that is obviously missing.

(i)   LGM / hp

(ii)   Presser UK Limited
       199 Knightsbridge
       London SW7 1RJ
       Tel: 071 586 5733
       Telex: 22498
       Fax: 071 586 9474

(iii) Linda Morgan (Mrs)

(iv)   Miss Juliette Rocache
       84 Ave du General de Gaulle
       91160 Longjumeau
       France

(v)   Yours sincerely

(vi)   Managing Director – Administration

(vii) Thank you for your letter of 6 May which has been passed on to me by Mr Webb.

       Mr Webb has asked me to inform you of your conditions of employment regarding Social Security arrangements. In cases like yours where we provide work experience facilities for overseas students, an individual is not covered by UK Social Security as he/she is not considered as an employee.

       If you have any questions to ask on this or any other matter, please do not hesitate to get in touch.

5 Useful expressions

STARTING A LETTER

Thank you for

We acknowledge receipt of	your letter	*of*	2 May.
Further to		*dated*	
With reference to			

I am writing to	*inform*
	advise you that ...
	tell

INFORMING

This is

| *I am pleased* to | *inform* you that ... |
| *I regret* | *advise* |

MAKING A REQUEST

Would you please	
Would you be so good as to	let me know as soon as possible.
Kindly	

I would be grateful
It would be appreciated } if you could ...

ENDING A LETTER
If you require any further information please do not hesitate to contact us.

I look forward to hearing from you } *soon.*
} *in the near future.*

We look forward to visiting you again shortly.
An early reply would be greatly appreciated.

Practice

b. Complete this fax using some of the 'useful expressions' above.

```
        FACSIMILE NUMBER  :  64 8 356 1874

TO  :  MR STRAZZULLA

TOTAL NUMBER OF PAGES INCLUDING THIS  :  1

- - - - - - - - - - - - - - - - - - - - - - -

¹_____ a recent order of ours
arrived in a damaged condition and has been
pillaged.

We duly made a claim on the insurance
purchased by you but ²_____ that the
claim has not been settled.

Settlement has been delayed for several
reasons but principally because GLOBAL
Transport has gone into liquidation.

We have recently learnt that IPP, our present
insurer, had accepted our claim and paid
compensation to GLOBAL even though they were
in liquidation. However, none of this money
has ever been passed on to us.

³_____ contact GLOBAL or their
liquidators to attempt to recover the money
owing to us.

⁴_____.

Yours truly,
```

68 Liable to vs Liable for vs Responsible to vs Responsible for

1 If something is *liable to* happen then it is likely to happen:
If customers are late paying you're *liable to* face a cash flow problem.

1.1 If you are *liable to* legal action then you are in a position whereby legal proceedings can be started against you:
You are in breach of contract and legally *liable to* the loss of the contract fee.

1.2 *Liable to* also means 'officially due to be paid':
All imports are *liable to* duty.

2 If you are *liable for* something you are legally *responsible for* it:
My partner and I are jointly and severally *liable for* any debts.

3 If you are *responsible for* someone or something then you have the necessary authority and control:
She's *responsible for* making sure orders are processed on time.

3.1 If you are *responsible for* a situation then you are the cause and are answerable for it:
I'm not *responsible for* this mess; it's not my fault.

4 You are *responsible to* someone who is directly above you in the organisation and to whom you are accountable:
I'm just a supervisor and I'm *responsible to* Mr Trent, my line manager.

Practice

In your job:

1. Who are you responsible to?
2. What are you responsible for?
3. If you refuse to carry out an instruction at work what is liable to happen?

69 Likely to vs Bound to

1 Both these expressions refer to probability

most likely	*bound to* (99% certain)
↓	*likely to* (+ 75%)
	may (50%)
least likely	*unlikely to* (less than 15%)

They're being taken over by the market leader so the price of their shares is *bound to* go up.

If you go to Britain you're *likely to* go inside a pub.

Albania is *unlikely to* join the Common Market in the near future.

Practice

Comment on the probability of these situations (for your country or others).

1. Videophones will replace standard telephones in most offices.
2. The majority of clerical staff will work from home.
3. The rouble will replace the dollar as the world's major hard currency.
4. The maximum rate of interest a bank can charge will be set at 5 per cent p.a.
5. Telexes will no longer be sent.
6. All firms will, by law, have to provide child-minding facilities for working mothers.
7. The majority of senior managers will be women.
8. The retirement age will be 55.

There is no key to this exercise.

70 Linking Words

Whether in speech or in writing, you help people to understand your message by clearly connecting one idea to another. The words and phrases that do this are like signposts on a journey and make it easier for the listener/reader to find his/her way.

1 Sequencing

1.1 This extract lists the advantages of using the services of an advertising agency for a small firm. Note how the ideas have been sequenced.

First of all, an agency can bring substantial resources to a campaign. The experience of its staff is gained through working for many clients and involves a wide range of product fields. *Secondly,* a major agency will have contacts with the main media companies and is in a good position to know of new developments likely to affect a client's business. *Thirdly,* there is intense competition between agencies which helps ensure agency staff give of their best. This rivalry may, *in addition,* lead to a cheaper cost to the client. *Finally,* an external organisation is in a good position to look at a firm's advertising needs from the outside, in an objective light.

1.2 When describing a procedure we can use *First of all, then, when, after, next...*

HOW TO USE THIS PHOTOCOPIER

First of all, connect the machine to a power supply and switch on. *Then* leave the machine to warm up for a couple of minutes. *When / After* the WAIT light has gone off, lift the cover and place your original on the glass plate. *Next,* close the cover and select the number of copies you require. *Finally,* press the COPY button. The machine will automatically make the number of copies requested.

2 Adding information

We have already seen the use of *in addition* (1.1). Here are two other ways of adding ideas:

Third World governments are having serious problems owing to the rise in the dollar and galloping inflation. *Furthermore / Moreover,* the interest on their debt represents a constant drain on their resources.

Note that these words are typical of a formal style.

Practice

a. This chart illustrates the basic steps in decision-making. Write a short paragraph to accompany the chart, using appropriate linking words.

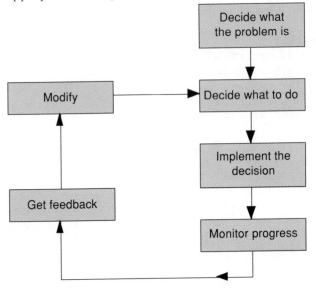

b. THE STAGES OF A CAMPAIGN.

Below are a number of events leading up to an advertising campaign. They are not in the right order.

Write out the correct sequence using the appropriate linking words.

_____ senior representatives of both the agency and the client meet for a more detailed briefing, a definition of the image and thoughts on the target public.

_____ the campaign is released on TV, radio, billboards and selected magazines.

_____ the creative teams are briefed, the media are chosen and an initial concept is selected.

_____ approval by the Board the exact budget is agreed on and the finishing touches are put to the campaign.

_____ the advertising manager for the client company meets the agency's account executive for a preliminary discussion. They talk about objectives, possible media, and the approximate budget.

_____ they have finished working on a campaign outline they submit the overall campaign strategy to the client company's Board of Directors.

3 The following text is an extract from a report. It is about a fairly technical subject – the construction of container handling facilities at a port – but it can be read by the non-specialist. As you read, decide whether the words in *italics* introduce a reason/result, a contrast or an example. Write the numbers in the space provided.

CONSTRUCTION OR ADAPTATION: THE CHOICE FOR A SMALL PORT

Background

This paper concerns a small port in the Eastern Mediterranean handling over 500,000 tons of cargo, and the choices it faced in coping with greater containerisation of cargo traffic. *Although* (1) the alternatives described were specific to the port, the general problem, *i.e.* (2) how to cater for a significant change in the mode of handling cargo at minimum cost, is faced by many ports in developing countries.

The costs and benefits are in S.D.R.s (Special Drawing Rights), the measurement used by the I.M.F. to measure the value of a 'basket' of currencies, and *thus* (3) avoid the effects of changes in the value of a single currency.

reason / result: _____
contrast: _____
example: _____

The Problem

The port consists of several piers for loading minerals, and a number of quays that can accommodate four medium-sized vessels. One of the piers is no longer used for loading minerals *owing to* (4) the exhaustion of the mineral deposits and the quays, *because of* (5) their narrow and light construction, are not suitable for handling containers carrying heavy equipment.

The problem faced by the port was how to cater for the increasing trend towards containerisation. *Since* (6) the port had a long undeveloped shore line, a traditional solution consisting of reclaimed land of about 3.5 ha and the construction of a new 270m quay, in 11.5m depth of water was considered. The estimate for reclaiming land was above the normal cost for such work on *account of* (7) the lack of suitable construction materials. Construction time was estimated to be more than three years *due to* (8) interruptions caused by ship movements. *Consequently* (9), *despite* (10) being visually impressive and operationally attractive, this solution proved to be unjustified financially *as a result of* (11) the rather modest rate of projected shipping increases over the next ten-year period.

reason / result: _____
contrast: _____
example: _____

An alternative solution

Therefore (12), a lower cost solution, preferably implemented in a shorter space of time, had to be found and attention was turned to the unused pier. Structurally, it was in good condition and was suitable for second generation container ships.

However, (13) there was a problem; the pier was only 13m wide and it was necessary to widen and strengthen the existing structure. It was also necessary to obtain additional vehicles to move containers over longer distances than is usual in a container port. Other structures (*for instance,* (14) sheds and warehouses) were to be the same as for the conventional scheme. Construction time was estimated to be less than two years and cost estimates for the modified pier were low enough to make it a viable solution.

reason / result: _____

contrast: _____

example: _____

3.1 Other ways of making a contrast

No satisfactory rules for motivating an organisation's personnel have ever been found. *Nevertheless/Nonetheless/Even so,* it is the duty of every manager to provide the incentives to motivate staff to do their best.

Some people see privatisation as a good thing *while/whereas* others see it as the unjustified sale of a collective asset.

It is easy to confuse 'motivation' and 'incentive'. Motivation is essentially an attitude of mind and is internal. Incentive, *on the other hand,* is an external reward to encourage an improved performance.

Practice

c. Complete the following short newspaper article using:

however   as a result   despite   due to

BPL's printing division yesterday announced its first annual loss for 23 years and said that, [1]_____, it would not be paying a dividend for the current 12 months.

BPL's problems have been created by substantial disruption and strain on resources [2]_____ the opening of a large new factory, increased competition and high interest rates.

[3]_____, the other two BPL divisions were trading profitably [4]_____ suffering tighter margins.

d. Complete this paragraph using:

however   because of   as a result   furthermore

Not too long ago, many American firms had little or no interest in exporting [1]_____ the complexities involved. Today, [2]_____, international business represents a major part of their total sales volume and profits. By selling world-wide, they can improve economies of scale in production, marketing and distribution. ³_____, the exporter can spread fixed costs over more products which reduces production costs and increases profits. ⁴_____, lower costs can mean a lower sales price that can, in turn, open up new markets.

e. This is the final part of the report on page 132. Complete it using appropriate expressions of *result* and *contrast.*

<u>Conclusion</u>
¹_____ of its higher capacity the quay solution would generate higher benefits from about year six onward. ²_____ it must also be pointed out that the pier solution is much less expensive and would be operational at least one year earlier, ³_____, benefits would flow sooner.
⁴_____ the quay would have a rate of return of 10 per cent that is unacceptable in a country where the opportunity cost of capital is usually considered to be in the region of 12 per cent. ⁵_____ the pier solution, with a rate of return of about 16 per cent, would seem to be preferable.

f. Below is a memo on the subject of office re-organisation. Choose the correct linking words.

FROM   J.A. King   Date 5 Oct
TO   A. Tolsen   RE Staffing

I have several suggestions concerning office reorganisation. ¹(*First / As a result / Nevertheless,*) I propose that we move Mrs Sinclair into the accounts department to help Mr Banks ²(*consequently / since / although*) there have been a number of complaints from staff that pay slips have been late and certain payments have not been processed as soon as they should have been. ³(*In addition / Secondly / Despite this*) Mr Banks has been requesting extra staff for some time.

⁴(*Secondly / Consequently / However*) I suggest we take on a temp over the summer period to handle incoming telephone calls and enquiries in the mail order section. ⁵(*Owing to / Moreover / Although*) the volume of orders has not increased the new computerised system has proved to be more time-consuming than anticipated. ⁶(*Consequently / For example / Next*) Mrs Kereasky and Mrs Davies have had more work to do than they can cope with.

⁷(*However / Thirdly / Thus*) I recommend that we take on a new order clerk in the sales department. A number of errors have been made recently ⁸(*owing to / despite / while*) a lack of available staff at peak times.

I am aware that these changes will involve extra expense. ⁹(*Finally / On the other hand / Furthermore*) they will, I believe, save money in the long run in terms of increased efficiency.

71 Make vs Brand vs Trademark vs Logo vs Patent vs Copyright

Brand and *make* are very similar words and refer to the names of products.

1 *Make* tends to be used to refer to the name of the firm that produces the product. The product itself is usually one that requires assembly.
Indesit is a *make* of washing machine.
Mercedes is a German *make* of car.
There are hundreds of *makes* of micro-computers.

2 A *brand* is not necessarily the name of the manufacturer:
Unilever markets many *brands* of washing powder and foodstuffs.
Supermarkets often sell goods under their own *brand*.
Camel is a famous *brand* of cigarettes.

> **2.1** However, the expression *brand name* identifies a group of products sold by the same firm:
> Miele is the *brand name* of a line of household appliances.
>
> **2.2** Note the expression *brand new* (= completely new).

3 The *trademark* is the word or symbol that a manufacturer always uses on a product or range of products to distinguish them from others. It is usually registered and protected by law.

4 The *logo* is the symbol, design or special way of writing a company uses on its products, notepaper, advertisements, etc. This word is very similar to *trademark*. However, we would probably prefer the word *logo* when referring to an emblem or purely pictorial representation.

5 Any intellectual property can be protected. Most firms will take out a *patent* for industrial designs or inventions and *copyrights* can be obtained for literary, musical or artistic work. The *Paris Convention for the Protection of Industrial Property* sets minimum standards and is recognised in about 100 countries.

Practice

Comment on the following.

For example

Coca-Cola and *Coke* are registered trademarks.

72 Make vs Do

The choice of *make* or *do* is best learnt as part of a fixed expression and not from an analysis of the meaning which is often given as:

do (= activity as in 'I'm doing my best'.) or
make (= creation as in 'The firm makes aircraft engines'.)

In many cases such an analysis is far from clear.

1 The following is a list of common expressions that could be used in a business context.

Make	Do
an application	business
arrangements	an experiment
a cancellation	someone a favour / a good turn
a choice	a job
a complaint	justice to
a concession	repairs
an effort	wonders
a loss	the + noun + ing
a mistake	(e.g. *do* the filing)
an offer	something for a living
a phone call	
preparations	
progress	
a request	

2 If you *make do* with something you content yourself with what is second best:

We haven't got any champagne so we'll have to *make do* with sparkling white wine.

Practice

You may need a dictionary for this exercise.
Make or *do*? Organise these words into columns.

a suggestion	a profit	a decision	research
an enquiry	the typing	a speech	an investment
an appointment	damage	business	a bid

73 Meetings

1 Study the meanings of these words. Decide which ones to use to replace the blanks in the practice section. (You may need to change the form of the word slightly.)

AOB:	any other business, items not originally included on the agenda.
adjourn:	stop a meeting for a short time
agenda:	a list of points or *items* for discussion
casting vote:	if there is a deadlock (e.g. three for and three against a motion: the chairperson may vote to ensure that a decision is made
consensus:	a general agreement on a subject
convene:	call a meeting
minutes:	the written record of a meeting
motion:	a proposal to be discussed and voted on
proxy:	a proxy vote is made on behalf of someone else (if permission has been obtained)
power of attorney:	permission to act on someone else's behalf

Practice

a. Complete this paragraph using the words and phrases above.

Before the Chairperson [1]_____ a meeting he/she should circulate an [2]_____ so that everyone knows what items are to be discussed. At the beginning of the meeting the [3]_____ of the previous meeting are confirmed. Then, those present discuss each [4]_____ on the [5]_____ and try to reach a [6]_____ view. If an issue is important a vote may be taken; those absent may have given [7]_____ to someone present and can therefore vote by [8]_____. In the event of a deadlock the Chairperson may record a [9]_____ so that a decision is made.

2 The word *meeting* can be combined with many different verbs. You can:

adjourn
attend
call
cancel
convene ⎫ *a meeting*
hold
interrupt
postpone

3 **Useful expressions**

There are many things that can be said at a meeting. Here are some useful expressions that can be used.

STARTING A MEETING
Shall we begin?
The first item on the agenda is...

MAKING YOUR POINT
I would like to point out that....
In my opinion...

TAKING THE FLOOR
If I could just come in here...
I'd like to go back to...

AGREEING
I agree that...
I would go along with you on that.

DISAGREEING
I'm sorry, I disagree...
I agree with you to some extent, but...

CORRECTING MISUNDERSTANDINGS
I don't think I quite made myself clear.
That's not quite what I meant.

ASKING FOR MORE INFORMATION
Could you be a little more specific?
Could you give us further details?

AVOIDING RESPONSIBILITY
I don't have all the information to hand...
I can't comment on that at this stage...

POSTPONING
Can I come back to that (later)?
Let's leave that until (later/next week..).

COMING TO THE END OF A MEETING
So to sum up...
Is there anything else you want to discuss?

Practice

b. Here are some more expressions that can be used during a meeting. Match them to the headings in 3 on p.137.

1. Sorry to interrupt but....
2. Let's get this meeting under way.
3. I really don't think that's on.
4. Is there any other business?
5. I'd like to emphasise the fact that....
6. I couldn't have said it better myself.
7. We seem to be talking at cross purposes.
8. It's very difficult to make a decision now.
9. I'm not sure I understood the point about....

74 Money

1 In Great Britain the currency used is the pound sterling. (£)
In the USA (and many other countries) the currency is the dollar. ($)

£1 = 100 pence (p): $1 = 100 cents (¢)

Note that the sign goes **before** the figure.

(→ 36 Currencies)

2 When speaking about sums of money we say:

$1.35	*a dollar thirty five* (or *one thirty five*)
$3,000	*three thousand dollars*
five cent coins	*nickels*
ten cent coins	*dimes*
twenty-five cent coins	*quarters*
fifty cent coins	*half dollars*
50p	*fifty p, fifty pence* (NOT * pences)
£1.99	*one (pound) ninety nine*

Note that we do not add 'and' between the figures representing pounds/dollars and pence/cents.

Nor do we mix figures and words; the following are wrong:

NOT * £39 ninety nine   £Twenty five   457 dollars

3 The separation of units of a thousand can be made by using a comma (,) or with a blank:

FF 365,027,968.80 = *three hundred and sixty five million twenty seven thousand nine hundred and sixty eight francs eighty centimes*

4 It is customary to place the currency sign before the figure:

DM16.7bn   *FF140m*   *L1,200bn*   *HK$2,500*   *Y9,000*   *£250*

5 A sum of money is used with a verb in the singular:

These days £50,000 *is* not a large sum of money.
Why *was* US$115.69 paid in addition to the ocean freight?

6 It is now common to see the abbreviation *K*:

$100K (a hundred thousand dollars)

Practice

Write these out as you would say them.

1. $1.45
2. £8.50
3. $199,000
4. £352.29
5. $75.50
6. £225,000,000
7. 89p
8. $354.50

75 Money Movements

1 There are many verbs which can be used to describe upward or downward movements of money or numbers in general:

UP		DOWN	
boost	go up	go down	decrease
increase	rise	drop	fall

1.1 Small movements could be expressed using:

ease up/down   *edge up/down*   *firm*   *creep up*   *slip back*

1.2 More dramatic movements would need these verbs:

UP	*jump*	*rally*	*rocket*	*soar*	*surge*
DOWN	*collapse*	*plunge*	*plummet*	*slash*	*slump*

2 It is also possible to use an adverb:

Sales in Japan rose *slightly*.

Sales in Scandinavia went up *steadily*.

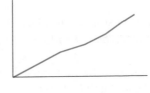

Sales in Great Britain went up *sharply*.

3 Some of these verbs have corresponding nouns:

an increase   *a rise*   *a boost*   *a surge*
a decrease   *a drop*   *a fall*   *a collapse*   *a plunge*   *a slump*

These words are followed by *in:*

There was a sharp *increase in* sales tax.
Following a *slump in* demand we had to shut down a plant.

4 If there has been little or no movement we could say that:

The market has been
} morose.
slack.
sluggish.
gloomy.
stagnant.
steady.

Sales
} peaked.
levelled off.
bottomed out.

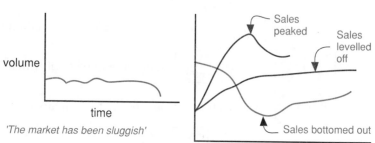

Sales
peaked

Sales
levelled
off

volume

time

'The market has been sluggish'

Sales bottomed out

4.1 If there has been more activity:

The market has been
} active.
buoyant.
firm.

4.2 A record high or low figure can be referred to as an *all-time high* or *an all-time low.*

5 There are a number of verbs of restriction which are useful when talking about reductions:

Expenditure has been *cut (back)/curbed/scaled down/trimmed.*

Practice

a. Decide whether the following statements represent *no* movement at all, a *slow* movement or a *rapid* one. Write N, S or R.

1. The plummeting dollar has boosted American exports. ( )
2. Sales have been stagnant. ( )
3. There has been a surge in the number of complaints. ( )
4. Imports have risen somewhat. ( )
5. There has been a slight increase in production costs. ( )
6. The glut in the market has caused prices to slump. ( )
7. Home sales have slipped back. ( )
8. Prices are likely to remain steady overall. ( )
9. The price of gold eased back by the end of the day to $423 an ounce. ( )
10. Coffee futures edged up yesterday. ( )
11. Euro-Disney shares went up sharply to 113p. ( )

b. Complete the passage using an appropriate expression to replace the graphs.

Last year was a bad year for commodity prices. The commodity

price index [1] throughout January and February

reaching an [2] in mid-March. Prices then started to

[3] and [4] until the end of April, when they

[5] again with disastrous results for commodity

producers. Despite a [6] in May the situation

worsened again in June and prices [7] once more to

another [8] at the end of July. Prices remained stable

for the rest of the summer and even [9] during the

period September–November, before [10] yet again at

the end of the year.

76 Must vs Have to vs Need vs Should

1 *Must* is used to refer to either present, general or future obligation. It does NOT change form (* musting and * musted are impossible) and it cannot be used with *to*.

Candidates, male or female, *must* be engineering graduates.
All employees *must* have a medical check-up every year.
We *must* try to improve our results next year.

> **1.1** *Must* is used when an order is imposed by an *official authority* (as for example, in a legal arrangement) or when an obligation is *self-imposed*.

Prices *must* be firm and not subject to escalation for any reason.
Helmets *must* be worn on the shop floor.

I *must* remember to write to Mr Parker, I keep forgetting.
I *must* say that I don't agree with you on this point.

1.2 *Must not* is used to indicate that something is forbidden:

Passengers *must not* smoke during take-off.
Unauthorised personnel *must not* go beyond this point.

2 *Have to* suggests a more external obligation than *must*.
Compare:

(a) Sandra *has to* find another job, her firm has closed down.
(b) Sandra really *must* get another job. Her present salary is much too low.

In (a) 'objective' circumstances have forced Sandra to find another job.
In (b) the statement is the speaker's personal recommendation.

3 The difference between *must* and *have to* is not always obvious and they are often interchangeable:

The articles of association state that our auditors *must/have to* provide a valuation of the company's shares every six months.

Anyone receiving a crossed cheque *must/has to* pay it into a bank account.

4 *Do/does not have to* is used when there is no obligation:

She's an EC citizen so she *does not have to* have a work permit to find employment in another EC country.

If your current account stays in credit you *do not have to* pay bank charges.

4.1 The question is *Do/Does + subject + have to:*

Do we have to do all this paperwork?

5 *Must* is preferred when a point needs emphasis and in speech, the word is stressed:

We *must* face the fact that the world's natural energy reserves are running out – before it's too late.

In a modern company, management *must* realise that secretaries are now in a position to make decisions that have traditionally been taken by executives.

6 When referring to a past necessity, *had to* is used:

Increases in the price of raw materials meant that we *had to* raise our prices last year.

Sales were failing and we *had to* rethink our marketing strategy.

6.1 The negative form, meaning 'there was no necessity', is *did not have to:*

We used to be a nationalised industry with a monopoly of production and *didn't have to* worry about competition.

6.2 The question form is *did + subject + have to:*

Did you *have to* lower the price?

7. *Will have to* is used for future necessity:

Next year we *will have to* reduce staffing levels.

Practice

a. Read this advice given by the Department of Trade and Industry to overseas businessmen wishing to export to the UK. What rules *must* they observe? What *must* they *not* do? When do they *not have to* pay duty?

Customs Duties

Manufactured goods from EC member countries are admitted free of duty. Most goods originating in member countries of the European Free Trade Association (EFTA) are also admitted duty free subject to evidence of origin.

For other countries, rates are given in the official 'Customs & Excise Tariff & Overseas Trade Classification in the UK', published by Her Majesty's Stationery Office.

Excise duties are imposed mainly on tobacco, hydrocarbon oils, liquor, beer and wine.

Tariff classification

Importers are required to state on the customs entry form the tariff classification or the duty liability of the goods they import. Failure to do so may result in overpayment of duty which could go undetected.

Temporary importation

Facilities exist for a number of goods to be temporarily imported free of import charges. These include:

> Commercial samples
> Goods for test, experiment or demonstration
> Goods for approved exhibitions
> Professional equipment
> Tourist publicity material

Restrictions

Generally, the importation of firearms, ammunition, endangered species, most live animals, meat and poultry, therapeutic substances and narcotic drugs is prohibited without authorisation.
For certain goods originating, in specified countries an import licence issued by the DTI is required.

b. When you started your present job you probably had to fill in a number of forms and follow an administrative procedure. What exactly did you have to do?

■8■ *Need* is a semi-modal; i.e. like other modal verbs it is followed by the infinitive without 'to' and can go before the subject in a question:

You *needn't* come into the office tomorrow.
Need we go to the meeting? (formal style)

But, unlike other modals, it is also used as an ordinary verb:

You *don't need* to come into the office tomorrow.
Do we *need* to go to the meeting? (neutral style)

> **8.1** In positive statements, the ordinary verb form is used when a need is imposed externally:
>
> You *need* to obtain a visa in order to visit China.
> (NOT * You need obtain...)
>
> **8.2** *Need* can be followed by a *gerund* or *to be + past participle:*
>
> If the government wants to encourage the creation of small businesses, interest rates *need* ⎱ *to be cut.*
> ⎰ *cutting.*
>
> **8.3** Note the difference in meaning between *needn't have + past participle* and *didn't need to + verb.*
> Compare:
>
> We *needn't have made* anyone redundant; after all, the order book was full. (i.e. some people lost their jobs even though it was unnecessary)
>
> We *didn't need to make* anyone redundant; luckily the order book was full. (i.e. no one lost his/her job because it was unnecessary)

Practice

c. Rephrase each statement using *need.*

1. It isn't necessary for you to get a consular invoice.
2. The procedure is too complicated and should be simplified.
3. Is it really necessary to fill in these forms in quadruplicate?
4. It wasn't necessary to take a taxi because we had arranged for him to pick us up at the airport.

5. There was no point sending a technician, so we didn't. They repaired the machine themselves.
6. We took on extra personnel, but there was no reason to because we're overstaffed already.
7. I wasted two hours redesigning the layout of the company magazine and it wasn't necessary at all.

9 *Should* is used to express a moral obligation or duty, and to make recommendations; it expresses a weaker obligation than *must:*

All developed countries *should* contribute a proportion of their GNP in aid to the Third World.

We *should* try to involve staff more in decision-making.

9.1 The negative form is used to criticise:
Managers *should* not accept bribes, in my opinion.

9.2 As *should* is used to give advice, it is not surprising to find it in sentences containing the verbs *suggest* or *recommend* or in a sentence beginning *If I were you:*
I suggest that we *should* meet next week to discuss terms and conditions.

If I were you I *should* sell those shares as soon as possible before you lose a lot of money.[1]

9.3 *Should* is also used in clauses following adjectives such as *advisable, essential,* etc:
It is *advisable/essential/important/necessary/vital* that she *should* be present.

9.4 To make a criticism of an action that took place in the past, *should have + past participle* is used:
I *should have sold* my shares before the Stock Market crash.

(→ 108 Should vs Would)

Practice

Before you do this exercise revise the use of *may*
(→ 26.)

d. Read the ***Conditions of Service*** and decide whether an employee *may, must* or *should* do the following things:

For example:
1. Every employee is obliged to give his/her services uniquely to the firm.
Every employee must give his/her services uniqely to the firm.

[1] In the US, **would** is more common.

CONDITIONS OF SERVICE

1. Every employee is obliged to give his/her services uniquely to the firm.
2. Employees are required to live within a radius of 80 kms from the place of work.
3. All employees are required to contribute 6 per cent of their gross salary to the company pension scheme.
4. Although no specific holiday periods are laid down, staff are expected to take their main holiday during the summer months.
5. Sick leave is allowed and paid according to current government regulations. There is an annual maximum of 90 days' sick leave with pay.
6. It is essential that notification of sickness be sent together with a medical certificate after 48 hours' absence.
7. Retirement is compulsory at the age of 65. However, employees are entitled to retire on reaching the age of 60, subject to appropriate notice being given.
8. The employer and/or the employee are entitled to terminate an appointment after one month's notice given on either side.
9. It is understood that an employee applying for another post will keep the company informed.
10. Employees have the right to appeal against dismissal.

---

77 Naming and Greeting

1 It is often difficult to recognise first names and surnames and know exactly how to address people.

For example, it may not be easy to know which is the first name and which is the surname for these people:

Hui Chzi-Hon　　*Boutia Eynour*　　*Romain Poteau[1]*
Mohammed el-Khalifa

1.1 In English, when giving or writing your name it is best to put the first name before the surname, even if this is not what you normally do.

---

[1] Chzi-Hon, Eynour, Mohammed and Romain are the first names. Hui, Boutia, el-Khalifa and Poteau are the family names.

2 A person from another country will often be unable to tell whether a name is masculine or feminine. When signing a letter it is therefore a good idea to indicate your status by using Mr/Mrs/Miss or Ms[1] as appropriate.

> Yours truly,
>
> *Jane Wyman*
>
> Jane Wyman (Mrs)
> (Marketing Manager)

3 The titles *Mr/Mrs* etc. are not used with the first name only; therefore *'Hello, Mr John' is incorrect.

4 When talking to or writing to someone who you do not know well it is better to use the surname: e.g. 'As *Mr Balloch said...*'; *'Dear Mrs Weston'*. When you know someone better you can start using the first name. Exactly when depends on people and circumstances. In the USA, it is common to use the first name relatively quickly.

5 In speech, use *Sir* or *Madam* only if you are, or wish to put yourself, in a position of inferiority. For example, a waiter would say, 'Would you like to order now, *sir/madam?*

Greeting

1. When meeting someone for the first time say *How do you do?* The reply to this is *How do you do?*
It is common to say *Pleased to meet you.*

2. If someone asks *How are you?* he/she wants to know about your health or mood. Common replies include *Fine thanks./very well[2]/OK./All right./So so./Awful.* It is polite to ask the same question with *And you?*

3. Some greetings depend on the time of day and the social context:

RELATIVELY FORMAL

Good morning. (up to 12.00)
Good afternoon. (from 12.00 – 18.00)
Good evening. (from 18.00 – about 22.00)
Goodbye. It was very pleasant meeting you.

Note that we only say *Good night* when leaving someone in the evening or in the small hours.

---

[1] Ms (pronounced / mz /) does not reveal the marital status of a woman. [2] We often reply positively even when we feel terrible, especially in a formal situation.

RELATIVELY INFORMAL

Hi! / Hello. / Morning.
See you. / So long. / All the best. / Take care. /Bye. (informal)

Practice

Match the greetings and the responses:

1. Good night.	a. Hello.
2. How do you do?	b. No problems.
3. How are you?	c. Yeah, see you tomorrow.
4. Hi.	d. Thanks, it's great to be here.
5. How was the flight?	e. How do you do?
6. Welcome to Greece.	f. Fine thanks. And you?

78 Nationality Words

1 With the name of each country there is also a name for the nationality and the language:

She's from *Portugal,* she is *Portuguese* and speaks *Portuguese.*

Note that all countries, nationalities and languages begin with a capital letter.

2 When referring to one individual or several people from a particular country we use *a* and *the:*

He's *an Italian* entrepreneur.
The Italians are famous for their textiles.

3 Nationality words have a certain regularity as can be seen from the examples below: sometimes the name of the language is different.

COUNTRY	NATIONALITY/ LANGUAGE	THE PEOPLE (Singular)	(Plural)
-an			
America	American[1]	an American	the Americans
Belgium	Belgian[2]	a Belgian	the Belgians
Egypt	Egyptian[3]	an Egyptian	the Egyptians
Germany	German	a German	the Germans
Hungary	Hungarian	a Hungarian	the Hungarians

[1] Technically, the Americans speak English though some people talk of American as if it were significantly different. [2] The languages are Flemish or French.
[3] The language is Arabic.

COUNTRY	NATIONALITY/ LANGUAGE	THE PEOPLE (Singular)	(Plural)
Norway	Norwegian	a Norwegian	the Norwegians
Russia	Russian	a Russian	the Russians

-ese

China	Chinese[1]	—	the Chinese
Japan	Japanese	—	the Japanese
Portugal	Portuguese	—	the Portuguese
Vietnam	Vietnamese	—	the Vietnamese

-i

Iraq	Iraqi[2]	an Iraqi	the Iraqis
Israel	Israeli[3]	an Israeli	the Israelis
Pakistan	Pakistani[4]	a Pakistani	the Pakistanis
Saudi Arabia	Saudi[5]	a Saudi	the Saudis

-ish

Britain	British	a Briton	the British
Denmark	Danish	a Dane	the Danes
Finland	Finnish	a Finn	the Finns
Poland	Polish	a Pole	the Poles
Scotland	Scottish[6]	a Scot	the Scots
Spain	Spanish	a Spaniard	the Spanish[7]
Sweden	Swedish	a Swede	the Swedish
Turkey	Turkish	a Turk	the Turks

-sh, ch

England	English	an English(wo)man	the English
France	French	a French(wo)man	the French
Holland	Dutch	a Dutch(wo)man	the Dutch
Ireland	Irish[8]	an Irish(wo)man	the Irish
Wales	Welsh[9]	a Welsh(wo)man	the Welsh

Argentina	Argentine[10]	an Argentinian	the Argentinian
Czechoslovakia	Czech	a Czech	the Czechs
Greece	Greek	a Greek	the Greeks
Switzerland	Swiss	—	the Swiss
Thailand	Thai	—	the Thais

[1] The languages are (among others) Cantonese and Mandarin. [2] The language is Arabic. [3] The language spoken is Hebrew. [4] The national language is Urdu. [5] The language is Arabic. [6] English is the main language. A small minority speak Gaelic. [7] 'The Spaniards' is less common. [8] The nationality is Irish. The main language is English, but some people speak Gaelic. [9] Welsh is spoken by a minority. English is the main language. [10] Spanish is spoken.

Practice

Answer the following questions

a.

Name six countries in	The Middle East.
	Latin America.
	Eastern Europe.
	The Far East.
	Africa.

b. What countries belong to the EC?

c. What language(s) do they speak in:

Switzerland	The Netherlands	Algeria
Mexico	Singapore	Ivory Coast

d. *Fujitsu* is a *Japanese* firm. Its headquarters are in *Japan*. What can you say about the following:

Olivetti	ICL	Philips	Nestlé
Perrier	Saab	Nokia	Daimler-Benz AG

79 Noun formation

1 Nouns can be formed in a variety of ways, notably from verbs. Some of the common suffixes are:

promo**tion**	deci**sion**	manage**ment**	deliver**y**
exhibi**tion**	conclu**sion**	employ**ment**	enquir**y**
weak**ness**	reliabil**ity**	engineer**ing**	distributor**ship**
effective**ness**	productiv**ity**	train**ing**	partner**ship**
prefer**ence**	perform**ance**	break**age**	
refer**ence**	insur**ance**	stor**age**	

2 A frequent way of forming nouns is by adding *-ing* to a verb. The noun or noun phrase may be in subject or object position:

Training is essential for a flexible labour force.
Breaking into a foreign market needs careful preparation.
I dislike *writing long reports*.

3 Nouns referring to people can be formed with *-er, -or, -ian, -ee, -ant, -ist*

employ**er**	supervis**or**	technic**ian**	train**ee**
bookkeep**er**	audit**or**	electric**ian**	employ**ee**
consult**ant**	typ**ist**		
account**ant**	machin**ist**		

Practice

a. Complete each sentence with the appropriate word. If you do not know the correct form, use a good dictionary (e.g. *The Longman Dictionary of Business English* and/or the *Longman Dictionary of Contemporary English*).

1. REMIT   Please return the form together with your _____.

2. APPLY   The ad attracted 230 _____.

3. LEAK   The batteries were damaged because of acid _____.

4. DEBT   A _____ is someone who owes money.

5. CONSIGN   The _____ is the name of the person goods are sent to.

6. ROTATE   Job _____ is sometimes used as a way of training managers.

7. CONFUSE   The transfer pricing policy has led to a lot of _____.

8. CORRESPOND   All _____ should be marked 'Strictly confidential'.

9. SIGNIFY   We have yet to see the _____ of the merger on our operations.

10. INVEST   An _____ in a unit trust is a good idea for a small careful saver.

11. SPONSOR   _____ is a good investment as an image-builder.

12. MASTER   It is very rare to achieve complete _____ of a foreign language.

b. *Situations vacant:* Complete each job advertisement with the title of the post. The first letters of the words are given. If in doubt, use as dictionary.

1.

BUSINESS SYSTEMS CONS_____

required to advise a small firm in evaluating, developing and implementing new office technology.
These developments are

2.

EUROPEAN   LIAISON
&
RESEARCH OFF_____

Applicants should be suitably qualified in economics or a related discipline

3.

INTERNATIONAL OIL INDUSTRY

SENIOR NEG_____

This new position has been created as a result of recent reorganisation and

4.

GRADUATE SURV_____

You are aiming to develop your career in the property industry. We are looking for someone who

5.

Suitable Distr_____

sought to promote sales of wooden household articles in The Netherlands on an exclusive basis

6.

ACCOUNT DIR_____
Advertising

We're a £7m agency with plans to triple our billings over the next five years. We're looking for a bright, young person to

7.

```
Software Eng_____ s and
Technical Prog____ s
```

Vacancies available for graduates with at least two years' experience in any of the following languages:

Fortran **Algol** **C**
Pascal **Cobol** **Ada**

4 Some nouns are identical to the verb (though not always in pronunciation). This is a selection:

delay   supply   sponsor   claim   benefit
offer   budget   lack   support   share

Words which change their stress include:

NOUN	VERB
_trans_fer	trans_fer_
_im_port	im_port_
_ex_port	ex_port_
_pro_duce	pro_duce_
_re_cord	re_cord_

Practice

c. Make nouns from these verbs and insert them into the letter below. Use each word once. Be careful of plurals.

sell   record   enquire   promote   deliver   advertise
exhibit   complain   expire   agree   perform   distribute
decide   compete   manufacture

This is just to note the ¹_____ made at our last meeting.

(a) We need to make a greater effort in terms of ²_____ in order to combat the increasing ³_____ from other ⁴_____. To this end we will be running a new ⁵_____ campaign at the International ⁶_____ in November.

(b) A ⁷_____ will be kept of all ⁸_____ and these should be followed up systematically.

(c) All ⁹_____ must be made promptly to ensure we minimise customer ¹⁰_____.

(d) A new ¹¹_____ ¹²_____ will be negotiated on ¹³_____ of the present contract. In return for a better ¹⁴_____ on your part we will allow a further 0.5 per cent commission on total ¹⁵_____.

80 Noun Combinations

Two or more nouns can be combined in a number of ways:

1 's possessive

When two nouns are connected by an *'s* they often correspond to a sentence with *have*, e.g.

the M.D.'s office	=	The M.D. has an office
the firm's strategy	=	the firm has a strategy
Mr Blake's secretary	=	Mr Blake has a secretary

1.1 In general, we use *'s* when the first noun is a person (e.g. *an executive*) or a group of people (e.g. *a committee*):

an executive's responsibilities   the committee's decision

In many cases, the second noun can easily be transformed into a verb:

the report's conclusion	=	the report concluded
the committee's decision	=	the committee decided

1.2 The *'s possessive* is also used when the first word refers to a time:

next week's meeting   today's paper

or a place (+ *superlative expression):*

the city's tallest building   Germany's biggest factory

1.3 Note too the *'s* when referring to sums of money + *worth:*

We bought 10 million dollars' worth of cocoa on the spot market.

1.4 When the possessive pattern includes several words, the *'s* is added to the word which is immediately before the main noun:

I'll see you in an hour or *so's* time.
That's someone *else's* seat.

2 *Noun used as adjective*

It is very common to use nouns as adjectives by placing them before other nouns. The last noun is the most important; the first noun tells us something about it and often answers the question 'What kind of...?'

a recruitment ⎫
a marketing ⎬ *policy*
an insurance ⎭

Here are some common examples:

an assembly line	*a bank account*	*export growth*
stock control	*factory prices*	*a trade deficit*
a department store	*a disk drive*	*wealth tax*

2.1 When a noun is used as an adjective it is nearly always singular:

a *slide projector*   (= a projector for showing slides)
an *instruction manual*   (= manual which gives instructions)
a *hotel chain*   (= a chain of hotels)

2.2 Numerical adjectives are also singular, e.g.

a *50-pound note*   a *three-day week*   a *four-star hotel*
a *10-dollar bill*   a *five-man team*   a *six-lane freeway*

2.3 However, the *s* is kept in the following expressions:

a *needs analysis*   a *clothes store*
an *accounts department*   a *sports car*
a *savings account*   a *sales policy*
the *futures market*   an *overseas branch*
a *means test*   a *works manager*
a *customs officer*   a *goods train*
a *prices and incomes policy*

3 -of phrases

3.1 We tend to use the '*of* structure' with inanimate nouns or abstract ideas:

They sued us for *breach of contract.*
A final *draft of the amendments* will be circulated soon.
It was the *beginning of the end.*
She's written a book on the *history of advertising.*

3.2 *Of* is also used with words such as *bit, piece,* etc. to indicate 'a certain quantity' or 'one of a group':

I've a *bit of good news* to tell you.
I'd like a *piece of information.*
Do you have a *sheet of paper?*

4

Sometimes it is possible to use two of the constructions to express the same relationship:

a *reduction in price*   =   a price reduction
an *account at a bank*   =   a bank account
the *company's strategy*   =   the strategy of a company
an *executive's responsibilities* =   the responsibilities of an executive

On other occasions only one structure is possible:

a *disk drive*   (NOT *a drive of disk / a disk's drive)
an *assembly line*   (NOT *a line of assembly / an assembly's line)

Mr *Blake's secretary*   (NOT *the secretary of Mr Blake / Mr Blake secretary)

a letter of credit	(NOT *a credit letter / a letter's credit)
a breach of contract	(NOT *a breach's contract / a contract breach)

Practice

a. Match each noun in the left column with the appropriate one from the right.

For example: press release

press	circle
television	capital
venture	form
quality	flow
takeover	margin
application	rate
exchange	chart
profit	bid
balance	release
retail	commercial
pie	outlet
cash	sheet

b. Each of these words *bank, work, pay* and *trade* can combine with *three* only of the following. What are they?

force	fair	union	holiday	loan	note
place	rise	mark	award	man	claim

c. Rephrase these descriptions:

1. a motorway with four lanes
2. a bank loan worth fifty million francs
3. a team with six men in it
4. a week made up of thirty-nine hours
5. a project lasting six months

d. Only one of the following (a), (b), or (c) is an acceptable noun combination. Choose the correct one.

1. (a) an expense's account
   (b) an account of expenses
   (c) an expense account
2. (a) a gifts' voucher
   (b) a voucher of gifts
   (c) a gift voucher
3. (a) a Bill's Lading
   (b) a Bill of Lading
   (c) a Bill Lading

4. (a) last month's figures
    (b) the figures of last month
    (c) last month figures
5. (a) Mr Young's assistant
    (b) the assistant of Mr Young
    (c) Mr Young assistant
6. (a) career's opportunities
    (b) opportunities of career
    (c) career opportunities
7. (a) a shoe's store
    (b) a store of shoes
    (c) a shoe store
8. (a) a letter's resignation
    (b) a letter of resignation
    (c) a resignation letter
9. (a) a five-year's plan
    (b) a plan of five years
    (c) a five year plan
10. (a) a settlement of pay
    (b) a pay's settlement
    (c) a pay settlement
11. (a) the company's future
    (b) the company future
    (c) the companies future
12. (a) a breach of contract
    (b) a contract's breach
    (c) a contract breach
13. (a) our sale policy
    (b) our sales policy
    (c) our policy of sales
14. (a) The AGM of last year
    (b) last year AGM
    (c) last year's AGM

5 Sometimes three or more nouns are combined. However, it is not good practice to combine more than three because it can be difficult to work out the meaning. For example, does:

management team members

refer to (i) members of a management team *or* to (ii) team members who are part of management *or* to (iii) members of management who form a team?

The answer is likely to be (i) but it is difficult to know without a context.

Other examples of three word compound nouns include:

public relations department   (= a department dealing in public relations)

machine tool store	(= a store for machine tools)
parts replacement guarantee	(= a guarantee for the replacement of [spare] parts)
car production costs	(= costs involved in the production of cars)
air traffic controller	(= a controller of air traffic)

Longer noun phrases can be made, such as:

a Social Security rebate claim form	(= a claim form for Social Security rebates)
an advertising agency design studio	(= a design studio in an advertising agency)
a winter sports insurance premium document	(= a document about insurance premiums for winter sports)

However, it is not a good idea to combine so many nouns. Four should be an absolute limit.

6 *Prepositional phrases*

A phrase consisting of *noun + noun* can often be reformulated by using a prepositional phrase or a relative clause:

a conference centre	= a centre used for conferences
a bank loan	= a loan made by a bank
a research project	= a project which involves research
a container ship	= a ship for containers
a market survey	= a survey of the market
a price reduction	= a reduction in price

Practice

e. What do we call them?

Supply the names corresponding to the following definitions.
For example: The department which deals with invoices and pay roll.
The Accounts Department
1. An account in which you can deposit money and earn interest. The opposite of a *current account.*
2. A list which gives details of prices.
3. A visit which lasts two weeks.
4. A chart which shows the positions people occupy in an organisation.
5. A team of people who try to increase sales.
6. A person whose job it is to ensure goods do not enter a country illegally.
7. A trip which is undertaken for business.
8. An analysis of needs in relation to training.

9. A survey which does research into the behaviour of consumers.

10. Forecasts which relate to the storage of raw materials.

f. Rewrite the following using a prepositional phrase or a relative clause.

For example: a telephone message: a message which is taken over the telephone

1. a trade fair
2. a hotel guest
3. export sales figures
4. construction machinery
5. income tax
6. a 10 year bank loan
7. a buyer credit report
8. a computer screen protector
9. an export credit guarantee
10. consumer opinion poll results

g. Complete the letter using the following noun combinations:

enrolment form	*conference timetable*	*leather industry*
Footwear Trade Fair	*conference date*	*Exhibition Centre*
design specialists	*Conference Organiser*	
export opportunities	*Industry Training Board*	

Dear Sir/Madam

We are pleased to invite you to the 12th [1]_____ to be held at the National [2]_____ from 6–13 June.

This annual event, organised by the Boot and Shoe [3]_____ brings together [4]_____, manufacturers and retailers involved in the [5]_____, both at home and abroad. It is therefore the ideal moment to learn more about [6]_____.

Please find the [7]_____ on the enclosed document. A reminder will be sent nearer the [8]_____. In the meantime you are invited to complete the [9]_____ and send it back by 30 April. In the event of over-enrolment your place will be assured.

Luang Pang
([10]_____)

81 Packaging

Good packaging is essential because it ensures that goods arrive at their destination in good condition. Therefore, the choice of packaging must suit the product, the means of carriage, handling facilities and any changes in climate during transport.

In some countries, import duties are assessed according to the gross weight of shipments, which includes packaging. Therefore, the heavier the packaging the higher the duties will be.

Practice

a. Label the pictures.

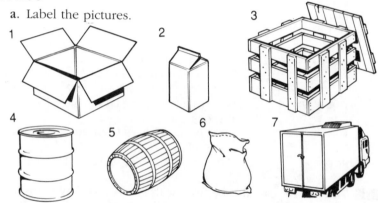

b. Match the consignments to the type of packaging.

1. drum	grain
2. sack	diesel engines
3. refrigerated container	wine
4. crate	beef
5. barrel	sulphuric acid

c. Match these expressions to the symbols.

use no hooks   *radiation*   *this way up*
keep dry   *dangerous chemicals* *fragile*

1.   2.   3.

4.   5.   6.

82 Passive vs Active

1 Passive verb forms are made with the verb *to be + past participle*.

Tea *is* grow*n* in Sri Lanka.
Microprocessors *are* produc*ed* in Silicon Valley.
Skoda cars *are* manufactur*ed* in Czechoslovakia.
Uranium *is* min*ed* in Australia.

2 The form of the verb *to be* (together with *have* or *will*) indicates the tense:

PRESENT SIMPLE	Coffee *is* grown in Kenya.
PRESENT PROGRESSIVE	The production line *is being* automated.
PAST SIMPLE	He *was* appointed a year ago.
PAST PROGRESSIVE	The matter *was being* discussed when he arrived.
PRESENT PERFECT	*Has* Mr Welsh *been* informed?
PAST PERFECT	She arrived an hour late but it was all right as the meeting *had been* cancelled.
FUTURE SIMPLE	The shop steward *will be* informed of any changes.
FUTURE PRESENT	The product *will have been* launched by the end of the year.
INFINITIVE	400 workers *are to be* laid off in the Autumn.

3 The passive can also be used with modal auxiliary verbs:

Do you think the plan *can be implemented* fairly soon?
A new switchboard *could be installed*.
Premiums *might be increased*.
He said more information *would be obtained*.
The top copy *must be signed and returned* immediately.
She *should have been consulted* earlier.

4 To see WHY we use the passive compare these sentences:

The Personnel Manager *interviews* candidates.
Candidates *are interviewed* by the Personnel Manager.

The auditors *inspect* the accounts once a year.
The accounts *are inspected* by the auditors once a year.

In each sentence the grammatical subject provides the topic of the sentence. The focus of attention changes from *The Personnel Manager* in the *active* sentence to *Candidates* in the *passive* sentence and from *The auditors* to *The accounts*. The word *by* tells us who performed the action.

5 Sometimes we are not interested in **who** performs an action or it is not necessary to know. Compare:

They *hold* the meeting on Monday morning.
The meeting *is held* on Monday morning.
Someone *delivers* essential components to the factory.
Essential components *are delivered* to the factory.

It would be very unusual to add 'by them' or 'by someone'.

Practice

a. Match the product and the country of origin. There may be more than one answer.

For example: Wine is produced in France and the USA.

Beer		
Cocoa		Japan
Gold	brew	China
Perfume	grow	South Africa
Rice	manufacture	The USA
Ships	produce	France
Tobacco	build	Scotland
Wheat		Ghana
Wine		
Whisky		

b. Rewrite the following sentences in order to make the word in *italics* the topic. Decide whether or not it is important to include *who* performed the action.

1. We are offering *an attractive price reduction.*
2. They completed *the survey* last month.
3. The company provides *free medical insurance* for all employees.
4. She sent *a copy of the report* yesterday.
5. Someone has translated *the contract* into Arabic.
6. A team of consultants is investigating *the problem.*
7. We will offer *an attractive salary* to the person appointed.
8. In normal circumstances, the exporter should clear *the goods for export.*
9. They have cancelled *the 14.45 flight to Rome.*
10. They were holding *talks* last night at the Union's headquarters.

6 The passive is very often used when we describe a **process** or a **procedure** because we are less concerned with **who** has done something than with **what** is done. For example, read this description of an export transaction involving a British firm and an Australian one:

First of all, the goods *are sent* to a port and *loaded* on board ship. They *are inspected* and if everything is fine, a 'clean' Bill of Lading *is signed* by the captain and a copy *sent* to the exporting firm. Then a Bill of Exchange requiring the Australian firm to pay on a future date *is drawn up* by the British firm and *presented*, together with the insurance certificate and the B/L, to a British bank. Next, the documentation *is sent* to the Australian bank. At this stage the B/E *is accepted* by the importer who is now *given* the B/L and is able to collect the goods when they arrive and pay his/her bank on the due date.

Note that *is/are* do not have to be repeated when the second verb (e.g. *loaded/ presented)* follows 'and'.

Practice

c. The life story of a cheque. See page 165.

Imagine a man called Mr White owes Blacks plc a sum of money. If he has an account at Bank B and the firm an account with Bank A what happens to the cheque he makes out? Complete the blanks with the following verbs:

credit   send   draw   exchange   deduct   pay
sort   put   send on

First of all, when Blacks plc receives the cheque it [1]_____ into Bank A and [2]_____ to the firm's account. Then, at the end of each working day all the cheques which [3]_____ on other banks [4]_____ and [5]_____ to Bank A's headquarters. Here they [6]_____ into piles together with cheques from other Banks (B, C, D, etc.) and [7]_____ to the clearing house where all the cheques [8]_____. Bank B's headquarters now sends Mr White's cheque back to Bank B (where he has an account) and the sum [9]_____ from his account.

7 Changes of state and completed actions are described using the *present perfect passive:*

He *has been promoted* to the post of Sales Manager.
The photocopier *has been repaired*.
The disciplinary procedure *has been modified*.
The meeting *has been cancelled*.
The offices *have been redecorated*.

The life story of a cheque

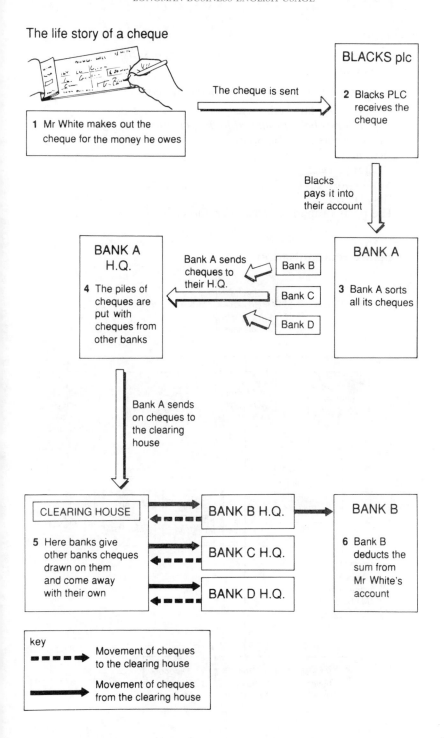

1 Mr White makes out the cheque for the money he owes

The cheque is sent

BLACKS plc

2 Blacks PLC receives the cheque

Blacks pays it into their account

BANK A H.Q.

Bank A sends cheques to their H.Q.

Bank B

Bank C

Bank D

BANK A

3 Bank A sorts all its cheques

4 The piles of cheques are put with cheques from other banks

Bank A sends on cheques to the clearing house

CLEARING HOUSE

5 Here banks give other banks cheques drawn on them and come away with their own

BANK B H.Q.

BANK C H.Q.

BANK D H.Q.

BANK B

6 Bank B deducts the sum from Mr White's account

key
- - - ► Movement of cheques to the clearing house
——► Movement of cheques from the clearing house

Practice

d. There has been a reorganisation at the *Starspot* advertising agency in Manchester.

Look at the two organisation charts and complete the following:

For example: Mrs Hall _____
Mrs Hall has been promoted to the position of Media Head.
Mr Chambers and Mrs Shaw _____
Mrs Patel _____
Mr Hunt _____
A new position of _____
Miss Jay _____
The posts of market researcher and creative researcher
_____

Before reorganisation

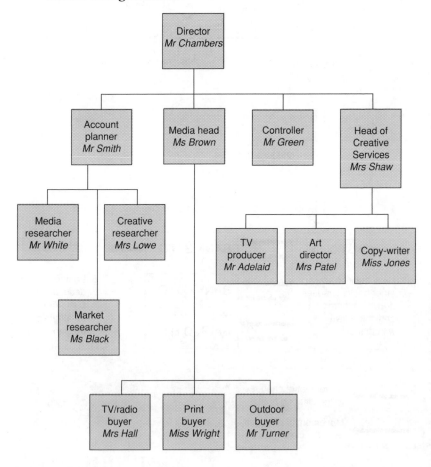

After reorganisation

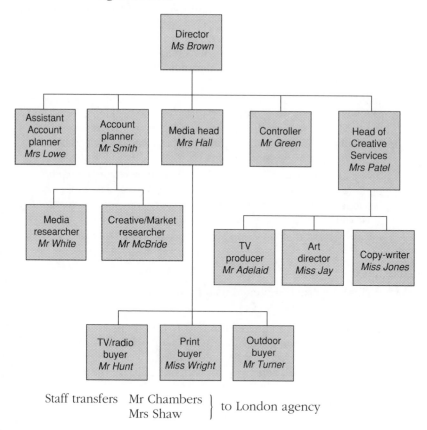

Staff transfers   Mr Chambers ⎫
            Mrs Shaw   ⎬ to London agency

8 Some verbs can have two objects, e.g.

They have sent *him a brochure*.
They showed *me their new machine*.
She offered *us the contract*.

When these sentences are transformed into the passive it is usual to begin the sentence with a personal pronoun:

He has been sent a brochure.
We were shown their new machine.
We were offered the contract.

9 When writing in a formal business style, more emphasis is placed on the message itself than the writer. In other words the style is *impersonal*.

An impersonal style is achieved by using the passive and, in particular, by beginning sentences with *It...*

Here is an example from the minutes of a meeting held in an advertising agency:

Blank Space presented four designs for the proposed new packet. The first of these *was considered* to be too dull and the second and the third *were rejected* because *it was felt* they were too similar to those of our competitors. The design which *was chosen* emphasises the value for money aspect of the product.

It was recommended that considerably more research *should be undertaken* to test consumer reaction. *It was agreed* that this *would be done* by Dr Williamson and his team. A report *would be presented* in November when the MD had returned from Malaysia.

It was decided that the fee for Dr Williamson *would be fixed* at £5,000.

Practice

e. Re-write each sentence using a personal pronoun and a passive construction.

1. Nobody told me a decision had been taken.
2. The committee gave him a week to reach a decision.
3. Mr Weston asked her to send a telex.
4. The board will send you an official reply by the end of next week.
5. She showed them how to pack the goods.
6. The firm paid me my expenses.

f. Below are the words that were spoken during a meeting. Using an impersonal construction, re-write what was said as you would for the minutes.

For example:

'I think we should introduce a self-assessment procedure.'
It was thought a self-assessment procedure should be introduced.

1. 'So we all think that expenditure on entertainment is excessive.'
2. 'Both Mr Williams and myself feel we should spend more on training.'
3. 'I hope we can do more to attract suitably qualified staff.'
4. 'I think it would be a good idea to extend the probationary period.'
5. 'We all agree we need to respect schedules.'

6. 'I feel, and so do many of us, that low prices do not always attract customers.'

7. 'I suggest that we should improve our corporate image.'

g. The following is a tapescript of what was said at a meeting. Read through the transcription and then complete the minutes appropriately.

JOHN MORTON   Now the first item on the agenda is...er...the projected sales of our *Newlook* line on the UK market. Jennifer, could you tell us what you think?

JENNIFER ADAMS   Well, everybody I've spoken to feels the whole *Newlook* range is market-tired and needs a whole new marketing approach. What do you think?

LUCY POOLE   I agree. Take the *Gem* mixer, most people consider it to be completely out of date. In my opinion we should launch a fully integrated food processor which can function as a juice extractor, slicer, mixer, sauce maker and so on.

PETER MOSS   Good idea.

JOHN MORTON   Yes, I think so too. And I recommend we package the whole thing attractively and advertise it heavily in women's magazines and so on. But first of all, we should test it out on the market to judge consumer reaction.

JENNIFER ADAMS   Who by?

JOHN MORTON   Oh, the *Starspot* agency is reliable.

JENNIFER ADAMS   OK so I'll produce a package design before the end of the month and I'll present a full report to the MD of what we've discussed when he gets back from Germany.

Jennifer Adams presented reactions to the *Newlook* line. In general ¹_____ that the range was market-tired and a new ²_____.

In particular, the *Gem* mixer ³_____. After some discussion ⁴_____ that a fully integrated food processor ⁵_____.

⁶_____ that the equipment ⁷_____ and ⁸_____ in women's magazines after appropriate test marketing. ⁹_____ that this ¹⁰_____ by *Starspot*.

Finally, a new package design ¹¹_____ by the end of June. A full report ¹²_____ on his return from Germany.

83 Past Perfect vs Past Perfect Continuous[1]

Look at this passage:

In 1991 Jane Wilson decided to use the money she *had inherited* from her father – a rich farmer – in the commercial rather than agricultural sector. After she *had paid* death duties (a tax on inheritances) she invested the capital in premises on the outskirts of London and set up a recruitment agency for firms wanting to headhunt promising young executives. By 1993 her turnover *had grown* to £3 m and she moved to new offices in the City. A year later she married the man she *had hired* as her PA and from that moment her business started to go into decline.

1 The *past perfect (had + past participle)* is used to show that one thing in the past happened before another thing in the past. In the above passage she made the decision to invest after she had inherited the money; her business had grown before she was able to move to more expensive premises; she hired a man and subsequently married him.

> **1.2** It is not always necessary to use a *past perfect* if the order of events is obvious or made clear by a linking word like *before* or *after*.
> *After* she paid death duties she invested most of the capital.
> (she *had paid* is possible, but unnecessary)
> Our research scientists thoroughly tested the drug *before* it was launched onto the market.
> (*had tested* is possible, but unnecessary)

2 The order of the two parts of the sentence is not important:
Before we concluded the deal we *had spent* thirty hours in delicate negotiations.
We *had spent* thirty hours in delicate negotiations before we concluded the deal.

3 The *past perfect* is used in reported speech after *said* or *told:*
She told me she *had dealt* with the problem already.

4 The *past perfect continuous* is used when we want to emphasise the duration of the event which preceded another:
I *had been trying* to get through for an hour before I was finally able to speak to him.
I*'d been thinking* of moving for a long time and then I got a job at ICL.

[1] Sometimes called Past Perfect Progressive.

4.1 Compare these two sentences:

(i) When I saw him he *had been redesigning* the packaging.
(ii) When I saw him he *had redesigned* the packaging.

In sentence (i) the activity is perhaps unfinished;
in sentence (ii) it is definitely finished.

Practice

a. Use the *past simple,* the *past perfect* or the *past perfect continuous* to complete this passage about a particularly tiring day at work.

Last Monday morning at 9.30, after I ¹(*deal with*) the mail, I ²(*go*) to a finance meeting but our accountant ³(*not prepare*) the relevant figures so that ⁴(*be*) a waste of time. Then I ⁵(*see*) Polly. Apparently, she ⁶(*ask*) to see me all week about a personal problem. I ⁷(*spend*) an hour with her. She said she ⁸(*see*) the Personnel Manager already but he ⁹(*tell*) her to see me! She explained that she ¹⁰(*have*) a lot of trouble with Mr Harris who apparently treats her unfairly. After that I ¹¹(*see*) three customers, one of whom ¹²(*say*) he ¹³(*not receive*) an order and I ¹⁴(*have to*) investigate that. I ¹⁵(*find out*) that the despatch department ¹⁶(*not send*) it off. A 'computer error'. Then I ¹⁷(*go*) to a planning meeting. Sales ¹⁸(*be*) a lot worse than we ¹⁹(*forecast*) probably because our competitors ²⁰(*launch*) a very similar product just three months prior to our own. And so it went on. I ²¹(*leave*) the office at 7.00 physically and mentally worn out. And when I ²²(*get*) home I suddenly ²³(*realise*) that I ²⁴(*not eat*) all day.

b. This passage is about a success story in an area of Britain particularly affected by high unemployment.

Use these verbs and decide whether to use *the past simple, past perfect* or *past perfect continuous* in each case.

grab	lose	be (x 5)	launch
become	listen	disappear	encourage
spend	close	have	join

In 1982 Ironworks ¹_____ its huge steel plant in the industrial heart of the North East. This ²_____ not an isolated moment of disaster for the region as jobs ³_____ since the mid-70s, but it ⁴_____ a major blow to the local economy and by 1984 over a quarter of the town's men and woman ⁵_____ their jobs.

It ⁶_____ into this economic climate that Phillipa Miles and Tony Peters came with the firm conviction that there ⁷_____ a gap in the slimming foods market waiting to be filled. Peters [8]_____ years in marketing with a food manufacturer, Miles [9]_____ a successful career in international advertising. The financiers [10]_____. The local Industrial Development Agency which [11]_____ set up to help create businesses in the area also [12]_____ the project. Immediately 350 jobs for redundant iron workers [13]_____ available in the manufacture of low calorie foods and drinks. Originally aiming for a turnover of £1.5m, that figure has grown to more than 10 times that amount, with a phenomenal growth of 35% a year. By 1990, Peters [14]_____ a large slice of the slimming foods market in the UK. And in 1991 they [15]_____ a new product-line – low calorie crisps and snacks. These products really hit the market after Peters and Miles [16]_____ forces with Robert James, Managing Director of the Northern Brewery. As a result of this partnership they now have access to the vast £2.5 billion-a-year pub food market and their slimming snacks may well turn out to be a feast.

84 Past Simple[1] vs Present Perfect

1 The *present perfect* unites past time and present time:

Prices *have risen* by 10 per cent over the past year.

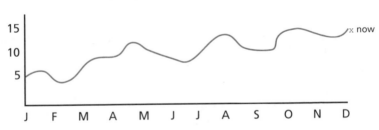

I *have been* in my present job for three years.

Three years ago   now

working in the same job.

[1] Sometimes called Simple Past.

The economic situation *has improved*.

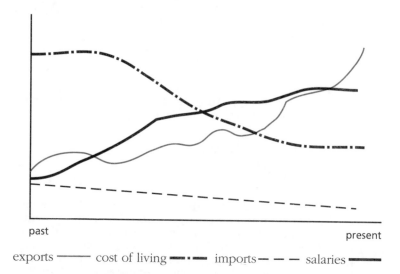

past   present

exports ——— cost of living ▬▪▬ imports — — — salaries ▬▬

In these examples the situations described began in the past and have continued up until now.

2 The *past simple* is used with time expressions referring back to a finished period of time:

I **saw** Mr Roberts *yesterday*.
I **was** in Venezuela *three weeks ago*.
She **worked** in Japan for *four years, from 1985 until 1989*.
I **met** Ms Turner *when I was in Melbourne*.
As I **wrote** in *my letter of 5 May...*
We **did** not **produce** semi-conductors *in the sixties*.

3 If the time expression means 'at any time up to now' the *present perfect* is used:

It's the first time I *have ever flown* by helicopter.
We *have sold* 25,000 units *so far*.
She *has never been* to Algeria.
To date, they *have succeeded* in gaining 15 per cent of the market.
We *have* not *contacted* them *for over* a year.
Unemployment *has not been* so low *since 1982*.

4 Study this letter. The verbs in *italics* are all in the *present perfect*. As you read, answer these questions:

When did they move to new premises?
When did they decide to close the office in Brussels?
When did they make arrangements for more telephone lines?

Dear Sirs,
We are writing to inform you that we *have moved* to our new premises at the following address:

> 300/12–13
> Suttshiarn Square
> Rachadapisake Street
> Huay Kwang
> Bangkok

We *have decided* to close our Brussels office owing to a decline in our European activities. As a result, Mr Bhumibhark *has returned* to Thailand and is no longer our director for Benelux countries.
Our P.O. Box and TLX number *have not changed*. At present, we have only one telephone line at our disposal but *have made* arrangements for more lines to be installed shortly.
Please contact us at the above address in future correspondence.

The answer to the questions is 'Don't know'. The verbs give us information about the present situation and **not** when the events took place. But it is important **now** to know about these events.

5 Compare this letter:
Do any verbs refer to events which took place at a specified moment in the past? Are there any associated time expressions?

Dear Mr Murphy,
I am pleased to confirm the phone conversation we *had* last week. I *have* now *received* your letter placing a trial order for 3 000 flashlights. As requested we *have sent* you a pro-forma invoice and are waiting for the Letter of Credit.
I *spoke* to Mr Muller yesterday and you will be pleased to learn that he *has agreed* to a 5 per cent discount on any repeat order.

Yes, *had* and *spoke*. Yes, there are associated time expressions: *last week* and *yesterday*. These refer the reader to the events which took place in the past.

Practice

a. Look at the charts and then complete the text with the appropriate time expressions.

so far this year *never*
since 1988   *at the end of December*
over the past month *during the past 12 months*
last month   *a year ago*

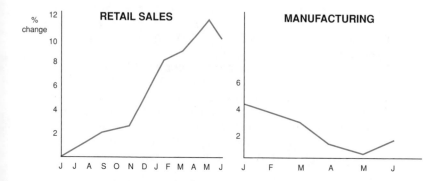

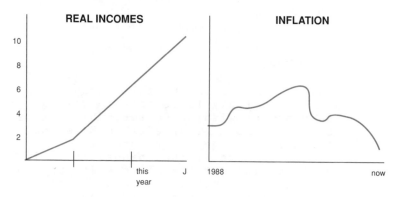

We have ¹_____ had it so good! ²_____ the nation's consumer spending has increased by 10 per cent. However, despite this encouraging news, the volume of retail sales fell back by 2 per cent ³_____, though it was still 6 per cent higher than ⁴_____.

The real incomes of those in work are still rising. Average earnings in the private sector were 8 per cent higher than they were ⁵_____. This compares with retail price inflation which has not been as low ⁶_____.

⁷_____, industrial output has continued to decline but the volume of production has shown an encouraging rise of 1 per cent ⁸_____.

b. Read this newspaper article and choose the correct verb form in the brackets.

Figures published today by the Department of Trade show that unemployment [1]*(fell/has fallen)* by 0.9% over the last three months. According to the Minister, this decrease can be explained by the government's successful economic policy which [2]*(led to/has led to)* more job creation in small businesses. In addition, these statistics show that so far this year the production of manufactured goods [3]*(increased/has increased)* by 1.5% and exports [4]*(rose/have risen)* by 2.1%. Figures for the same period last year [5]*(were/have been)* 0.9% and 0.4% respectively.

A week ago the Prime Minister [6]*(announced/has announced)* a drop of 0.5% in interest rates. Since then the Stock Market [7]*(reacted/has reacted)* accordingly with the FT 30 Index now standing at 1772. Last night, at a banquet given in the Guildhall in the City of London, the Minister [8]*(underlined/has underlined)* the importance of using this opportunity to boost private investment in industry.

c. Choose the *present perfect* or the *past simple* in each case. Use the following verbs:

explain   be   ask   meet   tell   send

Dear Sue,

While I [1]_____ in Italy recently I
[2]_____ lucky to be able to make an
appointment with Mr Carlucci of Fontana
S.A. We [3]_____ briefly in Milan on
the day of my departure and he
[4]_____ some of the changes in their
distribution network. In particular, he
[5]_____ me that I should deal with
him directly and not worry about
complicated administrative procedures.

I am now back in the office and I
[6]_____ him our catalogue and samples
as he seems interested in placing a
firm order. In addition, I [7]_____
Miss Parker to make sure he receives
the latest list of prices by the end of
next week. If there are any further
developments I will let you know.

---

d. Choose the *present perfect* or the *past simple*. Use the following verbs:

*appear   say   prevent   keep   write   praise
have   be*

Dear Martin,

Thank you for your phone call yesterday. It is true that I ¹_____ not ²_____ to you for quite some time. This letter should try to put you in the picture.

As I ³_____ on the phone the launch of the X100 cloth cutter in Singapore last winter ⁴_____ rather low-key. Competitors' machines are manufactured locally and aggressively marketed at attractive prices. Up until now, imported machines ⁵_____ subject to 30% duty and 25% sales tax. So we find it difficult to gain market share.

To date, the major disadvantage for us ⁶_____ our inability to find a motivated agent to push our products. We ⁷_____ our profit margin low to make the price to the customer reasonable but so far this ⁸_____ us from discounting or granting high commission rates. And yet the trade press is favourable. An article which ⁹_____ in last month's *Textile Technology* ¹⁰_____ the X100 highly.

All for now. I hope you ¹¹_____ more success in your part of the world. Keep in touch.

85 Past Simple[1] vs Past Continuous[2]

1 We use the *past continuous* when we want to emphasise the duration or continuity of a past event:

During the late 80s technology *was changing* and more sophisticated databases *were becoming* available.

I *was living* in Mali in 1991 and sadly lost touch with a lot of people back home.

She *was working* on the report all night.

2 It can also be used for repeated actions:

When he worked here, he *was* always *making* mistakes.

3 The *past continuous* and *past simple* are often used together in a sentence; the *past continuous* describes an event in progress which was interrupted by another:

I *was* just *leaving* the office when he *called.*

My car *broke down* while I *was driving* from Barcelona to Madrid.

4 Note the form of this polite request:

I *was wondering* if you could give me a lift.

There is no idea of past time here.

5 The past continuous form *was going to* is used to refer to events planned in the past but which did not take place:

I *was going to* write to you yesterday but I didn't find time.

(For more information on the past simple → 84.)

Practice

This is an extract from the Chairperson's speech at the Annual General Meeting. Change the verbs in the brackets, using the *past continuous* or *past simple*.

...... and if you remember at that time our sales [1](*go down*), we [2](*lose*) market share, we [3](*not invest*) enough in Research & Development, we [4](*not train*) our staff in order for them to use the new technologies that [5](*become*) available. In addition, our competitors [6](*put*) a lot of effort into their own new products and [7](d*ictate*) market trends. Then, at about the time I [8](*became*) your Chairman, we [9](*decide*) that we [10](*have to*) do something. So, we [11](*make*) the decision to make a three-for-one rights issue, we [12](*expand*) our Training Department, we [13](*commit*) more money to R & D ......

[1] Sometimes called Simple Past. [2] Sometimes called Past Progressive.

86 Pay vs Pay for vs Pay off

1 The verb *pay* is commonly used in these expressions:

Make a deposit of £20 now and *pay the balance* in three equal instalments.
Did you *pay* the bill?
We'll *pay* the invoice at the end of the month.
She *paid* $300 (i.e. a sum of money)
Have you *paid* the consultants their fee? (i.e. paid someone)
Companies have to *pay* Corporation Tax.
We are *paying* 7% interest on the loan.

1.1 Note the use of the passive in:

I *am paid* £35,000 a year.

But we can also say:

The job *pays* well.

This means that the remuneration is high.

1.2 A business or a deal *pays* when it brings a profit:

A successful entrepreneur has to make his business *pay*.

1.3 If a course of action *pays*, then it brings a benefit of some kind:

It sometimes *pays* to hide the truth.
It *pays* to keep on the right side of the Director.

2 You *pay for* something which is purchased:

He *paid for* the coat in cash.

You can also *pay for* someone when you meet someone else's debt:

He didn't have any money so she *paid for* him.

2.1 Note the word order:

He *paid* $600 for the printer.

2.2 To *pay for* can also mean that something must be suffered as a consequence of failure:

We are *paying for* under-investment now in lost orders.

2.3 Note the collocation *pay the penalty*:

We didn't think the Indian market was important and we are *paying the penalty* as our competitors have got there first.

3 *Pay* is also a noun and refers to the money received as wages or salary:

The *pay* is higher in the US.
The workers were given a *pay* rise.[1]
The company owes me three months' *back pay*. (i.e. salary owing)

[1] (In AmE you would simply say **a raise**).

4 If you *pay off* a debt you reimburse the money owed completely:

I'm lucky, I've already *paid off* my mortgage.

4.1 If a course of action *pays off*, it is successful:

It was a risky investment but it *paid off* in the end.

4.2 The noun is *payoff* (also spelt pay-off), meaning 'reward':

It's a long-term venture – there's no immediate *payoff*.

Practice

a. Complete these sentences using a form of *pay*.

1. 'How much did you _____ the plane ticket?'
'I'm not sure, I think I _____ $1,100.'
2. Do you have to _____ high social charges in your country?
3. We managed to _____ the start-up capital after only twelve months.
4. We're now having to _____ the mistakes of the previous management team.
5. When I worked at ILC, I _____ £25,000 plus profit-sharing.

87 Payment

1 In the export trade a *pro-forma invoice* is a quotation made to a potential purchaser giving details of prices, quantities, discounts, etc.

2 Payment may be made *on invoice* or *on statement. Payment on invoice* may be before, at the same time or after goods are delivered. *Payment on statement* is made when the buyer receives a *statement of account* at a later date. The latter method is used when purchases are made on a regular basis.

3 A regular customer may have an *open account* with payment typically at 30, 60 or 90 days. In effect this is a trade credit with the risk of non-payment carried by the exporter.

4 The *confirmed letter of credit* is the most frequent way of
financing international trade. Imagine a transaction between
two firms *Imco* S.A. and *Exco* plc. The payment procedure is as
follows:

a. The importer (*Imco* S.A.) fills in an application form asking
his or her bank (the issuing bank) to open a L/C in favour of
the exporter (*Exco* plc) . On the form, details are provided of
the consignment, its value, trade terms (e.g. FOB, CIF),
shipping dates and the length of time the credit will be
available.

b. *Imco's* bank next notifies its agent (the confirming) bank in
the exporter's country that a credit has been opened. The agent
bank in turn notifies *Exco* plc.

c. *Exco* plc sends off the goods (before the credit has expired!)
and sends the shipping documents (the Bill of Lading,
insurance certificate, consular invoice, certificate of origin,
certificate of quality etc.) to the agent bank.

d. The agent bank checks the documents, sends them to *Imco's*
bank.

e. *Imco's* bank checks the documents and, if everything is
correct, pays the agent bank and debits *Imco's* account. Finally
it sends the documents to *Imco* so that *Imco* can claim the
goods.

Practice

a. Complete this chart in order to demonstrate the above
procedure visually.

```
 _____ IMCO        IMCO'S _____
|                        BANK               |
|                                           |
commercial                                  pay-
contract                                    ment
|                                           |
|_____ EXCO        AGENT  _____|
                         BANK
```

5 Another means of payment involves the *Bill of Exchange*. The
exporter draws the B/E and gives it to his or her bank, together
with the various shipping documents. These are sent to the
importer who pays for the consignment, receives the shipping
documents and can collect the goods when they arrive. This is
a *Documents against Payment* transaction with the importer
paying immediately or *at sight*.

Alternatively, payment can be deferred to a later date. In this case, when the importer receives the B/E he or she writes 'accepted' on it. His or her bank sends it to the exporter. When the importer has paid his or her bank, the sum of money is transferred to the exporter's bank account, usually 30, 60 or 90 days after the bill was drawn. This is known as a *Documents against Acceptance* transaction.

6 A supplier can use the services of a *factor* to ensure rapid payment. In return for a fee, the *factor* pays the supplier a percentage of the invoice immediately and the remainder when the customer pays.

7 If a supplier wishes to receive the payment more quickly, the bill can be *discounted,* that is to say, sold to the bank immediately in return for a fee.

Practice

b. Using the above information, put these sentences into the right order to form a coherent paragraph.

1. When the credit period has expired, the importer pays his or her bank and the sum is then transferred to the exporter's account.

2. Often, however, the payment is Documents against Acceptance and he or she is given a period of credit.

3. The exporter sends the Bill of Exchange ('draws' it) to his or her foreign customer together with the invoices and necessary documentation.

4. In a Documents against Payment transaction the importer pays for the goods and receives the documents needed to collect the goods.

5. In this case, the exporter's bank sends the B/E and shipping documents to the importer.

6. He or she must accept the bill (otherwise he or she will not be able to claim the goods on their arrival). Accepting a bill is a proof of receipt of goods in law.

88 Personal vs Personnel

These words are often confused but their meaning and pronunciation are very different.

1 *Personal* means 'belonging to someone or destined for someone's attention':

You can leave your *personal* property in the locker provided.
Don't open any letters marked *'personal'*.

1.1 *Personal* is also used to refer to an individual's ideas or preferences:

Whether employee participation is good or bad is largely a matter of *personal* opinion.

2 The *personnel* in a business is the staff employed:

We haven't got the *personnel* to cope with the administrative work efficiently.

2.1 The *personnel* department deals with the staff, keeps records and deals with any *personal* problems.
This department is sometimes called Human Relations or Human Resources.

Practice

Complete the sentences.

1. All our _____ have to wear a badge, for security reasons.
2. We believe in providing a _____ service to all our clients.
3. An interviewer shouldn't ask _____ questions during an interview; the family situation is irrelevant.

89 Phrasal Verbs

1 We often use words like:

about	across	away	by	down	in	off
on	out	over	round	through	under	up

with verbs like:

ask	be	break	call	carry	come	find
go	get	give	keep	look	make	put
run	set	take	turn			

These combinations: *carry on, give up, put off*, etc. are known as *phrasal verbs*. They are common in speech as informal alternatives to one-word verbs.

1.1 Phrasal verbs are often difficult to understand because the meaning is often very different from the individual meanings of the two words. For example, the meaning 'continue' cannot be guessed from the individual meanings of *carry* and *on*. The examples here are just some of the meanings that can be derived from *call, get, look, put, take and turn*.

The verbs in parentheses are approximate synonyms.

1.2 Call

The chairman decided to *call off* the meeting as few members could be present. (= cancel)

She was able to *call up* the information she needed from the computer database. (= access)

1.3 Get

The new machine hasn't arrived so we'll have to *get by* without it. (= manage)

He's enthusiastic and ambitious: he's sure to *get on*.[1] (= succeed/make progress)

The lines were busy and I wasn't able to *get through*. (= speak to someone on the phone)

1.4 Look

They will *look over/through* the applications and make a short-list of the best candidates. (= examine)

Look up the name of the company in the Yellow Pages. (= find)

Look me *up* the next time you're in New York. (= visit)

Business hasn't been too good recently but things are *looking up* now. (= improving)

1.5 Put

It's a good idea to *put aside/by* a sum of money to cover unexpected expenditure. (= save)

The committee rejected every proposal she *put forward*. (= suggested)

Some days, I *put in* thirteen or fourteen hours. (= do/work)

He *put in* a claim for an extra payment. (= submitted)

Don't *put off* until tomorrow what can be done today. (= delay/postpone)

The government has *put* an embargo *on* all imports. (= imposed)

I'll *put* you *through* to extension 242. (= connect)

They've *put up* the price of spare parts from $10 to $12. (= raised)

The bank is refusing to *put up* the money. (= provide)

1.6 Take

Sales started to *take off* a couple of months after the campaign had begun. (= rise rapidly)

[1] BrE only

She *takes on* more work than she can cope with. (= accepts)

We're going to *take on* another supervisor: Mrs Rigg can't cope on her own. (= employ)

The shareholders of XYZ plc would like the company to *take over* its main competitor. (= gain financial control of)

They want me to *take over* as Chief Financial Controller when Mr Ramsey retires. (= assume responsibility)

I won't *take up* any more of your valuable time. (= occupy)

1.7 Turn

We decided to *turn down* their offer of a joint venture because we weren't ready to expand into another market. (= reject/refuse)

Despite fears to the contrary, the new line *turned out* to be a huge success. (= proved)

She *turned up* late for the seminar. (= arrived)

Practice

a. Rewrite these newspaper headlines using a more colloquial phrasal verb.

TML GAINS CONTROL OF REXON
ANDERSON REFUSES TOP CITY POST
BANK OF ENGLAND PROVIDES TUNNEL FINANCE
TRANSPORT TALKS CANCELLED
MEXICO RAISES COPPER PRICES
TEXTILE WORKERS SUBMIT 15% WAGE CLAIM
BUSINESS IMPROVING IN LUXEMBOURG
SISA DELAYS CAPITAL INCREASE

2 There are two types of *phrasal verbs*: those without an object and those with.

2.1 Without an object

He *turned up* late.
Go on, we're listening.
My car has *broken down*.

2.2 With an object

Please *fill in* this declaration.
I'll *fix up* a meeting for next week.
They have *put off* the launch until next season.

2.3 If the verb has an object, the *particle* (*in, up, off,* etc.) can be placed after the object:

Please *fill* this declaration *in*.
I'll *fix* a meeting *up* for next week.
They have *put* the launch *off* until next season.

2.4 Sometimes the particle cannot be separated from the verb. For example:

We'll *look into* the problem and see if we can find a solution. (= investigate)

cannot be reformulated as:

*We'll *look* the problem *into* and see....[1]

3 Some verbs can take two particles followed by an object. Examples include:

They're trying to *back out of* our agreement so we may threaten them with legal action. (= withdraw from)

His plan *came in for* a lot of criticism. (= attracted)

The design never *came up to* expectations and was abandoned. (= equalled)

We hope to *come up with* a solution in the near future. (= find/ produce)

We should try to *cut down on* spending. (= reduce)

Let's *get down to* business. (= start)

I'll *get on to* Mr Wilkins and give you his reply shortly. (= contact)

I find it difficult to *get on with* Mrs Grimes; she's so bad-tempered. (= have a friendly relationship with, see eye to eye)

I've finally *got round to*[2] reading the report; it's been on my desk for four months. (= eventually found the time to do something)

It's difficult to *keep up with* new developments. (= follow)

I *look forward to* a successful conclusion. (= anticipate with pleasure)

We're well behind schedule and will have to work very hard to *make up for* lost time. (= compensate for)

The failure of the system can be *put down to* insufficient Research & Development. (= explained by/attributed to)

She's dissatisfied with her present work and has *put in for* promotion. (= applied for)

I've had to *put up with* a lot of harassment. (= tolerate)

I hope you'll *stand up for* me. I know he will want to criticise everything I've done. (= defend)

Practice

b. Change the verbs in *italics* by using phrasal verbs.

Not long ago I [1]*applied for* a post as Regional Sales Manager at ABC plc. The job sounded interesting and the salary would have enabled me to save a sum of money at the end of each

[1] This is because *into* is a preposition and not an adverb.   [2] (AmE: **gotten around**)

month. I would also have been encouraged to ²*accept* more responsibility than in my present job where I knew promotion was blocked and it was impossible for me to ³*make progress.* My application was ⁴*refused.* I never really understood why but it is true that during the interview I didn't ⁵*see eye to eye* with Mr Pike, the Sales Director. It was obvious he wanted to ⁶*employ* a younger person and aggressively challenged every idea I ⁷*suggested.* The interview itself only lasted a quarter of an hour. However, this failure ⁸*proved* to be for the best. I stayed in my job at XYZ plc and have just learnt that we are going to ⁹*gain financial control of* ABC plc. This gives me particular satisfaction because I've been ¹⁰*investigating* the changes in the organisation chart. It seems that Mr Pike will now be working under me.

I do not like hurting people and I'm ¹¹*anticipating* a good working relationship. However, if he wants to ¹²*succeed* in his new position he will have to ¹³*accept* many extra duties which he may not particularly like. If he doesn't like these duties he will just have to ¹⁴*tolerate* them.

90 **Policy vs Politics**

1 *Policy* has two main meanings.

> **1.1** An agreed set of principles which form the basis of any decision:
>
> Our *policy* is to keep inventory as low as possible.
>
> **1.2** An insurance certificate:
>
> You should always read the small print of your insurance *policy.*

2 *Politics* refers to the activity of government and the political parties in opposition:

Politics has been defined as the art of the possible.

The adjective is *political.*

Practice

Complete the blanks:

The international manager must understand the effect of
¹_____ on business. A change in bilateral ²_____
relations can change strategic ³_____ and modify
investment decisions.

91 Prefixes and Suffixes

1 New words can be formed by adding a beginning or an ending to existing words. Here are some examples of prefixes for verbs. Write the prefix alongside its area of meaning:

(a) again _____ (b) badly _____
(c) too much _____ (d) the opposite _____
(e) too little _____ (f) do much better _____

de	brief nationalise regulate value	*over* *under*	charge estimate pay spend
mis	count inform judge time spend use	*re*	build do organise use
out	bid do last perform vote		

2 Common verb suffixes include *-ise* (AmE: *ize*), *-ify*, *-ate*:

legal**ise**	national**ise**	modern**ise**
privat**ise**	rational**ise**	subsid**ise**
clar**ify**	class**ify**	just**ify**
not**ify**	simpl**ify**	ver**ify**
calcul**ate**	collabor**ate**	investig**ate**
negoti**ate**	oper**ate**	regul**ate**

Practice

a. Find the verbs in **1** and **2** that correspond to the definitions. *For example:* to make something clear = *clarify*

1. to do again
2. to make something simple
3. to give someone wrong information
4. to check
5. to use something in the wrong way
6. to work with someone
7. to make someone pay too much
8. to make something legal

9. to privatise
10. to put something into a category
11. perform much better
12. tell someone something

3 Many nouns can be formed from phrasal verbs:

to cut back	=	a cutback
to break down	=	a breakdown
to set back	=	a setback
to take over	=	a takeover
to spin off	=	a spinoff
to shake up	=	a shake-up
to write off	=	a write-off

3.1 Sometimes the *particle* (*back, off,* etc.) is the first part of the word:

a downswing	an upsurge
a downturn	an upgrade
a downtime	an upturn

an inflow	an outcome
an intake	an outlay
an input	an outlet
	an outlook
	an output

Practice

b. Complete the sentences using the verb in brackets together with a suitable particle or verb.

1. Hopes of a recovery suffered a sharp _____ yesterday with the announcement of a steep rise in inflation. *(set)*
2. If the two companies merge we can expect a _____ in the organisation chart. *(shake)*
3. There has been an encouraging _____ for the Union meeting. *(turn)*
4. The plant's _____ is about 3,000 tonnes of iron ore a week. *(out)*
5. We may have to reduce this year's _____ of trainees. *(in)*
6. Could I have the _____ of expenditure on promotion by the end of the week? *(break)*
7. The scheme needed an initial _____ of £2m. *(out)*
8. There has been an encouraging _____ in sales after a disastrous first quarter. *(up)*
9. An unexpected _____ of the office reorganisation was a decrease in the consumption of electricity. *(spin)*

c. What do these words mean?

a *co*-founder
an *ex*-President
a *post*-dated cheque
a *counter*-proposal
an *anti*-trust law

92 Prepositions

Prepositions are used to relate things or people in various ways to time, place, direction and distance.
It is difficult to use prepositions correctly as most of them have a variety of uses and meanings.

1 Time

About (approximately)

The job will take *about* a week.

Around (approximately)

She'll be there *around* 5 o'clock.

At (point in time)

We've got the results *at* last. (after a long period of waiting)
I suggest we meet *at* 4.30.
Please send us your comments for the end of May *at* the latest.
We close down *at* Christmas.

Beyond (limit in duration)

It's impossible to extend credit *beyond* the 60 days agreed.

By (limit in time)

The plane leaves at 10 so we must be at the airport *by* 9 a.m.

From (starting point in time)

The exhibition will be open *from* 1 June.

In/During (between two points in time)

They went bankrupt *in* 1989. (some time between January and December)
I didn't send my application *in* time to be considered. (it arrived too late to be considered)
They employ students *in* the summer vacation.
There was full employment *in* the 1960s.
The office is shut *during* the holidays.

On (point of time)

The video conference is *on* 3rd April.
Please be *on time* (at the right time, not late.)
The quality circle meeting is *on* Wednesday.

Through (direction inside time)

I'll be staying in Chicago May *through* June. (AmE)

I worked all *through* my lunch-break.

To (future direction)

It's seven minutes *to* three.

There are only two weeks *to* the symposium.

The office is open from 9 *to* 5.30 (= until)

Practice

a. Look at Mr Grant's diary.

Use suitable times and prepositions to complete these statements:

1. The sales report must be ready _____.
2. His sales conference is _____.
3. His train to Birmingham leaves _____.
4. He's seeing Mr da Silva _____.
5. Mr Arestrup will be staying _____.
6. _____ Monday 12th he'll be working _____ his lunch break.
7. He's meeting Mrs Winter _____.
8. The office will be closed _____ Easter.

MON 5 *Sales report. Must be ready no later than 3 p.m. for typing*	**MON 12** *Working lunch Mr. Leclerc 12.00 – 15.00*
TUES 6 *Sales conference*	**TUES 13** *Mr. Arestrup leaves*
WED 7 *Train – Birmingham 14.57 Euston Station*	**WED 14** *Mrs. Winter 11.00 approx*
THURS 8 *Mr. da Silva 10.00 sharp*	**THURS 15** *Office shut*
FRI 9 *Mr. Arestrup arrives*	**FRI 16** *Office shut*
SAT 10	**SAT 17** *"*
SUN 11	**SUN 18** *Easter Sunday*

2 Place

About (approximate position)

I've left the folder lying *about* somewhere.

Around

The Accounts Department is *around* the corner.

At (place)

He spent Saturday afternoon *at* work.

He's staying *at* the Dorchester.

I'll meet you *at* Gatwick airport.

At (direction)

We've aimed our campaign *at* the young urban professional.

Beyond (limit in direction)

We cannot transport the goods *beyond* the Pakistani frontier.

By (close to)

The warehouse is *by* the canal.

From (source)

The video recorders are imported *from* Taiwan.

In (three dimensional space)

San Francisco is *in* California.

The money is kept *in* the safe.

On (two dimensional line or surface)

California is *on* the Pacific coast.

The file is *on* the desk.

The calendar is hanging *on* the wall.

Through (direction between two points in space)

It can take ages to clear goods *through* customs.

Once we're *through* Rome we'll be able to drive faster.

To (movement, destination)

I have to go *to* Rabat next week.

The taxi will take you *to* the airport.

Practice

b. Complete the letter on the next page with suitable prepositions.

Dear Olie,

This is to confirm that I will be staying [1]_____ Sydney [2]_____ October 15 [3]_____ October 21 [4]_____ the *Pacific* hotel. Could you please arrange for somebody to pick me up [5]_____ the airport?

I have [6]_____ last received the report [7]_____ the marketing division [8]_____ New York. These are the most important points you should know:

a. The *Dolce Vita* promotion should be completed [9]_____ 20 September [10]_____ the latest. Sales figures will be sent [11]_____ you when they are available.

b. The launch of the *Pacific* sun lotion has been a success. Over 11,000 will have been sold [12]_____ the end of September.

c. 15,000 merchandising units are being shipped [13]_____ Australia [14]_____ November as requested.

d. We are having problems with our operations in Latin America. It is proving difficult to get goods cleared [15]_____ customs rapidly. Many clients are insisting on credit terms [16]_____ the usual 30 days.

e. Current marketing plans are to be finalised following receipt of all relevant data [17]_____ John Price. As I understand it, the idea is to aim more of our products [18]_____ the lower middle-class income group.

f. The next Joint Marketing meeting will be held [19]_____ 4 November. We will start [20]_____ 9.00 a.m. and hope to finish sometime [21]_____ midday.

See you soon,

Lee

3 Other prepositions of place
Look at the diagram of the Conference Centre.

The reception area and auditorium are *on* the ground floor.
The lifts are *on* the left, the entrance to the bar is *on* the right. *Next to* the bar are the stairs which go *down* to the basement.

The telex room, telephone booths, library and exhibition area are on the first floor. The telex room is *behind* the stairs, just *along* the corridor *to* the right. The telephone booths are *next to* the library and the exhibition area is *across* the landing *in front of* you.

On the second floor there are a number of rooms used for meetings and *above* them *on* the third floor there is a television studio which is used for video-conferences.

At the top of the building there is a roof restaurant with a fine view *over* the city.

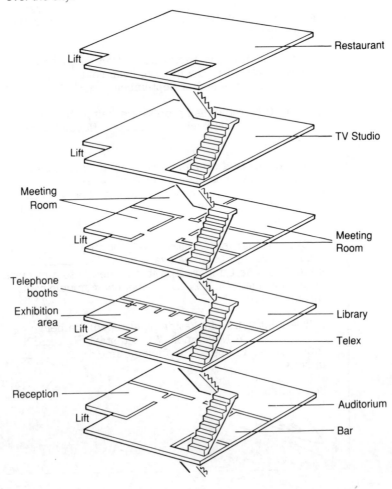

Practice

c. Look at how prepositions are used in this talk introducing a visit round a factory. Then label the plan using information from the passage.

Welcome to Randall Components. Before we go on our guided tour let me just show you this plan of the factory. We are standing here in the reception area and as you can see directly *opposite* us is the Administration Block which has four floors. *On* the ground floor we have the main entrance and production department offices. *On* the first floor we have the R & D department offices and *above* them the Sales and Personnel sections. *At* the top of the building there are the offices used by the senior executives.

To the right of this building you can see the assembly workshop and *behind* that the delivery bay and car park[1]. *To* the left of the Administration Block we have the stores and *next to* them a smaller and a larger warehouse.

To get to the canteen and the First Aid Centre you have to go *out of* this building, go *across* the road and walk *down* a path *along* the river bank. After about 30 yards *on* the right you come to a single-storey building which is our staff restaurant.

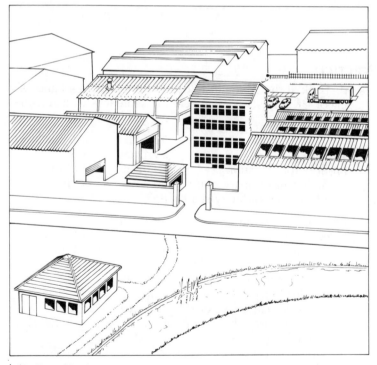

[1] (AmE: **parking lot**)

4 Numbers

Prepositions are often used when referring to the movement of figures:

At the end of May sales stood *at* £125m, having risen *from* a previous low point of £98m. Then in June they went *up to* just *above* £130m but in July and August went *down to below* £120m. In September this fall continued and sales decreased *by* another £1.5m.

above and *below* can be replaced by *over* and *under*.

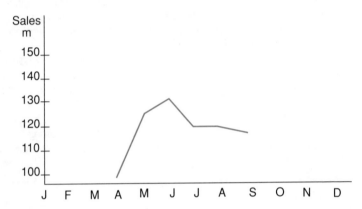

Practice

d. Look at the table illustrating the financial highlights of a major UK firm. Then complete the sentences with suitable prepositions.

	This year	Last year
Turnover	£9,424m	£8,387m
Profit before taxation	£2,027m	£1,851m
Earnings per ordinary share	20.9p	17.1p
Dividends per ordinary share	8.45p	7.5p
Capital expenditure	£2,107m	£1,973m
Fixed assets	£11,500m	£10,714m
Capital and reserves	£7,557m	£7,090m

1. Turnover went up _____ £1,037m.
2. Dividends rose _____ 7.5p _____ 8.45p.
3. This year, earnings per share are just _____ 21p.
4. Last year, profit before tax stood _____ £1,851.
5. This year, it is just _____ £2,000m.
6. Capital and reserves increased _____ £467m _____ just _____ £7,550m.

5 Complex prepositions

5.1 Many prepositions are made up of two or more words.

according to	*apart from*	*as for*
except for	*further to*	*out of*
instead of	*on to*	
regardless of	*up to*	

5.2 Some complex prepositions contain a noun between two prepositions:

by means of	*in addition to*	*in case of*
in favour of	*in spite of*	*in view of*
on account of	*on behalf of*	*with reference to*
in accordance with	*in consultation with*	*in line with*
with effect from	*in touch with*	

Practice

e. Complete this fax using the following:

in line with	*instead of*	*in favour*
further to	*up to*	*on account of*
regardless of	*with reference to*	
as for	*in touch with*	

---

¹_____ your recent request I have
been ²_____ Robert Macdonald
³_____ the making of a promotional
videocassette.

He is ⁴_____ shooting the film in
London ⁵_____ Los Angeles as you
originally suggested ⁶_____ the
expense.

⁷_____ me, I think L.A. would be a
much better location ⁸_____ the cost
and ⁹_____ what our C.E.O. wants. In
any case, we have a budget of
¹⁰_____ $100,000 so I don't see the
point of making false economies.

Regards,

---

6 Prepositional phrases
All the phrases below are frequently used:

against { acceptance / documents / payment }

at { your disposal / our expense / a profit/loss / short notice / your risk }

beyond our control

by { mistake / return of mail / monthly instalments / law }

a cheque *for* £x
value *for* money

in { advance / banking / bulk / your name / good condition } *in* { arrears / debt / demand / due course / duplicate } *in* { force / full / transit / stock }

on { approval / arrival / business / delivery / display } *on* { closer inspection / request / the phone / a regular basis / sale } *on* { loan / schedule / trial }

out of { date / order / stock / work }

through the usual channels
to your satisfaction

under { orders / pressure / separate cover }

within { the hour / a fortnight. }

Note too the expression: accurate *to within* a certain sum of money):
The figures are accurate *to within* the nearest $10,000.

Practice

f. Use the correct preposition to complete each sentence.

1. Requests for re-imbursement should be made _____ the proper channels.

2. Please complete the form _____ triplicate.

3. I am sending our catalogue _____ separate cover.

4. Please find enclosed a cheque _____ £675.

5. She's away _____ business.

6. Any defective items will be repaired _____ our expense.

7. You'll have to take the stairs; the elevator's _____ _____ order.

8. I'm sorry but the Director is unable to see you _____ such short notice.

9. He's been _____ a lot of pressure and that may explain his behaviour.

10. She works _____ aeronautics.

11. You won't find better value _____ money anywhere.

12. At present we are _____ _____ stock but should be receiving new items _____ due course.

93 Present Perfect vs Present Perfect Continuous[1]

1 Compare:

(a) *We've talked* about a different approach.

(b) *We've been talking* about a different approach.

In (a) the implication is that this discussion has now finished. In (b) the emphasis is on the continuity of these discussions. It is likely that they will go on talking.
Similarly:

(a) *He's written* his speech for the AGM. (It is completed)

(b) *He's been writing* his speech for the AGM. (He hasn't finished it yet)

(a) *She's learnt* how to use the off-set printer. (She can use it now)

(b) *She's been learning* English for 10 years. (This process is never complete!)

2 The *present perfect continuous* cannot be used with verbs describing states or beliefs, e.g. *know, understand, believe,* etc.

I've known Mr Koo Hon Syn for years. (NOT * I've been knowing...)

(→ 84. **Past simple vs present perfect**)

[1] Sometimes called Present Perfect Progressive.

Practice

In your work situation:

What projects have you been working on?
What major decisions have been taken recently?
What have you been trying to do without success?
Who have you spoken to today?
Have you written to anyone recently?

94 Present simple[1] vs Present Continuous[2]

1 Look at sections A–E below.
Decide which section concerns:
(i) temporary situations
(ii) regular events
(iii) permanent states or situations
(iv) actions happening now
(v) changing and developing situations

What tense is used in each case?

A.

Unilever *is* an Anglo-Dutch company which *produces* food products and detergents. It *operates* in over 70 countries and *employs* about

---

[1] Sometimes called Simple Present.   [2] Somtimes called Present Progressive.

300,000 people. It *has* a subsidiary, UAC International, which *specialises* in paper, plastics, speciality[1] chemicals and packaging.

B.

Would you like to hold, Mr Bloom *is speaking* on another line?
They*'re repairing* the machine right now. It should be ready for use in a couple of hours.

C.

Mr Jones *is* a stockbroker and *works* for a major firm in the City of London. He *gets up* at 7.30, *has* breakfast then *drives* to the local station where he *takes* a commuter train. After a short train ride he *arrives* at work at 9.00, *says* 'hello' to colleagues, *sits* at his desk and *reads* any telexes that have arrived.

D.

Western economies *are changing.* More and more people *are working* in services instead of manufacturing industry and the number of women in the labour force *is increasing.*

E.

I'*m walking* to work this week as my car *is being* serviced.

Mrs Kaur is ill so I'm *dealing with* her correspondence.

If you have analysed each section correctly your answers are: A (iii) (present simple); B (iv) (present continuous); C (ii) (present simple); D (v) (present continuous); E (i) (present continuous).

Practice

a. Decide which category, (i) – (v) above, each of the following sentences belongs to. Then choose a verb and decide whether it should be in the *present simple* or *present continuous.*

manufacture	*receive*	*have*	*look*	*stay*	*interview*
include	*try*	*expand*	*answer*	*hold*	*change*

1. I _____ at the Continental Hotel whenever I'm in Hong Kong.
2. ABC plc _____ a wide variety of adhesives.
3. Consumer research has identified a new trend; more and more people _____ to *Sunkist.*
4. The prices _____ full insurance cover.
5. Our firm _____ fast; 35% growth in only two years.
6. We _____ a departmental meeting every fortnight.
7. A receptionist _____ all incoming calls and _____ routine enquiries.

[1] (AmE: **specialty**)

8. We _____ branches in most major cities.
9. Mr Prescott _____ the candidates right now.
10. We _____ for a new Media Sales Manager.
11. Our engineer _____ to detect the cause of the fault.

b. *Simple* or *continuous*?

P & S [1]*(be)* a chain of department stores with branches in many cities in the UK. Each store [2]*(sell)* a variety of goods from textiles to kitchen utensils to furniture, P & S [3]*(employ)* over 3,000 people and [4]*(have)* a turnover of over £75m. The firm [5]*(grows)* rapidly and at present [6]*(recruit)* more highly qualified personnel to run its new branch in Maidstone, Kent.

2 Some verbs, especially those describing states, beliefs, or verbs which make a declaration are never, or rarely, used in the present continuous.

Examples include:

Mantex *owns* over 50% of the shares.

The box *contains* 144 packets.

The consignment *weighs* 44 kilos and *measures* 2' x 1' x 1.5'.

C & F *means* that insurance is not included in the price quoted by the exporter.

Our records *show* that you owe us £694.

They *believe* in free trade.

I *realise* that there has been a breakdown.

I don't *understand* how the profit margin is calculated.

I don't *know* what time I'll arrive, it *depends* on the traffic.

We *assure* you that your request will receive our best attention.

I *promise* to deal with the matter myself.

I *wish* to make my position clear on this point.

I *regret* to announce a 12% decrease in profitability.

I *suggest* we look at the figures very carefully.

3 With some verbs it is sometimes possible to use either the *present simple* or the *present continuous* as in:

I *am looking* forward to seeing you.

I *look forward* to seeing you.

I *am enclosing* a detailed quotation.

I *enclose* a detailed quotation.

I will be in Rio next week and *am hoping* to meet Sr Gomez then.

I will be in Rio next week and *hope* to meet Sr Gomez then.

In each case, the use of the *present simple* can be seen as a declaration. Note that the *present simple* makes each sentence slightly more formal in tone.

4 The *present continuous* is used to refer to *arrangements* (i.e. present plans for the future):

Next year we *are investing* more in office automation.
She *is flying* to Jakarta next week.

Practice

c. Put the verbs in the brackets in either the *present simple* or *present continuous:*

We ¹*(have)* a great deal of difficulty with this order and I ²*(admit)* that the delivery date is unlikely to be respected. However I ³*(realise)* that you need rapid delivery and we ⁴*(do)* our best to ensure that the goods will arrive by the end of April.

In the circumstances I ⁵*(agree)* that payment terms should be modified. I ⁶*(suggest)* a reduction of 2.5 per cent on the unit price.

I ⁷*(assure)* you that we will take the necessary steps to avoid any future delay and ⁸*(promise)* to supervise the satisfactory completion of your orders personally.

d. Put the verbs in the correct form.

We ¹*(have)* offices in most European capitals and ²*(think)* of opening another in Budapest shortly. I ³*(think)* this will help us to improve our performance in Hungary. In addition, we ⁴*(try)* to do better in Romania and Bulgaria but ⁵*(doubt)* whether this will be possible in the near future.

I ⁶*(confirm)* that I ⁷*(spend)* a couple of weeks in Germany in the spring and will be able to meet you in Berlin during the first week of April. In the meantime I ⁸*(send)* our latest report on the situation in Eastern Europe under separate cover. If you ⁹*(need)* any further information please let me know.

95   Price vs Rate vs Charge vs Fee vs Commission

1 The *price* is the amount of money you have to pay (usually for goods) in order to buy them:

What is the *price* of a carphone?
Share *prices* are quoted in the *Financial Times.*

1.1 *Price* is also a verb. If you *price* something you decide how much a purchaser will have to pay:

We've *priced* the new model at $1,300.

1.2 To *price yourself out of the market* is to offer your goods at such a high price that everyone will buy your competitors' products:

If we don't work to a lower profit margin we'll be *pricing ourselves out of the market.*

2 The *rate* of interest or taxation is the percentage level:

Interest *rates* have stabilised at around 15%.
The basic *rate* of income tax in 1990 was 25%.

2.1 We can also refer to the *rate of exchange* (or *exchange rate*) of a currency:

Tourist *exchange rates* are published in most newspapers.

2.2 *Rate* can refer to an amount of something within a period of time.

The *rate* of unemployment fell in some European countries in the late 80s.

2.3 In insurance, the amounts charged to cover a risk are expressed as a percentage:

A *rate* of £1.75 per cent.

This means that you have to pay £1.75 for every £100 of the sum for which the goods are insured.

2.4 *Rate* can also indicate the speed or frequency at which something happens:

We're losing skilled workers at the *rate* of three a month.

3 *Charge* is used mostly in the context of paying for services:

There will be a *charge* for confirming the letter of credit.
No extra *charge* is made for maintenance.

3.1 *Charge* is also a verb:

We *charge* for delivery. (= There is a delivery *charge*.)
The bank *charged* me 12% commission.

3.2 If something is *charged to an account* it is put on the bill for payment later:

Please *charge* the bar bill *to my account.*

3.3 Occasionally, services are *free of charge*.

You may use the telephone in your room *free of charge*.

4 A *fee* is payable for services provided by the legal profession, consultants, accountants, etc.:

In the US, a lawyer is paid a contingency *fee* which is a proportion of the damages granted by the court.

4.1 When permission is granted to use intellectual property there may be a *fee*. It is also possible to refer to a *registration fee* and a *booking fee* when a charge is made for a reservation.

5 A *commission* is a payment to an agent or middleman, calculated as a percentage of sales made:

5.1 Salesmen are often paid a fixed salary plus *commission* on sales made:

A higher **commission** increases the incentive to sell.

5.2 *Commission* is used as a synonym of *charge* in the context of banking:

There is a small **commission/charge** for handling standing orders.

Practice

Complete these sentences.

1. The American Bar Association has warned lawyers that their _____ were getting so high that the profession might _____ itself out of the market.
2. Please pay the conference _____ directly to the Registrar.
3. As a salesman, the more goods you sell, the more _____ you make.
4. We were _____ £850 for repairs to the switchboard.
5. What is the _____ of an overhead projector?
6. We're now producing the new model at the _____ of 100 a day.
7. There is a small _____ to cover handling costs.
8. A bear is a speculator who expects share _____ to fall.
9. The _____ of inflation is over 10%.
10. Could you _____ this to my expense account?

96 Principal vs Principle

1 *Principal* means 'most important':

The **principal** reason for our success has been our ability to manage risk.

1.1 The noun *principal* has two meanings:
(a) a person who authorises someone else to be an agent.
(b) the amount of a loan, not including the interest.

2 A *principle* is a guiding rule of behaviour:

We work on the **principle** that, in business, you can't afford to be sentimental.

Practice

Complete the sentences.

1. The interest shall be payable at the same time as the
   _____ at a rate of 12.5% per annum.
2. I refuse on _____ to mix work and family life.

97 Questions

1 *Yes/No* questions

All these questions use an *auxiliary* in *initial position* and are
Yes/No questions requiring a positive (yes) or negative (no)
response.

Is Carlos from Mexico?	Yes, he is.
Are you coming with us?	No, I'm not.
Do you export to Korea?	Yes, we do.
Does your firm have a language policy?	No, it doesn't.
Have the goods arrived at the frontier?	No, they haven't yet.
Has she finished typing the report?	Yes, she has.
Did they give a discount?	No, they didn't actually.
Should we have complained?	Yes, definitely.
Will they want to negotiate the price?	No, they probably won't.
Can you write in COBOL?	No, I can't.

2 *Wh*-questions

We use this question form when we are asking for information:

Where should I put it?
When does she want me to phone?
Who is in charge of purchasing?
What shall we do?
Which is the most profitable line?
Why is she always late?
Whose is this briefcase?

The question word is placed before the auxiliary verb.

2.1 When we use a verb in a simple tense (present or past)
we have to use the auxiliary *do/does/did*:

Where do you live?
When does she want it?
Who do you work with?
Where did you get it from?
Why did they come?

■3■ Negative questions

We use a negative question when we suspect the answer will be 'No' having first thought it would be 'Yes':

Can't you get there earlier? (I think it's possible.)
Didn't you tell them about the deal? (I thought you would.)
Won't 8 o'clock be too late? (I suspect it will be.)
Aren't you going to the conference? (I thought you were.)

■4■

When *who, what* or *which* is the *subject* of a sentence, an auxiliary is not used:

Who wants a lift to the station? (NOT * Who does want...)
What happened at the meeting? (NOT * What did happen..)
Which costs more? (NOT * Which does cost more?)

Practice

a. All of the following are grammatically wrong. How should they be said?

1. Is coming Mr Perez?
2. Do you be ready?
3. Do you can help me?
4. Does she have completed the survey?
5. Why she is angry?
6. No possible to get here earlier? (two possible questions)
7. Did they sold the subsidiary?
8. We no met before?
9. What means 'price/earnings ratio'?
10. Why they came?
11. When it must be finished?

■5■ Questions with *how*

5.1 *How* asks a question about the way something is/was done:

How do you spell 'inuff'? E-N-O-U-G-H
How did you get here?

5.2 It asks a question about your feelings or opinion:

How did you feel about the deal?

5.3 It is used before another word to ask questions about: age, distance, frequency, time and quantity:

How old is Mrs Chow?
How far is the construction site from here?
How often does the quality circle meet?
How soon will you be able to give us an answer?
How many people attended the AGM?
How much would you want to spend?

Practice

b. Write the question which relates to the words in *italics*.
For example: She finished her interview *two hours ago*.
  When did she finish her interview?

1. Output has increased *by 7.5%*.
2. Betamix became a public limited company *in 1990*.
3. The departmental meeting is held *once a month*.
4. We'll get back to you *very shortly*. (two possible questions)
5. It cost *in excess of 2 million dollars*.
6. A consultant was called in *to look at our recruitment policy*.
7. I prefer *the second solution*.
8. There were *at least 500* enquiries.
9. It's *my* ticket.
10. The bank is about *100 metres from here*.

c. These are some questions that were asked during a
CONSUMER SURVEY. Provide the question words and (if
necessary) verbs.

---

1. _____ most of your groceries from?
a. Corner shop   b. Supermarket   c. Hypermarket?

2. _____ on groceries every week?
a. Under £50   b. Between £50–100   c. Over £100
d. Over £200

3. _____ of these dairy products _____
regularly?
a. Yoghurt   b. Low fat milk   c. Soft cheese
d. Cottage cheese

4. _____ pots of yoghurt _____ on average
each week?
a. None   b. One   c. Two   d. More than two

5. When buying your groceries, _____ choose a
particular store rather than another?
a. Convenience   b. Car parking   c. Selection of products
d. Prices   e. Service

6. _____ cook pasta?
a. 2 times a week   b. Once a week   c. Less than once
a month   d. Never

7. _____ a car in your household?
a. You   b. Your spouse   c. Other   d. No one

(→ 100. reporting questions)

98 **Remind vs Remember**

1 If you *remind* somebody you tell them so that they will not forget:

Remind me to phone Anne, will you?
I *reminded* him to take his passport with him.

2 If you *remember* something, you do not forget:

I must *remember* to phone Anne.
I have to write everything down, otherwise I won't *remember*.

2.1 If you *remember* something **now** about an event *in the past,* the second verb is in the *-ing* form:

I *remember* meet*ing* him but I've forgotten what we said to each other.

Practice

Complete the sentences.

1. Sorry, I don't _____ your name.
2. Could you _____ me to take a catalogue with me, otherwise I'll forget.
3. I _____ being introduced to him at a cocktail party in Madrid.
4. 'What was the exact figure?' 'I don't know, I can't _____.'
5. I've got to _____ her to take some important papers but I may not _____ to do so.

99 **Reporting Information**

We use reported speech when we want to relate what another person said, wrote or thought on a previous occasion.
We can report both statements and questions.
When we use reported speech we usually refer to a past situation but sometimes we may want to tell someone what another person is saying right now e.g. over the phone. We call this *immediate reported speech.*

1 **Immediate reported speech**
Look at this telephone conversation.

MR FORESTI   Could I speak to Mr Gardner please?
MRS WILLIAMS   Sorry, he's out – can I take a message?
MR FORESTI   Yes please. Ny name is Mr Foresti. Could you tell

him I'm sorry we haven't been able to send him the estimate he requested. Our technician is away at the moment.

MRS WILLIAMS   Right, I'll tell him when he comes in.

(Mr Gardner enters the office.)

MRS WILLIAMS   Mr Foresti, could you hold on a moment?

MR FORESTI   Yes.

MRS WILLIAMS   *(to Mr Gardner)* Mr Foresti is on the line. He *says* he's sorry he *hasn't been able to send* you the estimate you *requested* because their technician *is* away at the moment...

The reporting verb *says* is in the present tense. There are no tense changes required because the conversation is reported at almost the same time as the original conversation itself.

Practice

a. Catherine Miller and Peter Barker have just arrived at work. Catherine goes to the telex machine and sees there is a message.

WE HAVE RECEIVED OUR LONG AWAITED CONSIGNMENT OF DISPOSABLE CIGARETTE LIGHTERS IN GOOD ORDER. AFTER SUCH A LONG BREAK ON THE MARKET IT IS ALMOST A NEW LAUNCH BUT WE ARE HOPEFUL THAT WITH THE ADDED ADVANTAGE OF THE 'SPORTS' SERIES WE CAN REGAIN SOME OF THE MARKET.

WE ARE NOW INTERESTED IN PLACING A FURTHER ORDER FOR

PLAINFLAME ASSORTED LIGHTERS
20 CARTONS = 11520 LIGHTERS

SPORTS SERIES LIGHTERS
25 CARTONS = 14400 LIGHTERS

DELIVERY IN COLOMBIA: EARLY SEPTEMBER.
COLOURS AND DESIGNS AS PREVIOUSLY.

REGARDS

ROBERT KLEIN

This is what she might say. Complete the missing parts. There's a telex from Robert Klein. He says [1]_____ the consignment of lighters and [2]_____ that they can get back some of their share of the market. He says he is [3]_____ for 20 cartons of Plainflame lighters and 25 cartons of the sports series. That's good news. And he also says that he [4]_____ them to be delivered in Colombia in September.

2 Past reported speech

Imagine that Mrs Williams took Mr Foresti's message (see pages 209–210) while Mr Gardner was abroad. Mr Gardner is now back and it is two weeks later than the original conversation. The time context has changed. As a result, the reporting verb *said* is in the past tense and the tenses of the other verbs are different.

MRS WILLIAMS   There was a phone call from Mr Foresti while you were away.

MR GARDNER   Oh, what did he say?

MRS WILLIAMS   He *said* (that) [1]he *was* sorry he *hadn't been able to* send you the estimate you *requested* because their technician *was* away.

(Note that *at the moment* is no longer appropriate and is therefore omitted.)
In this example, the tense changes are:

Present   => Past simple
Present perfect   => Past perfect
Past simple   => Past simple

2.1 Past verb forms in direct speech are sometimes transformed into past perfect in reported speech to make it clear that one event preceded another.

DIRECT SPEECH: 'I saw him before the talks began.

REPORTED SPEECH: He *said* he *had seen* him before the talks began.

2.2 However, it is often unimportant to make this distinction between a past and an earlier past.

'She sent several telexes.'
He *said* she *sent* several telexes. (rather than *had sent*)

'The report showed that their policies weren't working.'
She *said* the report *showed* that their policies weren't working. (rather than *had not been* working)

2.3 Even if the reporting verb is in the past, there may be no tense change if we are reporting things which are still true at the moment of speaking:

'I'm 34 years old.'
She *said* she *is/was* 34 years old.

---

[1] **that** (pronounced /ðət/) is optional. In more formal contexts it is usually included.

'*Prices rise when demand is greater than supply.*'
He *said* that prices *rise* when demand is greater than supply.
'*I'm leaving the firm at the end of the year.*'
He *said* he *is/was leaving* the firm at the end of the year.'

Practice

b. Three days ago Sean O'Connor took a telephone call destined for a colleague Laura Greene who was at a management seminar. This morning he phoned her extension to give the message.

Look at what he wrote and imagine what he said. Begin: 'Hideki Asano phoned from Kyoto. He said that he...'

Telephone Message

FROM: *Hideki Asano*   FOR: *Laura Greene*

Hideki has spoken to business friend in Malaysia — interested in importing sports shoes. Name: Syarikat Dalia Baru Address: 64a Jalan Lamut, Damai Kompleks Kuala Lumpur Large quantities of American footwear now going to Malaysia — many more than to Singapore.

---

3 **Other tense changes**

'I'*ll* get in touch with you[1] as soon as I *can*.'	She said she *would* get in touch as soon as she *could*.
'I *may* be able to.'	He said he *might* be able to.

4 **No tense changes**

'Cheques *must* be countersigned.'	The accountant said cheques *must* be countersigned.[2]
'The bank *might* agree to extend the loan period.'	The bank manager said they *might* agree to extend the loan period.

[1] Both **shall** and **will** become **would**.   [2] **had to** or **have got to** is also possible.

'I *would like* to be a Systems Analyst.'	She said she *would like* to be a Systems Analyst.
'You *could* set up a franchise.'	He said we *could* set up a franchise.
'They *should* give the store a new image.'	He said they *should* give the store a new image.
'They *used to* have an office in Seoul.'	She said they *used to* have an office in Seoul.
'I *had* never *been* to Tokyo before.'	He said he *had* never *been* to Tokyo before.

5 Say vs Tell (→ 104. say vs tell)

These words are often confused.

Tell is followed by a word which indicates the person receiving the information.

Compare:

He *told me / him / them / the forwarding agent*, etc. that the goods had been inspected.

He *said* (that) the goods had been inspected.

5.1 It is useful to remember that *tell* is used when information is given:

Could you *tell* me the correct procedure?
She *told* him how to fill in the form.

5.2 *Say* reports the actual words used:

She *said* 'Allo' with a strong accent.

5.3 *Tell* is also used (with an object and an infinitive) for orders, commands or strong advice:

Would you *tell* her to hurry up?
Tell them to be more careful next time.
Please *tell* him not to overspend. (NOT *to not..)

6 Other reporting verbs

When writing the minutes of a meeting or a report it is good practice to use a variety of verbs in addition to *say* and *tell*. Look at the way the verbs *in italics* are used in the following minutes.

Minutes of the meeting held at the Head Office of Architech Consult on 7/2/92.

Present   Apologies: Peter Thornborough

Richard Harris (Chairman)
Amanda Bell (Chief Designer)
Donald McGregor (Human Relations)
Jonathon Coe (Accountant)
Wendy Adam (Designer)

Subject

Abidjan design project

The minutes of the last meeting were confirmed.

1 RH opened the meeting and *underlined* the importance of reaching a decision on the project.

Each person in attendance was invited to state his/ her position concerning the feasibility of the work in Abidjan.

2 AB (the initiator of the project) *pointed out* that it would be a major contract and *explained* that it should be accepted for the following reasons:

- the company would be able to expand into new areas
- it would enhance the company's reputation
- it would broaden the expertise of the company's specialists
- it would open up new international markets

3 JC *agreed* that the project was viable for the following reasons:

- the bankers were favourable and ready to provide finance
- raw materials were cheap and plentiful
- local labour was inexpensive
- the level of risk was within acceptable limits

He *claimed* that estimates from local sub-contractors indicated that profit margins would be high.

4 DM *stated* that there would be difficulties in controlling the project from a distance. Staff would have to spend considerable time abroad supervising progress on site. He also *mentioned* the problems they had encountered with a similar venture in Togo.

5 WA *outlined* her reasons for opposing the scheme. In her view it had not been thought through sufficiently by the client. She *emphasised* that further research was needed before going ahead.

6 RH closed the meeting and *announced* that he would make the final decision himself after due consideration of the issues.

Practice

c. This is the transcript of a meeting held to discuss the possible purchase of a piece of land on which to build a warehouse.

Write suitable minutes for circulation to all concerned.

MR TODD   Well, thank you ladies and gentlemen for being able to attend this meeting at such short notice. Unfortunately, Alison Moore couldn't make it because she's still in Taiwan.

I'm sure we all appreciate that we need to come to an agreement on this matter as soon as possible. Perhaps you could start, Charles, by reminding us of the options open to us.

MR GREEN   Yes, we've investigated four sites in all and the position now is that we've narrowed down the number of suitable sites to two, one near Burnsley, the other near Whitly. The others were either too small or too expensive. Both the Burnsley and the Whitly sites are very similar in surface area though the price of the Whitly site is considerably lower.

MR MARSH   Well, that is probably because the Whitly site is not so advantageous as far as communications are concerned. In my opinion, access to rail and road routes is too restricted to make it a viable choice.

MRS GRANT   I'm sorry but I think the Burnsley site is out of the question. I've actually visited the place myself and the amount of work that would be needed before construction would make it even more expensive. It needs levelling and compacting, it's not enclosed and the surface is unstable.

MR GREEN   Are you sure? I though it could be resurfaced quite easily.

MRS GRANT   Not according to the advice I've been given. And there's another thing. There are plans to build a motorway extension to Whitly within the next five years so in fact there won't be a problem in terms of road transport. Quite the opposite.

MR MARSH   Except that it's much farther north. And that would mean extra transportation costs.

MR TODD   Well look, I think the next thing is for us to commission a proper survey of the sites and particularly check Sheila's impressions of the Burnsley site. Then the next stage will be to contact a number of contractors and get tenders from them.....

100 Reporting Questions

1 Look at these examples:

'How much does it cost?'	She asked how much it cost.
'How soon can you deliver?'	He wanted to know how soon they could deliver.
'Where is your Head Office?'	He asked where their Head Office was.
'Why won't you give a discount?'	She wanted to know why they wouldn't give a discount.

Note the *tense* in reported questions (one step back in the past).

2 The *word order* is important:

	QUESTION	VERB PHRASE
He/she asked	*how much*	*it cost.*
wanted to know	*how soon*	*they could deliver.*

Note too that there is no question mark.

3 When reporting direct questions beginning with 'do' or 'does', *if* or *whether* are used:

'Do you know the gross weight?'
He asked him *if/whether* he knew the gross weight.

'Does the price include freight charges?'
He asked her *if/whether* the price included freight charges.

'Do you insure exports against political risks?'
He enquired *if/whether* they insured against political risks.

4 Questions beginning with a modal verb are transformed in a similar way:
'Can you type?'
She wanted to know *if/whether* I could type.

'Would you like to meet our Finance Director?'
He asked me *if/whether* I would like to meet their Finance Director.

5 Note that the past verb form is not always necessary. For example, it is possible to say:
He wanted to know where their Head Office is.
She asked how much it costs to fly to San Francisco.

This is because the address of the Head Office is still the same and the price of the ticket has not changed between the time the question was asked and the time of reporting.

Practice

a. Complete each question. Be careful of word order and verb forms.

1. 'Where is the nearest cashpoint?'
He asked me _____.

2. 'How long does it take to go from Heathrow to the City?'
She wanted to know _____.

3. 'What is the time difference between Boston and Los Angeles?'
She asked her _____.

4. 'Do you offer an introductory discount?'
She enquired whether we _____.

5. 'Can you use a spreadsheet?'
She wanted to know _____.

b. Complete the questions in an appropriate way.

Dear Sirs:

We have recently received an application from Ms Valturri for a managerial position in our firm.

She has given your name for reference purposes and I would be grateful if you would give us an appreciation of her general suitability. In particular would you let us know:

how long _____ in your firm;
what responsibilities _____ ;
how many people _____ under her supervision;
how well _____ colleagues;
how often _____ abroad;
how many foreign languages _____ speak

I assure you that this information will be treated in the strictest confidence.

Very truly yours,

Donald Getz

Donald Getz

---

101 Rise vs Raise vs Arise

1 If something *rises* it becomes higher:

Unemployment *rises* in a time of recession.

The past tense is *rose* and the past participle *risen*:

Prices *rose* from $1,300 a ton to $1,450 last year.
Prices have not *risen* as much this year.

> **1.1** The verb *rise* is intransitive, i.e. it cannot take an object:
>
> Interest rates will no doubt continue to *rise*.

2 The verb *raise* is transitive, i.e. it is followed by an object:

A country with a balance of payments problem can *raise* its interest rates to attract foreign capital.

> **2.1** The past tense is *raised*, as is the past participle:
>
> They *raised* their fees last year.
> The government has *raised* sales tax by 3%.

3 There are two nouns: *a rise* and *a raise* which have different usages.
In American English *a raise* is an increase in salary – in British English the word *rise* is used:

She asked for   *a raise.*   (AmE)
             a rise.   (BrE)

In both varieties of English, *a rise* is any kind of increase:

There has been *a rise* in fuel prices.

4 The noun *rise* may refer to the process by which a person became more influential and powerful:

His *rise* to the position of Vice-President took only five years.

5 There are two adjectives that can be derived:

Rising costs have contributed to our deficit. (= increasing)
He spoke to the audience from a *raised* platform.
(i.e. the platform was at a higher level than the audience)

6 If a situation *arises* then a new state of affairs comes into existence:

Problems *arise* when you try to introduce organisational changes too quickly.

> **6.1** The past simple is *arose* and the past participle *arisen*.
>
> **6.2** *Arise* may be used as a synonym of *result from*:
>
> Transport difficulties may *arise* from the proposed location of the warehouse.

�▓7▓ Other meanings and collocations

If a feeling or atmosphere *rises*, it becomes more intense:

Tension is *rising* in the country as a result of the invasion.

If you *rise to an occasion* or *a challenge*, you respond to it positively:

Everyone thought he would be nervous but he *rose to the occasion* and delivered a magnificent speech.

If something *gives rise to* a situation, it causes or creates it:

His resignation has *given rise to* a lot of speculation on his eventual successor.

On the rise means 'on the increase':

Absenteeism is *on the rise* again.

Raise is commonly followed by a number of different nouns:

The team *raised standards* of quality. (= improved)

They are trying to *raise capital/funds* from a number of sources. (= obtain)

Mr Chairman, I would like to *raise the subject of*... (= bring up)

There is mounting pressure from consumer groups to *raise the ban* on cheap imported electronic equipment. (= lift/remove)

Practice

a. Complete the sentences appropriately.

1. If a firm's costs go up then the price of its products will _____.

2. Please get in touch with me if the need _____.

3. I would like to _____ an objection to what has been suggested.

4. The issues you _____ in your letter are serious and merit attention.

5. If any further questions _____ please contact Mr Gordon Clarke in our engineering department.

6. Those in favour of the motion please _____ their right arm.

7. The staff's discontent _____ from the fact that they are underpaid and overworked.

8. Printing costs _____ last year by 14%.

9. We were able to _____ $100,000 through subscriptions.

10. Our expenditure on travel has _____ excessively.

b. Complete the passage with *rise* or *raise* or words derived from them.

The Unions state that because the cost of living ¹_____ by 8% last year, management should ²_____ wages by an

equivalent amount. However, such a [3]_____ means that
the prices of the company's products would have to be
[4]_____ in order to maintain adequate profit margins. It
should be clear that the Unions' demands give [5]_____ to
an inflationary spiral of [6]_____ costs, [7]_____ prices
and further wage claims, ultimately to nobody's satisfaction.

102 Salary vs Wages vs Perks

1 A *salary* is paid monthly and usually by bank transfer. We use
the word *salary* for monthly payments to professional
employees.

2 *Wages* are paid weekly to manual or unskilled workers:
In many countries workers are paid a legal minimum *wage*.
A *wage packet* is the envelope containing *wages*.

3 *Perks* (also known as *fringe benefits*) are extra payments made
in kind e.g. a company car, free accommodation etc.
In many job advertisements the combination of salary plus
perks is called a *remuneration package*.

(→ 43 Earnings vs Income vs Revenue)

Practice

Complete this extract from a job advertisement.

We are offering an attractive _____, including basic
_____ of 60K p.a., plus numerous _____ such as
subsidised accommodation, free medical insurance etc.

103 Save vs Spare

1 To save means 'to economise'. A number of things can be
saved: time, money and *effort* in particular.
Fax it over, it'll *save* time.
We *saved* thousands of pounds by sub-contracting the work.
I'll ask someone to do it for you so as to *save* you the effort.

1.1 *Save* can be followed by the prepositions *up* and *on*:
My wife and I are *saving up* for a new car.
We bought a diesel model to *save on* fuel expenses.

1.2 If someone *saves* you the trouble of doing something, they help you avoid an unpleasant task:

She gave in her resignation to *save* me the trouble of firing her.

2 Note how *spare* is used below:

If I get through my work OK this week I should have some time to *spare* on Friday. (= some time free)
She caught the plane with a few minutes to *spare*. (= a few minutes in reserve)

2.1 If you *spare no expense* you make no effort to reduce the money spent:

They've *spared no expense* in modernising their production lines.

2.2 To *spare* can mean 'to grant':

Could you *spare* me a few minutes of your valuable time?

2.3 *Spare* is also used as an adjective:

The guarantee includes the cost of *spare parts* and labour.
What do you do in your *spare time*?
I had a flat on the freeway and had to use the *spare tire*. (AmE).

Practice

Complete the following.

1. It would _____ time if you organised a videoconference rather than a trip to the States.
2. I've no time to _____ this week but I could see you next Tuesday.
3. The equipment is certainly cheaper but _____ parts might be difficult to obtain.
4. Their new offices are luxurious – they've _____ in furnishings and equipment.
5. A change in our suppliers _____ us hundreds of thousands of pounds.

104 Say vs Tell

1 *Say* and *tell* are both used to report information. They can be followed by *that* but it is not necessary.

She *says (that)* the procedure isn't working.
She *said (that)* the instructions for late shipment had been confirmed.

2 In a negative sentence or a question, *say* can be followed by a *when, where, how,* etc.:

He didn't *say how* we could achieve that goal.
Did he *say when* he would arrive?

3 With *tell* we must make it clear *who* received the information:

We told **them** (that) we couldn't make any more cuts.
I told **Frau Silberstein** (that) I needed the statistics straight away.

3.1 *Tell* (+ object) can be followed by an infinitive when giving orders or advice:

They have *told* us *to speed up* the procedure.
I *told* her *to get away* for the weekend and have a rest.

3.2 Note the word order if *tell* is followed by a negative:

She *told* me *not* to give her any confidential information.

(NOT * to not give)

(→ 99 reporting information)

3.3 There are a number of fixed expressions with *tell*:

tell the time   tell the difference (between)
tell the truth   tell someone the way

Practice

Complete the blanks with the correct form of *say* and *tell*:

1. He's just _____ me he's going to emigrate.
2. She didn't _____ when she would be available.
3. She wouldn't look me in the eyes and I got the distinct impression that she wasn't _____ the truth.
4. I _____ that I would do my best.
5. Did they _____ how much it would cost?
6. I _____ Mr. Lim not to worry.

105 Sell vs Sale vs Sales vs Seller vs Selling

1 If you *sell* something you put it on the market at a stated price:

They have agreed to *sell* us the property.
We have *sold* the last one in stock.

1.1 If something *sells*, it is bought by customers:

Our products *sell* in 25 countries.
The new videodisk is *selling* like hot cakes.

1.2 If something *sells* something else, it makes people want to buy it:

Good software *sells* computers.

1.3 If you *sell* an idea, you convince someone you are right:

He *sold* me on the idea of a new brand of snack biscuits.

1.4 If you *sell yourself short*, you do not present yourself to your best advantage:

If you didn't get the job it's probably because you *sold yourself short* at the interview.

1.5 *Sell* can be followed by *off*, *out* or *up*:

They're *selling off* their assets at bargain prices.

Here the implication is that the price is low because they need to sell quickly.

Sorry, we've *sold out*.
I'm afraid we've *sold out of* this model.

This means there are none left.

She's decided to *sell up* her business.

This implies she's selling everything in order to do something new.

1.6 *Sell* can be used as a noun in two expressions:
a *hard sell* is an aggressive way of selling, a *soft sell* is more gentle and persuasive.

2 The noun derived from *sell* is usually *sale*:

Many economies in the Third World depend on the *sale* of cash crops to obtain foreign currency.

2.1 Something can be *for sale* (property or an asset) or *on sale* (available for purchase in a shop):

The premises are up *for sale*.
Our latest model is *on sale* in most department stores.

2.2 A *sale* is organised by a shop when it wants to move stock quickly by offering goods at lower prices:

They're having a clearance *sale*.
The *sale* price is marked down 50%.

2.3 The *point of sale* is the place where a consumer actually buys an article:

We've recently spent £250,000 on *point-of-sale* advertising – display stands, posters and so on.

3 *Sales* are the quantity of goods sold over a given period of time:

Car *sales* have gone up in the third quarter.
Our *sales* grew by 120% in the first two years.

3.1 *Sales* can be used with a number of nouns:

sales
- clerk
- conference
- department
- man
- person
- talk
- target

3.2 An *after-sales service* organises the maintenance and repair of goods sold by a producer or distributor.

4 We do not usually use the word *seller* to refer to a person who sells a company's products. However, it can be used to refer to a private individual:

She's a *seller* of second-hand books[1].

4.1 If something is a *good seller* then it sells well:

The Ford Model T was a *best-seller* in its time.

5 *Selling* commonly occurs in three combinations:
selling price (the price at which goods are sold)
selling point (a feature which makes an article particularly
attractive)
unique selling proposition (the special feature which makes a
product a must for a potential
customer)

Practice

Complete the blanks with a suitable word or expression.

1. Good advertising can _____ even a poor product.
2. We've sold _____ of this particular line, but we can order some for you.
3. _____ have improved, particularly in Scandinavia.
4. They sell _____ their old stock in January.
5. EFTPOS means Electronic Funds Transfer at the point of

_____.

6. He's decided to sell _____ and emigrate.
7. My business is up _____ and I will _____ to the highest bidder.
8. If anything goes wrong, take it back to our _____ service.
9. The IBM PC was a world _____.
10. There's a _____ of summer clothes to make room for the winter collection.

[1] 'She **sells** second-hand books' is more usual.

106 Set up vs Establish vs Settle

1 If you *set up* a piece of equipment you install it ready for use:

I've *set up* the video so that you can show the clip.

1.1 If you *set up* a company, you take the necessary steps to create the business:

The bank lent us £200,000 to *set up* a small business.

1.2 *Set up* goes with *enquiry* and *investigation*:

The government has *set up* an enquiry to investigate the extent of insider trading on the Stock Exchange.

2 To *establish* tends to suggest a permanent position, e.g.:

The new design has already *established* a clear superiority over its rivals.

whereas to *set up* stresses the initial act of creation. This distinction is brought out in the use of the adjective *established*:

We have an *established* international reputation.
Soltran is the *established* market leader.
We have a well-*established* customer base.

2.1 *Establish* is frequently used in two collocations:

We have *established* a reputation for quality.
They want to *establish* contact with a firm interested in a joint venture.

2.2 *Establish* has another meaning similar to 'make the facts clear or known':

The enquiry *established* that the chemicals plant had been polluting the river.

3 *Settle* has none of the above meanings, though it is commonly confused with *set up*.
The main meanings are:

He *settled* the bill by credit card. (= paid the sum due)

I'll leave you to *settle* the details. (= make arrangements so that everything is finalised)

She chose to *settle* (down) in New Hampshire. (= become a permanent resident)

The dispute was *settled* with a minimum of lost production. (= resolved)

As legal costs are so high they agreed to *settle* out of court. (= end the dispute by offering compensation without a legal judgement)

Practice

Put a tick (✓) in the chart if the verb can be used with the noun phrase in the top column.

	a dispute	a business	an invoice	an overhead projector	contact	in business	an international reputation
set up							
establish							
settle							

107 Shall vs Will vs 'll

1 *Shall* is used mainly in British English.

1.1 One use is to make a suggestion or an offer:

Shall we start now?   (= Do you want us to start?)[1]
Shall I give you a hand?   (= Do you want me to ...?)

1.2 *Shall* is used to ask for advice or someone's opinion:

What *shall* we do about the complaint?

1.3 It is becoming old-fashioned to use *shall* as a future form. *Will* is more common:

I *will/shall* be in touch shortly.

The negative form is *shan't/won't*:

I ⎰ shan't ⎱ know until Friday.
  ⎱ won't ⎰

1.4 *Shall* is very common in contracts and indicates an obligation:

The guaranteed private credits *shall* be amortised in ten (10) years. Their rate of interest *shall* be the usual rate applied to export credits,to which the cost of credit insurance *shall* be added.

2 *Will* is used to make a prediction or refer to a future fact:

I think they *will* increase Social Security contributions.
The mayor *will* open the new site on 4 July.

It is particularly common in conditional statements:

If the pound is devalued, Britain's exports *will* be more competitive.

2.1 It can be used for a 'present' prediction:

It's 7 o'clock here so it *will* be 1 o'clock in Los Angeles.

[1] *Shall we* is also used as a 'tag' question after Let's. Let's make a start, shall we?

2.2 If you want to make a promise, you can use *will*:

I *will* send off the consignment as soon as the documentation is ready.

2.3 In a question, *will* asks about what someone else wants to happen or what someone else has decided:

Will it be OK if I do it tomorrow?
Will I be making the presentation?

2.4 The contracted form *'ll* announces a spontaneous decision, usually an offer of some sort. It is informal and is more typical of the spoken language:

'I haven't got time to have these papers photocopied.'
'Don't worry, I *'ll* do it if you like.'

In other cases it is simply the contracted form of *will*:

I *will/'ll* let you know on Friday.

2.5 The negative form is *won't*:

I *won't* be at the committee meeting next Wednesday.

(→ 56 future, → 65 Legal English)

Practice

Mrs Walsh has just arrived at work and someone has just phoned. Complete the dialogue with *will, shall* or *'ll*.

SECRETARY There's a Mr Bjork on the line who wants to speak to you.
MRS WALSH OK, I ¹_____ take the call in my office.
MR BJORK Mrs Walsh?
MRS WALSH Speaking.
MR BJORK Hello. My name is Mr Stefan Bjork. I represent Tinned Foods in Stockholm.
MRS WALSH What can I do for you Mr Bjork?
MR BJORK Well, I'm ringing about a delivery problem. Our latest consignment is over three weeks late.
MRS WALSH Oh dear, I'm sorry to hear that. I can't explain without checking in your file but it may be because of the seaman's strike. Anyway, I ²_____ call our Export Department and see what has happened.
MR BJORK When ³_____ you be able to give me a definite answer?
MRS WALSH ⁴_____ it be all right if I call you back tomorrow?
MR BJORK No, not really I ⁵_____ be in the office until some time next week.
MRS WALSH Oh, well when ⁶_____ it be possible to get you?
MR BJORK It's rather difficult to say.

MRS WALSH In that case, ⁷_____ I ask the Export
Department to fax you their reasons for the delay and
their suggestions?

MR BJORK Yes please and if there is any major problem I
⁸_____ ask my deputy Mrs Lof to get back in
touch with you.

108 Should vs Would

1 *Should* has a number of uses.

1.1 To say something is a good idea, to make a
recommendation:

I think you *should* change your advertising strategy. Your present
approach isn't working.

Special quotes or any important statements made during a phone
conversation *should* always be confirmed in writing.

1.2 To indicate that something is 'right' and desirable. There
is often an implied criticism:

If the government wants to encourage investment it *should* lower
the lending rate. (the lending rate is too high)

If something is undesirable we use *should not*.

They *should not* be charging us for carriage – we've already paid
for the transport.

1.3 To criticise a past action (with *have + past participle*):

We *shouldn't have* mentioned it, we *should have* kept quiet.

1.4 For rules and instructions:

Changes in company directors or premises *should* be notified to
the Registrar on form 288.

In this example the meaning is very close to *must*. The
sentence is potentially ambiguous; however it seems to be
closer to an obligation than just a recommendation.

1.5 As a replacement of *if* in a formal style:

Should you wish to make a booking, please contact our
Reservations Manager, Gillian Gregg.

1.6 To say that something is probable:

Mr Watson *should* be able to see you shortly, the meeting is
almost over.

1.7 After verbs such as *suggest, recommend, insist* in a
formal style:

She insisted (that) I *should* stay on for the demonstration.
He recommended that we *should* try the more expensive model.

1.8 After certain adjectives such as *surprised, important* or *essential* (in a formal style):

It is *essential* that all moving parts *should* be fitted with a safety guard.

2 *Would* is used:

2.1 To make a polite request:

Would you please let me have the details as soon as possible?

'Shall I shut the window?' 'Yes, if you *would*.'

2.2 To express a desire (as a polite equivalent of *want*):

I *would* like to make an appointment.

I *would* like to point out that there seems to be an error in our last invoice.

I wish they *would* reduce the rate of corporation tax.

Note that 'I *would* like to' can be replaced by 'I *should* like to'. However, the use of *should*, in this meaning, is becoming old-fashioned in British English and is rarely heard in American English.

2.3 With *like* to make an offer:

Would you like another cup of coffee?

2.4 To express a refusal (in the negative):

He was late today because his car *wouldn't* start.

She *wouldn't* think of doing overtime because she's afraid of paying more tax.

2.5 For imaginary situations:

How much *would* it cost to buy 10,000 British Petroleum shares?

What *would* happen, if we were taken over?

We *would* be a more successful firm, if we exported more. (but we don't)

They *wouldn't have* gone bankrupt, if they had diversified their product line. (but they didn't)

2.6 To talk about a past habit:

When we lived in Japan I *would* often have a few drinks in a bar before going back home after work.

2.7 Note that this sentence:

I *would* be grateful if you *would* send me the necessary forms.

is a polite request and it is therefore possible to have *would* after *if*. It is NOT possible in a conditional statement:

* If we *would* export more ....

(→ 61 If; 76 Must vs Have to vs Need vs Should)

Practice

a. Use *should* or *would*.

COMPANIES HOUSE
CARDIFF CF4 3UZ

The Directors
ITC Ltd
Inverness House
3 Aldwych
London WC2B 4CZ   10 February 1992

FIRST AND FINAL NOTICE

Dear Sirs

COMPANIES ACT 1985

My records indicate that the last annual
return received for your firm was made over
18 months ago.

The Companies Act requires that an annual
return [1]_____ be sent to me within 42
days of each AGM of a company.

Full accounts [2]_____ also be submitted.
They [3]_____ normally include a profit and
loss account, a balance sheet, an auditor's
report and a directors' report.

[4]_____ you please ensure that these
documents reach this office within the next
14 days.

If they were sent more than 21 days ago I
suggest that you [5]_____ contact me in
order that we may check the records for your
company.

Yours faithfully

Lisa Clarke

LISA CLARK (Mrs)

Registrar

b. Advice to Exporters.

Which of these *should* you do if you intend to export?
Which *shouldn't* you do? (Suggest alternatives)

1. Translate the product literature yourself.
2. Appoint an agent who is working for a competitor.
3. Make your agent pay for local advertising and promotion.
4. Quote 'Delivery Duty Paid'.
5. Insist on payment in sterling.
6. Obtain bank references for open account customers.
7. Insist on a confirmed letter of credit.
8. Type all documents individually.
9. Check whether the profit margin has been realised after deducting all costs and overheads.

c. If you were in charge of running the economy what five measures *would* you take as a matter or priority?

For example: I *would* abolish all exchange controls.

d. Comment on these situations using *should.*

1. The photocopier is always breaking down.
2. The cheque couldn't be paid into the account because the signature was missing.
3. The documentary credit couldn't be accepted because the total value of the consignment was greater than the amount authorised.
4. They only advertise in the trade press and fail to reach the average customer.
5. The original design was stolen by a competitor and commercialised. We didn't have a patent unfortunately.

e. What *would* you *have done?*
Read through this short case and think about how you would have dealt with this situation.

The coming year's sales programme was now complete and Francis Kennedy, sales manager of *Pinewood Products*, had just completed a three week trip auditing customer accounts and following up prospective clients (mainly furniture stores or department stores with a furniture department) contacted by his sales staff over the previous six months. To his surprise, Francis discovered that the majority of these sales reports were not based on any previous visit and had been completely made up. In fact his sales staff had only made 7 of the 24 reported visits.

109 So vs Such

1 *Such* is used before countable or uncountable nouns (with or without adjectives):

Italy is *such* a beautiful country – I'd love to work there.
I don't know how he keeps going – he has *such* energy!

2 *So* is used before adjectives, and not before nouns:

She's *so* enthusiastic about her work.

3 *So* and *such* are intensifiers – they make the adjective or determiner stronger in force:

Why did the job take *so* long?
Why did the job take *such* a long time?
There were *so* many applications for shares that they had to hold a ballot.
There were *such* a lot of applications for shares that they had to hold a ballot.

4 These words can both express a result but the pattern is different. Compare:

The bid was *so* high *that* we couldn't refuse.
It was *such* a high bid *that* we couldn't refuse[1].

    4.1 It is also possible, in more formal contexts, to say:

It was *so* high *a* bid *that* we couldn't refuse.

5 *So* can be used with an adverb.

He speaks *so* quickly *that* he is very hard to understand.

6 Neither *so* nor *such* can be used when the noun is preceded by *the, this, that* or a *possessive* (*his, your,* etc.)
NOT * Thank you for your such warm welcome.
NOT * We don't export there because of the so complicated procedures.

7 You said you would mark the display stands with the recommended retail price if we *so* wished.

In this sentence *so* is used as a substitution word in order to avoid repeating 'if we wished to *mark the display stands with the recommended retail price*':

I am writing to enquire whether you are able to be of assistance. If *so*, could you.please indicate what kind of help you can provide.
Here *so* avoids repeating *you are able to be of assistance.*

---

[1] NOT* A so high bid.

8 *So* is used when expressing an opinion or agreement

I think *so*   I hope *so*   I'm afraid *so*

I suppose *so* (a weak or reluctant agreement)

9 Note the polite request:

Would you be *so kind as* to arrange for me to be met at the airport?[1]

Practice

a. What could you say (using *so* or *such*) in these circumstances?

1. You're shocked at the price.
2. You find the service in your hotel very poor. You won't stay there again.
3. It's the fifth time you have had to explain to him.
4. You want to apologise.
5. The delivery you expected six weeks ago still hasn't arrived.

b. Reformulate these sentences in order to avoid unnecessary repetition.

1. Mr Owen said the payment could be made at a later date if we wished it to be made at a later date.
2. We can increase our production capacity but Mrs Cook doesn't think we can increase our production capacity.
3. They may demand a more attractive financing package. If they demand a more attractive financing package telex me immediately.

110 Some vs Any; Much vs Many; No vs None

All these words tell us about a quantity.

1 *Some* is used with both countable and uncountable nouns. It means 'a number of' / 'an amount of'.

Some people like working at night, but I don't.

We've been doing *some* research into the causes of the problem.

Would you like *some* whisky?

---

[1] (AmE: Would you be kind enough to ...)

2 *Any* is most commonly used in negative sentences and in questions:

I haven't got *any* change on me.
We haven't got *any* instruction manuals left.
Have you *any* luggage?
Is there *any* model you particularly like?

3 *Any* can indicate that *all* examples of the noun are to be included as in:

Any manager will tell you that flexitime is difficult to administer. (= all managers)
A telex can be received at *any* time of the day or night. (= all the time)
Choose *any* colour you like. (= it doesn't matter which colour)
Cars can be hired at almost *any* US airport. (= almost all US airports)

3.1 Note the use of *any* in sentences beginning with *if*:

If you have *any* queries to make, do not hesitate to contact us.

4 *Much* and *many* mean 'a large quantity' / 'number of' something. *Much* is used with uncountable nouns and *many* with countable ones: (→ 35 countable vs uncountable nouns.)

I haven't had *much* time recently.
Many decisions are made after *much* prior consideration.
Have you got *much* work to do?
Did you meet *many* people at the exhibition?

4.1 Both *many* and *much* can be substituted by *a lot of*. *Many* can be replaced by *a large number* (*of*) and *much* by *a great deal* (*of*).

5 *No* and *none* mean 'not one' / 'not any'

We've had *no* orders for the XL368 and it should be dropped from our catalogue.
They have paid *none* of their invoices.
None of the candidates *was* appointed.

(Note the singular verb form)

5.1 *Not any* is neutral in force; *no* is a little stronger and both can be followed by 'at all' for emphasis:

We haven*'t* received *any* orders recently.
We've received *no* orders (at all) recently.

Practice

a. Complete this letter using: *no none some any much many.*

Dear Mrs. Lambert,

Distributorship Agreement : BURO cartridges

Clinton West Jnr. has requested that I contact
you with reference to his agreement with you
for the sale of BURO cartridges in the USA. He
has tried on [1]_____ occasions to reach you
at work but has been repeatedly told that you
were absent.

This agreement provides for the payment to Mr
West of $0.005 for [2]_____ cartridge sold by
you, for monthly reports of sales made, and
quarterly payments computed with relation to
sales.

Since this agreement was signed, [3]_____
payments have been made but only at irregular
intervals. Not [4]_____ reports have been
sent (five in the last 18 months) and
[5]_____ commissions at all have been
received over the past year.

You are clearly in breach of contract and in
order to avoid [6]_____ legal action would
you please forward by return:

1. A report on sales of BURO cartridges to
date.
2. Payment by check of [7]_____ sums owing on
the said sales.

Your agreement with Mr West is over three years
old. For [8]_____ of the time you have chosen
to disregard its obligations. [9]_____ of my
client's letters has been answered in the
recent past.

Therefore, in order to avoid wasting
[10]_____ time, I am sending this letter by
telecopy and expect a prompt response,
certainly [11]_____ later than by the end of
this month.

Very truly yours,

Randolph T. Zick

Randolph T. Zick
(Attorney at Law)

111 So that vs To vs In order to vs So as to

There are a number of ways of expressing the reasons *why* things are / were/ will be done.

1 So that

This structure is followed by a present or a future verb form:

Companies build up buffer stocks *so that* they do not/will not run short of supplies.

It can also be followed by a modal verb:

Manufacturers must be aware of incidents involving the safety of their products *so that* they *may/can* take corrective action.

1.1 In sentences referring to past time *would* or *could* are used:

We set up there *so that* we *would* be able to use the excellent transport network.

We opened a branch in the Bahamas *so that* we *could* benefit from the tax concessions available.

We reduced our prices *so that* we *would* become more competitive.

2 To

We make regular safety checks *to reduce* the risk of an accident.
Procedures have been reviewed regularly *to cut down on* inefficiency.
I went to the bank *to get* a cash advance on my credit card.
The commission will be meeting *to investigate* complaints.

3 In order to / So as to

In a slightly more formal style *in order to* + *verb* or *so as to* + *verb* can be used:

The ministers met *in order to* discuss the harmonisation of levels of VAT.

They sponsored a number of cultural events *so as to* enhance their reputation.

Practice

Answer these questions in your own words.

1. Why do governments give subsidies to certain firms?
2. Why is there a World Bank?
3. Why are there import quotas in certain countries?
4. Why do firms use 'just in time' inventory control?
5. Why do some firms use the services of a factor?
6. Why are some goods shipped air freight and not by sea?

112 Spot vs Forward

These words refer to two different kinds of market for currencies or commodities.

1 On the *spot* market the buyer is required to pay cash and delivery is more or less immediate.

2 On a *forward* market delivery takes place at a stated time in the future, e.g. 30, 90 or 180 days. However, the price is specified immediately.

Dealings on forward markets are common in international trade where contracts have to be made well in advance of delivery, despite the fact that prices and rates of exchange are bound to fluctuate between the moment the order is made and payment is received.

For example, if a UK company has ordered machinery from Germany to be delivered in three months' time and to be paid for in Deutschmarks, it can be sure of the exchange rate in advance by purchasing Deutschmarks at the *forward* rate. The bank may quote a *spot* rate of DM2.918 = £1 and a *forward* rate of DM2.880 = £1. In effect, the British company promises to purchase the foreign exchange at a future date at DM2.880 = £1. In this way it can keep its sterling invested in the business and avoid any effective rise in price of the machinery resulting from a dramatic fall in the value of sterling against the Deutschmark.

Practice

Complete the sentence.

1. It is possible to buy commodities on the _____ market for immediate delivery or purchase at a _____ price for delivery in three months' time.

113 Still vs Yet vs Always vs Already vs No longer

1 *Still* emphasises continuity:

London is *still* a port even though it doesn't handle as much cargo as before.

Does she *still* live in New York or has she moved?

2 In negative sentences, *yet* means that something has not so far happened:

They have*n't yet* signed a tax treaty, but I think they will soon.

The position of *yet* can change:

They have*n't* signed a tax treaty *yet*.[1]

3 In positive sentences and before an infinitive, *still* and *yet* are interchangeable:

'Who's been nominated?'
'It's *yet/still* to be decided.'

4 *Always* means 'on all occasions'; it is the opposite of *never*.

We *always* use a translation agency for our foreign documentation.

5 *Already* means 'before now', 'sooner-than-expected':

'Do you know Mr Weisz?' 'Yes, we've *already* met.'
'Could you give me the figures by the end of the week?'
'I've *already* done them.'
'*Already*? I thought they would takes ages!'

6 If something *no longer* happens, it means it does not happen any more.

We used to export to Australia but we *no longer* have a market there.

Practice

a. Complete the following sentences and extracts with:

still   (not) yet   already   no longer   always

1. Thank you for your explanation but there are _____ a number of points that need clearing up.

---

[1] Note the difference in British and American usage:
Have you seen him **yet**? (BrE)
Did you see him **yet**? (AmE)

(→ 23   British English vs American English.)

2. 'Have you finished typing up the report _____?'
'No, I'm _____ typing it.'
3. There will _____ be conflicts in a firm, especially if younger people have little access to promotion.
4. There's no need to write. I've _____ spoken to him over the phone.
5. I regret to inform you that the STT laser printer is _____ available. However, the STT Mark II will soon be available from your local stockist.

b.

Our records show that payment of invoice no. 9735/IJ is [1]_____ outstanding. If you have [2]_____ paid please disregard this notice. However, if you have [3]_____ settled this bill, please send your remittance to Bower & Gregg, 112 East 59th Street, New York, NY 10022.

c.

We are writing to advise you that we have now adopted the new Harmonized System of Commodity Classification. As a result, a precise invoice description of goods being shipped is very important. Code or part numbers alone will [1]_____ be acceptable. Future consignments should now [2]_____ be accompanied by a complete and proper description of each item shipped.

114 Stocks and Shares

Although these words are often used as synonyms there is a difference in meaning.

1 *Stocks* are similar to loans and pay interest. In the UK, they are known as *debentures* (if issued by companies) or *gilts* if issued by the government. The interest is usually at a fixed rate. They are a safe investment as companies are obliged to pay interest and repay the capital whether or not the firm is making a profit. However, the return on the investment is likely to be lower than on *shares*.

2 *Shares* pay *dividends* rather than interest and enable the *bearer* to own a part of the company. If a company goes *bankrupt*, the *shareholders* will only be repaid after all the other creditors. As the term *equity* can be defined as what remains when all other claims on a company's assets have been met, s*tock* and *equity* are interchangeable terms.

There are many varieties of shares; these are some of the most important.

> **2.1** *Ordinary shares* give the bearer the right to vote, appoint and remove directors and the right to receive a dividend.

> **2.2** *Preference shares* give the holder the right to receive dividends before ordinary shareholders and priority if the company is liquidated. However, the dividend is fixed.

> **2.3** *Cumulative preference shares* entitle the bearer to be paid in arrears if a dividend is not paid in any one year.

3 *Stocks, shares* and *bonds* are known collectively as *securities*.

4 A *unit trust* is an organisation which enables small investors to own a wide *portfolio* of securities. These are bought by fund managers and divided into units of equal price which are offered for sale to the public. Each *subscriber* becomes the owner of a fraction of all the securities held by the trust. Dividends are paid at six month intervals.[1]

5 If an existing company needs to raise more equity capital it can make a *rights issue*. Shares are offered to existing shareholders (usually at a discount) in proportion to the number of shares they hold (for example, one share for every four owned).

6 A *bonus issue* (or *scrip issue*) does not increase a company's funds. Extra shares are given to shareholders in proportion to their holdings. In this way, retained earnings are converted into share capital and the *nominal value* of each share can be reduced.

7 A *takeover* occurs when one company acquires more than 50 per cent of the shares of another. When a *takeover bid* is launched the company wishing to buy tries to win the consent of the other firm's board. If the board agrees (because the offer price is high or the advantages obvious) the bid is *friendly*. If the bid is rejected, the takeover will be *hostile*. In this case, over a 60 day period, each side will hire banks and public

---

[1] Unit trusts exist in the UK only. They are not traded on the Stock Exchange.

relations specialists to put forward the case for or against the acquisition. The costs of a major bid can be very high but so can the increase in share prices. For example, in 1988 Nestlé bought Rowntree whose shares were quoted at £4.50 before the takeover. When the bid finally succeeded they were worth £10.75.

8 A firm may be acquired by its own managers. This is known as a *management buy-out.*

9 *Share valuation*

These calculations are commonly used to assess a share's performance.

$$\frac{\text{The company's total earnings}}{\text{The number of shares issued}} = \text{earnings per share}$$

$$\frac{\text{The share price}}{\text{Earnings per share}} = \text{price / earnings ratio}$$

$$\frac{\text{Dividend}}{\text{Current share price}} = \text{yield}$$

Practice

Using this information and your own knowledge find the connections between the words in the table.
For example: *a market maker* is a dealer in *securities* on the Stock Exchange.

unit	market	stock	bond
insider	management	equities	issue
bull	earnings	friendly	bid
takeover	Dow Jones	trusts	maker
hostile	securities	acquisition	rights
trading	gilts	buyout	index
ordinary	Hang Seng	broker	share
holder	debenture	preference	bear

115 Subject to

1 This expression is very commonly found in legal contracts and official documents. It expresses a condition. X will happen only if Y also happens:

This contract is binding *subject to* the fulfilment of the following conditions. (= If the conditions are fulfilled then the contract is binding.)

Standby tickets are *subject to* availability. (= If a standby ticket is available you can obtain one.)

2 It can also mean 'liable to':

Your recent allowance is *subject to* income tax.

3 In another meaning it can mean 'susceptible to/prone to':

The warehouse is *subject to* flooding.

or 'bound by' as in:

The activities of stockbrokers are *subject to* the rules of the Stock Exchange.

4 It is possible to follow *subject to* with a gerund:

Promotion is automatic *subject to* passing internal examinations.

This offer is valid *subject to* (your) signing the enclosed conditions of service.

You are entitled to retire at 55 *subject to* appropriate notice *being* given.

Practice

Rewrite these sentences using *subject to*. There may be more than one possible way of doing this:

1. Any cash bonus will be liable to income tax.
2. Our offer depends on the approval of the Board of Directors.
3. All textile imports are liable to a 15% tariff.
4. British citizens resident in France come under the jurisdiction of French law.
5. Our improved pay offer applies only if the strikers return to work.
6. This distributorship agreement is governed by the rules and regulations of the United Arab Emirates.
7. Whether we go ahead with the plan or not is dependent upon his confirmation.
8. Promotion is not automatic and is only made on condition that you demonstrate initiative and commitment.

9. You will receive 2% commission providing that you sell more than 5,000 articles a year.

10. If you complete the probationary period satisfactorily you will be transferred to the permanent staff.

116 Subsidy vs Grant vs Allocation vs Allowance

1 A *subsidy* is money paid by the government to a producer so that goods can be sold below the normal market price. The sum of money involved is likely to be quite high:

Within the EC, government *subsidies* are considered unfair competition.

The verb is *to subsidise*[1].

2 A *grant* is money made available (by the government or official body) to help finance a project, e.g. a course of studies or starting a small business. The sums involved are likely to be quite small:

IMX plc gave him a *grant* to undertake research in the USA.

The verb is *to grant.*

3 An *allocation* is a sum of money which is '*earmarked*' (= set aside) for a particular purpose.

We've already spent our budget *allocation* for sales promotion.
The Director has *allocated* £400,000 for re-training.

The verb is *to allocate.*

4 An *allowance* is similar in meaning to *allocation*. However, the word implies that money will be given on a regular basis:

The company gives me a car and a fuel *allowance.*

Practice

Complete the following.

1. She received a _____ from the Youth Business Initiative scheme and set up a small business.

2. I wine and dine potential customers using the money from my entertainments _____.

[1] (AmE: **subsidize**)

3. Why don't we _____ a sum of money from the reserve funds and spend it on further research?

4. We _____ our staff restaurant so employees only pay 40% of the real cost of a meal.

117 Take place vs Happen

1 Things which *take place* are organised and planned:

The China Write symposium is to *take place* in Shanghai.

2 Things which *happen* are unforeseen and uncontrolled:

The accident *happened* at 9.35.

2.1 *Happen* can also have the meaning of *result.*

I pressed the right button but nothing *happened*.

Practice

Complete the sentences.

1. What would _____ if we threatened to take them to court?

2. Next year's conference will _____ in Jeddah.

118 Telephone Language

Below are some useful expressions when speaking on the phone.

1 MAKING A CALL

'Hello, this is ...... Could I speak to ...?'

'Is ... available?'

'Can I leave a message?'

'Do you know the code / extension number?'

'Sorry, I didn't catch that, could you say that again?'

'Could I leave a message?'

'Sorry, wrong number.'

'We got cut off.'

2 RECEIVING A CALL

'44291' (your phone number)

'Altel International, can I help you?' (your company)

'Speaking' (when someone at the other end of the line has asked to speak to you)

'Would you like to leave a message?'

'Would you like him / her to call you back?'

'Hold on a moment please, I'm putting you through / I'll put you through.'

'The line's busy (AmE) / *engaged* (BrE). *Would you like to hold?'*

Practice

a. Three people are involved in this jumbled conversation, Mr Thomas of Jetset Services, Mr Chouaki of Sybil S.A. and a switchboard operator.

Put the conversation into the correct order.

1. His number's busy. Would you like him to call you back?
2. Yes, speaking.
3. Sybil S.A. Can I help you?
4. Right. Well, thank you for calling.
5. I'm afraid he's on the line at the moment. Do you want to hold or leave a message?
6. Hello, is that Mr Chouaki?
7. My name is Michael Thomas of Jetset Services. I've been trying to get through to you. I'm phoning to find out whether the display stands I ordered last week have been sent off.
8. No, it doesn't matter, I'll hold.
9. Mr Chouaki is free now, I'll put you through.
10. Yes, they've just been sent off and should arrive in the next couple of days. If there's any problem give me a call.
11. Hello, this is Michael Thomas of Jetset Services. Could I speak to Mr Chouaki in Customer Services, please?
12. No, I'll hold.
13. Thank you. Goodbye.
14. Oh good. Yes, I will, but I hope it won't be necessary.

b. Choose a word and find another that is associated with it in some way. Try and give a brief description.

For example: *a phone card* is necessary if you want to use a public phone box which does not accept coins.

switchboard	*reverse*	*enquiries[1]*	*phone*
conference	*operator*	*answer*	*distance*
call	*charge*	*collect*	*dial*
number	*long*	*card*	*ring*
directory	*hang*	*freefone[2]*	*up*

119 Tender vs Bid

These words can both be used as nouns or verbs.

1 A *tender* is a formal offer to supply or produce goods or services at a stated price, usually in competition with other *tenderers*:

The Arab Industrial Investment Company invites firms to **tender** for the construction of hospital units in Iran, Iraq, Qatar and Yemen.

The Crown Agents invite you to submit a **tender** for the supply of heavy engineering equipment to Gabon. All **tenders** must be submitted by 30 May.

2 The word *bid* is identical in this usage:

Tenderers are bound by the terms of their **bid** for a period of 60 days.

3 However, there are other uses where only one of the words is possible:

3.1 A *takeover bid*. (→ 114 **Stocks vs Shares**)

3.2 To *bid* at an auction sale.

3.3 A *bid price*: the price an individual is willing to pay for a stock or share.

3.4 To *tender* one's resignation. (= offer to resign)

3.5 *Legal tender*, bank notes and coins which are accepted in payment, e.g. Scottish banknotes are *legal tender* in England. Irish banknotes are not.

---

[1] (AmE: **inquiries**)   [2] (AmE: **toll-free**)

Practice

Complete the following sentences.

1. News of the takeover ——————— raised share prices by 15 per cent.

2. He ——————— over $50m for a painting by a little-known American artist.

3. She's decided to ——————— her resignation and look for a better position elsewhere.

4. You can't buy anything in Britain with an old ten shilling note. It's no longer ———————.

120 The

1 We use *the* to refer to nouns that have already been mentioned or when it is obvious what particular thing is being referred to:

We are sorry to receive your letter of 5 May informing us of an error in carriage charges. *The* error was due to an incorrect entry in our records which has now been rectified.

Thank you for your order of 26 October. Please find enclosed *the* pro-forma invoice you requested.

He bought a compact disk player and a portable TV from the store but took *the* TV back a week later.

The post hasn't arrived yet.

It takes 25 minutes to get to *the* airport from downtown.

Therefore *the* refers to things which are definite, specific or unique:

As *the* focal point for trade traffic throughout *the* region, Dubai is *the* gateway to commerce in *the* Middle East.

2 *The* is NOT used before a noun when the noun refers to something general and unspecific and is uncountable or plural:

Time is *money*.

Industry needs good *graduates*..

We never give *credit*.

Consultants specialise in giving *advice*.

Venture capitalists have to take financial *risks*.

She works in *banking*.

Sole traders may find it difficult to raise *capital*.

Microchips are used to make *computers*.

Banks provide *firms* with *finance*.

3 We use *the* to refer to organisations such as:

the police   *the* army   *the* fire brigade
the civil service   *the* Inland Revenue

4 We use *the* to refer to unique institutions:

The World Bank   *The* United Nations   *The* White House
The Stock Exchange   *The* Bundesbank[1]   *The* Kremlin

Abbreviations which have to be pronounced as single letters take *the* (e.g. *the* BBC, *the* EEC)
If an abbreviation can be said as a word *the* is omitted: (GATT, ARAMCO, COMECON, EFTA, ESSO, UNCTAD, OPEC, TASS, UNIDO, etc.)

Practice

a. Insert *the* wherever necessary.

1. He has no experience of _____ word processing.
2. She's a government tax inspector and works in _____ Treasury.
3. _____ exporters can receive help from _____ Export Credit Guarantee Department.
4. _____ business we set up last year is doing well.
5. _____ peseta went down against _____ dollar yesterday.
6. _____ EEC is made up of 12 member nations.
7. _____ credit enables _____ people to buy _____ goods now and pay later.
8. _____ personnel department organises _____ training.
9. _____ cash dispensers are machines which enable _____ customers to draw out _____ money quickly from their bank.
10. _____ advertising gives _____ information on _____ events and _____ services, _____ products and _____ prices. _____ aim is to persuade _____ consumers to buy.

[1] Note, however, that banks can be known by their name and **the** is omitted e.g. Barclay's, Citibank.

b. Read these extracts from business letters and complete the blanks appropriately.

For example:

....We enclose a pro-forma and request you to open a letter of credit for £9,225. As soon as we receive notification that *the letter of credit* has been confirmed .....

1.

.... and you will receive a commission of 10% on all sales of equipment in Brazil. _____ will be paid at three-monthly intervals .....

2.

.... we enclose a job description and an application form. Would you please send _____ back to us by 15th September ....

3.

Gentlemen:
We are pleased to advise you of our shipment of your order no. 80/190-09 for spare parts. _____ was sent on September 27th in carton no. 4376.

4.

Dear Sir

Statement 1 June

On 15 July we wrote to remind you that debts totaling $6569 were still outstanding. According to our records we have not yet received any settlement and I am therefore enclosing another copy of _____.

c. Place *the* where necessary in this extract from an official document.

undersigned, duly authorised by company, swears that above-mentioned goods have been inspected and certified by Osaka Chamber of Commerce.

d. Which of these can only be pronounced as single letters? Which are pronounced as a single word? Write *the* if necessary.

...... OPEC	...... TASS	...... EXXON	...... UN
...... UNESCO	...... OECD	...... NYSE	...... EEC
...... IMF	...... ASEAN	...... EMS	...... EFTA

5 *Countries and Nationalities*
The is used to refer to people belonging to a nation:

the Algerians	*the* Dutch	*the* Irish	*the* Portuguese
the Belgians	*the* English	*the* Japanese	*the* Russians
the Brazilians	*the* French	*the* Mexicans	*the* Spanish
the Chinese	*the* Germans	*the* Norwegians	*the* Swedes
the Danes	*the* Greeks	*the* Poles	*the* Vietnamese

(→ 78 Nationality words)

6 Plural names of countries, geographical areas or island groups take *the*:

the Caribbean	*the* Netherlands	*the* Ukraine
the Far East	*the* Pacific	*the* United Arab Emirates
the Middle East	*the* Seychelles	*the* West Indies

as do countries which include 'kingdom', or 'states':

the United Kingdom   *the* United States

7 *The* is NOT used before most countries, cities and places:

Italy	Laos	China	Sweden
Copenhagen	Lima	Belgrade	Edinburgh
Wall St.	Lake Michigan	Piccadilly Circus	Kennedy airport

But note: *The* Hague, *the* City, *the* West End (of London).

7.1 *The* is NOT used with the names of continents:

Africa	Asia	Australasia
Europe	North America	South America

But note: *The* Arctic, *the* Antarctic, *the* Indian sub-continent.

Practice

e. A geography quiz

1. Where is Beijing?
2. Where is Rotterdam?
3. Where is Chernobyl?
4. In what part of the world are:
   Jamaica?   Oman?   Tahiti?

5. What is the capital of Peru?
6. What is the capital of Holland?
7. What is the capital of Hungary?
8. What do England, Wales, Scotland and Northern Ireland belong to?
9. What countries produce:
   rice?   coffee?   iron and steel?
   perfume?   computers?

f. The table illustrates the change in the amount of money spent on international travel in selected countries.

Change in international travel spending
% change 1986–1991.

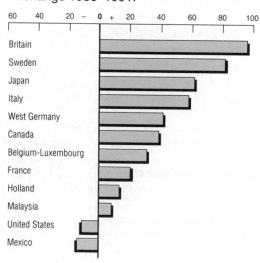

Complete this paragraph, using the information in the table. The first has been done for you.

People are travelling in even greater numbers. According to latest estimates [1]*the British* have almost doubled the number of overseas journeys in the five-year period under review. [2]_____ and [3]_____ rank second and third in the increase in foreign travel, with [4]_____ not far behind. However, [5]_____ and [6]_____ are not going abroad as often as they used to – the former, no doubt as a result of the fall in the dollar.

Other uses of *the*:

8 We also use *the* to refer to categories of things:

The food-processing industry employs many part-time workers.
The mark is a strong currency.
The telecopier is a useful piece of equipment.

Very often, an adjective is used with *the* to make a category or social group:

the rich   the poor   the unemployed   the well-to-do

These expressions are plural: *the* rich = rich people
However, a singular noun can also refer to a category of people:

the sole trader   the venture capitalist

Franchise agreements usually give *the* franchisor the right to inspect *the* franchisee's running of the business.

9 In noun groups with the word 'of', *the* is compulsory:

the Bank of England   the Board of Directors
the President of Exxon   the level of productivity

10 We use *the* in superlative expressions, where the noun is, by definition, unique:

Lloyds is *the* biggest insurance company in the world.
The Queen of England is probably *the* richest woman in the world.

Other cases when we do NOT use *the*:

11 *The* is omitted before certain 'places' used for their routine purpose:

He's *at work*. He's reading law *at University*.
She stayed *at home*. She left *college* a year ago.

12 It is NOT used with personal names:

Dr Miller	Lord Derby	Mr Spears
Sir John Squires	President Bush	Judge Spence
John Porter	Ruth Toye	Captain Kirk

13 *The* is omitted before means of transport (with *by*):

Come		bus
Go	*by*	car
Travel		train
		plane, etc.

BUT: We took *the* 8.15 from London Euston.
         The plane (a particular plane) is standing on the runway.

Note the omission of *the* with *flight* in sentences such as:

Flight BA 343 has been delayed.

14 *The* is NOT used before the names of meals, unless a particular meal is referred to:

have breakfast	at tea
before brunch	after cocktails
during lunch	stay for dinner/supper

BUT: *The* dinner we had at Maxim's was superb.

Practice

g. *The* or *no article*?

Expertly handling over 8.7 million tonnes of ¹_____ cargo a year, ²_____ Port Rashid is ³_____ Gulf's No. 1 port boasting ⁴_____ superb facilities and ⁵_____ easy communications by ⁶_____ road, ⁷_____ rail and ⁸_____ air. ⁹_____ red tape is cut to a minimum and there's no fuss when shipping ¹⁰_____ goods both in and out.
Close to ¹¹_____ city centre and with ¹²_____ Dubai's world-famous five start hotels near at hand, ¹³_____ Port Rashid is probably ¹⁴_____ most relaxing place in ¹⁵_____ world for ¹⁶_____ busy exporter to do ¹⁷_____ business.

h. Dear Dr Riccioli,
We are thinking of setting up a factory in ¹_____ India for ²_____ manufacture of ³_____ products made of ⁴_____ plastic and would like to start this venture with ⁵_____ technical co-operation. ⁶_____ plastics industry is still relatively underdeveloped and we would welcome ⁷_____ outside help.
⁸_____ market for items such as ⁹_____ tableware, ¹⁰_____ picnic sets, ¹¹_____ kitchen utensils and so on is a promising one, given ¹²_____ continuing consumer boom on ¹³_____ Indian sub-continent.
We have learnt from ¹⁴_____ Commercial Attaché at ¹⁵_____ French embassy in ¹⁶_____ New Delhi that you are ¹⁷_____ biggest manufacturer in this line. We are therefore making this approach to find out if you are able to provide ¹⁸_____ assistance technically or financially.
We look forward to hearing from you soon, as we wish to benefit from ¹⁹_____ World Bank's recent announcement of ²⁰_____ substantial loans for ²¹_____ joint ventures of this nature.

121 Travel vs Trip vs Journey vs Voyage vs Tour

1 *Travel* is both a NOUN and a VERB.
If you *travel* you go from one place to another, or to several places:

She has *travelled*[1] widely in the Middle East.

The noun is used without an article; we cannot say *a travel or *the travel:

Travel is said to broaden the mind.

2 We use the word *trip* to describe a visit there and back. It usually involves a stay in the place visited:

He often goes on business *trips* to Latin America.
(and returns to the office)
She told us about her recent *trip* to Amsterdam.
(she is now back)

3 A *journey* is usually for travel overland and often suggests a relatively long distance. There is no idea of a return contained in the word and no idea of a stay:

Ah! You've arrived! Did you have a good *journey*?

4 A *voyage* usually refers to water transport:

The Titanic sank on its maiden *voyage*.

5 A *tour* is a trip during which many places are visited:

In Rome they went on a city *tour* and saw most of the sites.

It can also refer to the inspection of a smaller area:

We went on a *tour* of the factory.

Practice

a. Complete the sentences using *travel, trip, journey, voyage, tour.*
1. The goods must have been damaged during the _____;
the weather was particularly bad in the Bay of Biscay.
2. Before your interview, Mrs Gould will take you on a
_____ of the site.
3. All reasonable _____ and accommodation expenses
will be paid.

---

[1] (AmE: **traveled**)

4. When we stayed in London we went on a day _____ to Cambridge.

5. The flight was OK but the tube _____ was awful; we were packed like sardines and I had to stand all the way.

6. Business people are now often rewarded with incentive _____; a holiday in Thailand, a Mediterranean cruise and that sort of thing.

122   Used to vs Be used to vs Get used to

1 *Used to* + verb is employed to talk about a situation or events as they were quite a long time ago. Whatever is described is no longer the case.

He *used to* work in Tokyo but now he has a job in Stockholm.
Sterling *used to* be tied to the gold standard but this was abolished in 1931.
When I was at college I *used to* read more than I do now.

1.1 The negative is *did not use to* or, more rarely, *used not to:*

Video conferences *did not use to* exist when I first started work.

It is also possible to ask questions:

Where did he *use to* live?

2 The pattern *be + used to* + | *noun phrase*
        get used to + | *verb + ing*

refers to a situation which is no longer strange:

Now I've settled in Germany I*'m used to eating Wurst.*
At first life here was very different but I've *got used to* it now.

2.1 If this process is still taking place we use *getting:*

I'm slowly *getting used to* the climate.
He's still *getting used to working* with so many different nationalities.

Practice

Imagine this conversation at an office party. Complete the missing parts with a form of *used to* and, where necessary, the correct form of *get up, work, start, live, use.*

A: ......How do you like your new life here? Are you settling in?
B: Yes, thanks but I find it a bit difficult to [1]_____ so early in the morning.

A: Early?

B: Well yes, back home I never ²_____ work before 9 o'clock, here it's 8 and I have to be up first thing in the morning.

A: Do you live far away then?

B: Yes, that's another difference – I ³_____ about 10 minutes away from the office so I never ⁴_____ public transport. Now I have about an hour's journey. And it's so tiring in the evening.

A: Oh well you'll soon ⁵_____ it.

B: That's what they say, but it's such a waste of time.

A: What about the work itself? I expect you've got a lot to do.

B: I enjoy it. I ⁶_____ under pressure so I don't mind – it's a challenge......

123 Verb Combinations (Infinitive vs -ing form)

It is very common for a verb to be followed by another verb. When this is the case it is often difficult to know whether the second verb is in the infinitive or terminated by *-ing*.

For example:

I *managed to get* there on time.
(NOT * I managed getting...)

I *suggest meeting* in Rome on 5 May.
(NOT * I suggest to meet)

It is not possible here to give a full list of verbs and the verb form used with them. However, the explanations below relate to verbs which commonly occur in business contexts.

■1■ Verb + infinitive

The following verbs take an infinitive:

afford	*appear*	*arrange*	*ask*	*choose*	*claim*
consent	*decide*	*demand*	*endeavour*	*expect*	*fail*
hope	*manage*	*offer*	*plan*	*proceed*	*promise*
refuse	*seem*	*tend*	*undertake*	*want*	*wish*

Examples:

Please *arrange to have* the goods collected at the docks.
I *hope to see* you in Amsterdam shortly.
We *plan to open* a new branch in Lima.
They *refused to give* us a refund.

We *undertake to replace* any damaged articles immediately.
We do not *wish to be* involved at this point in time.

2 Verb + -ing

This set includes:

admit	*advocate*	*anticipate*	*avoid*	*consider*
delay	*deny*	*involve*	*justify*	*mention*
mind	*miss*	*postpone*	*prevent*	*recommend*
risk	*save*	*suggest*		

I would not *advocate trying* to take short cuts.
Have you *considered using* a debt collection agency?
The proposed design would *mean changing* the automatic feed.
They *recommend buying* a more sophisticated model.
We *risk losing* an important market.
She walks to the office to *save spending* money on bus fares.

Practice

a. Choose the correct verb form in *italics*.

1. I avoid *to travel / travelling* during the rush hour.
2. Would you mind *to tell / telling* her straight away?
3. They have offered *to send / sending* a replacement.
4. I can't delay *to break / breaking* the bad news any longer.
5. We expect to *to receive / receiving* an answer soon.
6. People tend *to take / taking* long weekends during the month of May.
7. He promised *to contact/contacting* me as soon as he could.
8. He denies *to represent / representing* any of our competitors.

3 Verb + object + infinitive

Many of the following verbs express the general meaning of making people do things. This set of verbs includes:

advise	*allow*	*ask*	*appoint*	*challenge*	*enable*
encourage	*entitle*	*expect*	*force*	*get*	*instruct*
invite	*oblige*	*order*	*persuade*	*remind*	*require*
tell	*want*	*warn*			

The consultants *advised them to streamline* their purchasing procedures.
The Export Credit Guarantee Department *enables firms to insure* against non-payment.
A green card *entitles the holder to enter* the USA.
I will *get her to ring* you back.
We have *persuaded them to give* us extended credit.
He *expects us to put in* a lot of unpaid overtime.
They *are* now *requiring us to carry out* further tests.

Practice

b. What do the following enable you or the user to do?

a spreadsheet   a carphone   a laptop computer

What do the following entitle you or the holder to do?

a diplomatic passport   an American Express card
a patent

4 Verb + preposition + verb + -ing

An infinitive never follows a preposition but an *-ing* clause often does:

We *agreed on sharing* the costs.

I *apologise for being* late.

Success *depends on having* the right people in the right place at the right time.

Did you *succeed in raising* enough money?

She's *thinking of leaving* the firm.

5 Verb + object + preposition + verb + -ing

She *accused him of stealing* company property.

Please *forgive me for not writing* sooner.

There is nothing to *stop/prevent them from copying* our designs.

I would like to *thank you for coming*.

6 Expressions + verb + -ing

It's *no use/good expecting* them all to speak English.

There's *no point trying* to argue; they're totally inflexible.

It's not *worth sinking* more money into this project – it'll never work.

She *can't bear/stand waiting* in line.

Practice

c. Change the form of the verb in brackets.

Thank you for your enquiry and I apologise for [1]*(not reply)* earlier.

We are pleased to inform you that some of the articles you wish [2]*(purchase)* are in stock. However, some items are at present unobtainable. If you do not mind [3]*(wait)* we will endeavour [4]*(obtain)* them from other sources.

I advise you [5]*(order)* rapidly as these articles are extremely popular and we expect [6]*(sell)* most of them within a week. If you decide [7]*(order)* please let me know.

▇7▇ Special cases

Some verbs are followed by either *an infinitive* or *another verb + -ing*.

Sometimes there is NO change in meaning as in:

I *intend / propose **to deal*** with the matter soon.
I *intend / propose **dealing*** with the matter soon.

In other cases these *is* a change, as in these examples:

We do not *allow / authorise **smoking*** in our offices. (= in general)
She *allowed / authorised* him ***to smoke*** a cigar in the office. (= on this specific occasion)

I will never *forget **meeting*** Umberto Eco. (= I will always remember)
I often *forget **to put*** a stamp on the envelope. (= fail to remember)

I *mean **to see*** her later this month. (= I intend to)
I could get a better job but it would *mean **moving***. (= involve)

We *need **to invest*** more. (it is necessary to)

The whole procedure *needs **reviewing***. (= to be reviewed; the meaning is passive)

They *regret **putting*** up their prices. (= they wish they hadn't)
We *regret **to inform*** you that we have had to put up our prices. (= we are telling you this unfortunate news)

She *remembered **to lock*** the safe before she left. (= she didn't forget)
She *remembers **locking*** the safe. (= she locked the safe and has a clear memory of this)

They *stopped **sending*** us reminders after a while. (= they ceased)
She *stopped **to have*** a cigarette. (*to* = in order to)

Why don't you *try **giving*** your salesmen greater incentives. (= experiment and see what happens)
I once *tried **to learn*** shorthand. (= attempted/made the effort)

Practice

d. Change the form of the verb in brackets.

Re the proposed modification to the Airlite Cloth Cutter, I had hoped [1]*(improve)* the machine's precision but it appears to be rather difficult from a technical point of view and would involve [2]*(spend)* quite a lot of money. I personally feel it is worth [3]*(make)* the changes and I am sure we can afford [4]*(spend)* a little more on the design. What do you think?
Alister
PS. I almost forgot [5]*(contact)* Mrs Oyeru from SNTC. She says they have stopped [6]*(produce)* the Vacubrite equipment so it's

no good ⁷*(place)* an order with them. She suggested ⁸*(get)* in touch with Ugalima Pty and seems ⁹*(think)* they are of the right quality. Why don't you try ¹⁰*(give)* them a ring?

124 Verb + Noun Combinations

1 Very often a number of nouns can follow a verb.
For example: You can *run* a firm / a campaign / a car.
put forward a proposal / a suggestion / an idea.

2 In some cases, only one noun is possible.
For example, in the sentence:
The idea may never *get off the...*

the only word that could complete it is *ground*.

3 Here are some more examples:
The new regulations come into *force / effect* on 1st January.
Arbitration is often used to *settle a dispute.*
It took a long time but we have finally *come up with a solution.*
Can I *count on* your *support?*
Parliament has *passed a law* allowing full privatisation.
They haven't *reaped the benefits* of their restructuring operation.

Practice

You may need a dictionary. Answer these questions using the words below.

1. What can you raise?
2. What can you reach?
3. What can you allocate?
4. What can you make?
5. What can you clinch?
6. What can you suffer?
7. What can you draw?
8. What can you meet?

a decision	funds	headway	a deal
an objection	a loss	a setback	a matter
an understanding	resources	a conclusion	a customer
a concession	a requirement	an agreement	

(Each verb may go with one or more of these nouns.)

125 Very vs Too vs Enough vs Quite vs Rather vs Fairly

These words can be used to answer questions such as *To what extent? How?* or *How much?* They change the strength of the adjective or adverb they qualify.

Look at the table below and the report from a consumer magazine. Notice how the words in *italics* are used.

NAME	VOLUME OF DRUM (LITRES)	SPIN SPEED	EASE OF USE	SAFETY	PRICE	OVERALL IMPRESSION
ANICO	38.3	600	5/10	****	£520	too expensive, very small drum
CORONA	41.8	800	8/10	***	£475	recommended
GALACTIC	47.2	1000	7/10	*****	£450	very good value for money
MINOVA	40.9	550	4/10	***	£480	rather complicated control panel. Mediocre.
NUMAK	44.5	450	7/10	**	£550	too expensive, door may open during wash cycle.

We tested five machines and compared their performances with a variety of fabrics. In our opinion the drum of the ANICO is *not* large *enough* for a 5kg wash and compares unfavourably with a machine like the GALACTIC which takes a 5kg load *quite* easily. At £520 the ANICO is also *too* expensive for a machine which does nothing exceptionally well.

The CORONA is *fairly* cheap at £475 for a machine that washes well and spins at a relatively high speed. We do not recommend the MINOVA nor the NUMAK. The latter is far *too* expensive and unsafe, the former is *rather* difficult to use without consulting the instruction manual every five minutes. The best buy is definitely the GALACTIC. 1,000 revolutions per minute is a *very* high spin speed and useful in our wet climate! Our testers found it *quite* easy to use and the £450 price-tag makes it cheap *enough* for most budgets.

1 *Too* and *not enough* are opposites.

too expensive = excessively expensive
not large *enough* = insufficiently large
cheap *enough* = sufficiently cheap

1.1 *Too* can also be used with a quantifier, e.g.:

Too much short-term debt means that a company is vulnerable to sudden interest rate rises.

If there are *too few* opportunities for promotion, ambitious young executives will tend to leave the firm.

2 *Quite, fairly* and *rather* do not have absolutely fixed meanings and may depend on the intonation used. However, in general, *fairly* is weaker than *quite* which is weaker than *rather*.

not	−
fairly	
quite	expensive
rather	
very	
	+

In American English, you would replace *quite* and *rather* with *very*.

3 In British English, *quite* can also mean 'totally':

I *quite* agree. (= I completely agree.)

In American English, you would leave out *quite* or replace it with *really* .

Practice

Below is a comparative table for selected hotels in Hong Kong. Using *very, too, enough, quite, rather* and *fairly* write a paragraph for a business magazine with your recommendations for the business traveller.

NAME	SIZE	QUALITY OF SERVICE	DISTANCE FROM CITY CENTRE	FACILITIES	PRICE PER PERSON PER NIGHT
The Central	55	***	2 kms	**	HK$1,200
Lee Ho Fook	30	****	1 km	***	HK$1,950
The Hing Ming	75	***	5 kms	***	HK$1,350
The Empire	125	***	3 kms	**	HK$1,050
The Chang	106	**	in city centre	****	HK$2,150

126 **What vs Which**

There is a difference in meaning between *what* and *which* when they are used as question words.
Compare:

What advertising media are you going to use?

Which do you think has more impact, direct advertising or sponsorship?

What is used when the question is open: *which* is used when there is a narrow choice of answers.

Practice

Which is correct, *what* or *which?*

1. _____ are the reasons for declining sales?
2. _____ is better, purchasing or leasing?
3. _____ is your occupation?
4. _____ are your payment terms?

127 **Which vs That vs Who vs Whose**

1 These words join two separate ideas; note how the linking word replaces the pronoun in **bold.**

1.1 I am writing about our agreement.
It was signed on 5 May 1991.

I am writing about our agreement *which* was signed on 5 May 1991.

1.2 Thank you for the display stands.
We ordered **them** last week.

Thank you for the display stands *that/which* we ordered last week.

1.3 He's the man. **He** used to work for BTR.

He's the man *who/that* used to work for BTR.

1.4 I spoke to a woman yesterday. **She** said the order had been cancelled.

The woman *who/that* I spoke to yesterday said the order had been cancelled.[1]

1.5 IKP is a firm. **Its** reputation has been growing.

IKP is a firm *whose* reputation has been growing.

1.6 She's a woman. **Her** life has been spent getting to the top.

She's a woman *whose* life has been spent getting to the top.

[1] It is now rather old-fashioned to use **whom** although traditionally it is correct to do so.

2 Note that we do not need to use *who* or *that* or *which* when they are used as the OBJECT of a clause:

Thank you for the display stands *(which)* we ordered last week. (We can miss out *which*.)

The woman *(who/that)* I spoke to yesterday said the order had been cancelled. (We usually do not say *who* or *that*.)

Practice

a. On the basis of these examples, complete the table with *which, that, who, whose*.

REFERS TO PEOPLE	REFERS TO THINGS

3 *Which, that* and *who* can be used in a clause which is 'defining' – i.e. identifies what it is you are talking about:

A bonus is an extra payment *which/that* is made to an employee in return for additional work.

An underwriter is an insurer *who* is a member of the Corporation of Lloyd's.[1]

3.1 They can be 'non-defining' – i.e. they give extra, non-essential information:[2]

G.P. Vickers & Co. Ltd., *which* was advertised for sale in the Financial Times, has now been purchased.

Mrs Mills, *who* is the Commercial Manager of FCI group, made a statement to the press yesterday.

4 *Which* can introduce a clause which makes comments on previous information.

She is always interrupting, *which* I find extremely unpleasant.

Practice

b. Complete these using *who, whose, that, which*.

There are two ways for managers to think of workers. One is as a commodity to be bought for a fixed price [1]_____ will bring fixed rewards. The other is as a resource [2]_____ can be developed and [3]_____ commitment and involvement varies. There are many managers [4]_____ are in the process of switching from the former view to the latter,

[1] **That** is not possible. [2] Non-defining clauses are always separated by commas (,). The word ***that*** is never used to introduce a non-defining clause.

[5]_____ I think is probably in the right direction.

Safco Inc. is a small firm based in Washington D.C. [6]_____ makes souvenirs and promotional novelties. It is wholly owned by the president [7]_____ two sons are employed as vice-presidents. There are 17 other employees [8]_____ handle such tasks as book-keeping, sales and distribution. Home sales, [9]_____ last year reached over $8m, have been growing steadily ever since..

c. Give definitions of the following.

For example:
official receiver
An official receiver is the person *who* is appointed to supervise the affairs of a company in liquidation.
(If necessary, consult the *Longman Dictionary of Business English.*)

1. an attorney
2. a balance sheet
3. a penalty clause
4. counterfeit goods
5. a certificate of origin
6. a CEO
7. a buyback agreement
8. a merchant bank
9. a holding company

128 Wish

1 The verb *wish* in a formal style can substitute *to want, to desire* or *would like*. It is commonly found in commercial letters:

We *wish* to order an initial quantity of 50,000 items with a view to carrying out a market test.

We *wish* to invite you to participate in a joint venture.

1.1 However, *wish* cannot be directly followed by a noun; if there is a noun use *would like:*

I *would like* a catalogue and price list.
(NOT * I wish a catalogue and price list)

2 An object can be inserted between *wish* and the infinitive construction:

I *wish* the person-in-charge to be informed.

3 *Wish* can also be used to express a regret, either for a present or a past state of affairs. The tense of the following verb is *past* for a present meaning, and *past perfect* for a past meaning:

I *wish* I **knew** the answer. (but I don't)
I *wish* I **could** tell you. (but I can't)
He *wishes* he **had received** more information. (but he didn't)
She *wishes* she **had learnt** Spanish at college. (but she didn't)

> **3.1** Note that in a formal style *I wish I were* is possible:
>
> I *wish* I were a millionaire.

4 *Wish* can be followed by *would* when we want to express irritation with other people's behaviour:

I *wish* you *would* listen.
I *wish* they *would* keep their promises.
He *wishes* she *would* be more cooperative.

Note that it is impossible to say or write:
* I wish I would... * He wishes he would...etc.

5 Learners of English very often mistakenly use 'would' in the examples given in **3** above. (e.g. * I wish I would know the answer.)

It is helpful to remember that the verbs used after *wish* are those used in hypothetical statements beginning with *If only:*

I *wish/If only* I understood.
I *wish/If only* she had made a small concession.
I *wish/If only* they would abolish all the red tape.

Practice

a. Complete the blanks using *wish* or *would like.*

```
CONFIRM WE _____ AN INITIAL QTY OF
1,000 UNITS.
IF QUALITY ACCEPTABLE WE MAY _____
TO ORDER ANOTHER 1,000 AT A LATER DATE.
```

b. How do the people in the following situations feel?

1. The day before yesterday Nobuhiko Kawamoto sold 2,000 shares in Atsugi Nylon at Y1,600. He has just bought a copy of the *Wall St. Journal* and seen they are now trading at Y1,750.
2. Peter West has a colleague, Christopher Ford, who insists on smoking in the office and leaving his ashtray on his (Peter's) desk.
3. Jenny Green has just opened a small business selling English

Language Teaching books. This has been financed with a mixture of savings and a bank loan at 16.5%. She has just been reading a leaflet entitled 'Government Help for Small Businesses' in which she learns that there are loans for private entrepreneurs at 12%.

4. Luigi Marrocco's office is on the fourth floor and the photocopying room is on the first floor. Every day he has to go up and down the stairs at least thirty times.

129 Within vs By vs Until

1 If something is done *within* a period of time it is done before that period has ended:

I should have the figures ready *within* a week.

1.1 *Within* is also used for distance:

Our offices are *within* a couple of miles of the city centre.
(= not more than two miles away)

2 *By* is used for actions completed on or before a certain limit in time:

I should have the figures ready *by* next Tuesday.
(Tuesday at the latest)
Please give me the costings *by* Thursday. (Thursday is the limit)

2.1 *By* has other meanings:

NEAR	The delivery bay is *by* the paint store.
PAST	I drove *by* your offices the other day.
WITH A METHOD	You can get more information *by* phoning Steven Mark's on freefone[1] 423 5572.
WITH A MEANS OF TRANSPORT	He's arriving *by* helicopter.

3 *Until* means 'continuing up to a particular time':

Hong Kong will be a British colony *until* 1999.

3.1 *Not until,* is a synonym of *not before:*

'When will the new design be ready?'
'*Not until* the end of May.'

---

[1] (AmE: **toll-free**)

3.2 *Until* can also refer to past time:

He was obliged to wait *until* he had worked for six months before he was given a full contract.[1]

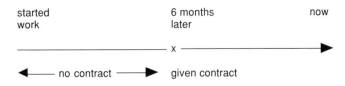

| started work | 6 months later | now |

x

◄─── no contract ───► given contract

Practice

Answer these questions using *within, by* and *until*. Ignore the questions that don't apply to you.

1. How far is your place of work from the city centre?
2. How do you get to work?
3. When will you get your next pay rise?
4. How long did you have to wait before getting your first promotion?
5. How can I get in touch with you on a Saturday?
6. How soon can you ship an order to Helsinki?

130 Would rather vs Had better

1 *Would rather* means 'would prefer to'.

It is often contracted to *'d rather*;
It is not followed by *to*;
Would cannot be replaced by *should*.

For example:

I'*d rather* deal with the second item on the agenda before the first.
I'*d rather* work abroad than in Great Britain.

1.1 *Would rather* can also be used when referring to other people. In this case we generally use a past verb form after the subject:

I'*d rather we* **dealt** with the second item on the agenda before the first.
I'*d rather she* **didn't make** a final decision before getting my report on the subject.

[1] Alternatively: He was not given a contract **until** he had worked for six months.

1.2 In a short, negative reply we do not need a verb:

'Do you want to have lunch before you go?'
'*I'd rather not.*'

1.3 Do not confuse *would rather* with *had better* (contracted to *'d better*) which is used to make a recommendation:

I think we *had better* try to reduce stock levels.

(NOT * *had better* to try)

2 The negative is formed by placing *not* after this expression:

You'*d better not* tell her – she'll complain if you do.

3 Note that * had rather and * would better are incorrect. However, it is possible to say *would do better to*:

He *would do better to* mind his own business and not interfere.[1]

Practice

a. State your preferences. Would you rather:

1. work in a large or a small organisation?
2. work for the state or private enterprise?
3. earn salary or commission?
4. live near your place of work or some distance away?
5. have a number of short holidays in a year or one long holiday?

b. What recommendations would you make in these situations? Use *had better*.

1. A visitor has to catch the last flight home. The airport can be reached by car or train. It is rush hour.
2. Item 4 on the agenda is, in your opinion, very important. The meeting is scheduled to end in 20 minutes' time.
3. It is lunch and you have had an apéritif and two glasses of wine. Your host offers you another glass. You need a clear head for the afternoon's negotiations.
4. A colleague is to spend one month in an English-speaking country soon. She says that her grammar and business vocabulary are not as good as they should be.

[1] (AmE: He'd be **better off to** mind his own business...)

Appendix One
Measurements
Linear measure

Metric

metric units		British equivalent
	1 millimetre (mm)	0.0394 in.
10mm	= 1 centimetre (cm)	0.3937 in.
10cm	= 1 decimetre (dm)	3.937 in.
10dm	= 1 metre (m)	39.370 in.
10m	= 1 decametre (dam)	10.94 yds.
10 dam	= 1 hectometre (hm)	109.4 yds.
10 hm	= 1 kilometre (km)	0.621 m.

British

British units				Metric equivalent
	1 inch (in.)			25.4 mm
12 in.	= 1 foot (ft.)			0.305 m
3 ft.	= 1 yard (yd.)			0.914 m
2 yds.	= 6 ft	= 1 fathom (fm.)		1.829 m
5.5 yds.	= 16.5 ft.	= 1 rod, pole or perch		5.029 m
4 perch	= 22 yds.	= 66 ft.	= 1 chain	20.12 m
10 chain	= 220 yds.	= 660 ft.	= 1 furlong (fur.)	0.201 km
8 fur.	= 1760 yds.	= 5280 ft.	= 1 (statute) mile (m.)	1.609 km
1 U.K. nautical mile* = 6080 ft.				1.853 km
1 international nautical mile (naut.m.)				1.852 km

*Note: nautical speed is usually measured in knots:
1 knot = 1 nautical mile per hour.

Cubic/solid measure

Metric

metric units	British equivalent
1000 cubic millimetres (mm^3)	
= 1 cubic centimetre (cm^3)	0.0610 cu. in.
1000 cubic centimetres (cm^3)	
= 1 cubic decimetre (dm^3)	610 cu. in.
1000 cubic decimetres (dm^3)	
= 1 cubic metre (m^3)	35.3147 cu. ft.

The *stere* is also used, in particular as a unit of
measurement for timber:

1 cubic metre	= 1 stere	35.3147 cu. ft.
10 dicisteres	= 1 stere	35.3147 cu. ft.
10 steres	= 1 decastere	353.1467 cu. ft.
		(= 13.0795 cu. yds.)

British

British units		*Metric equivalent*
	1 cubic inch (cu. in.)	16.39 cm^3
1728 cu. in.	= 1 cubic foot (cu. ft.)	0.0283 m^3
27 cu. ft. or 1 load of earth	= 1 cubic yard (cu. yd.)	0.7646 m^3
1 ton of shipping	= 40 cu. ft.	1.1327 m^3
1 register ton of shipping	= 100 cu. ft.	2.8317 m^3

Square measure

Metric

metric units		*British equivalent*
	1 square millimetre (mm^2)	0.0016 sq. in.
100 mm^2	= 1 square centimetre (cm^2)	0.1550 sq. in.
100 cm^2	= 1 square decimetre (dm^2)	15.5000 sq. in.
100 dm^2	= 1 square metre (m^2)	10.7639 sq. ft.
		(= 1.1959 sq. yds.)
100 m^2	= 1 square decametre (dam^2)	1076.3910 sq. ft.
100 dam^2	= 1 square hectometre (hm^2)	0.0039 sq. m.
100 hm^2	= 1 square kilometre (km^2)	0.3861 sq. m.

British

British units		*Metric equivalent*
	1 square inch (sq. in.)	6.4516 cm^2
144 sq. in.	= 1 square foot (sq. ft.)	0.0929 m^2
9 sq. ft.	= 1 square yard (sq. yd.)	0.8361 m^2
30¼ sq. yds.	= 1 square perch	25.29 m^2
40 sq. perch	= 1 rood	0.1012 ha
4 roods or 4840 sq. yds.	= 1 acre	0.4047 ha
640 acres	= 1 square mile (sq. m.)	2.5900 km^2
100 sq. ft.	= 1 square	9.2903 m^2
272¼ sq. ft.	= 1 rod of brickwork	25.2928 m^2

Liquid measure

Metric

metric units		British	U.S.
10 millilitres (ml)	= 1 centilitre (cl)	0.0176 pt.	0.0211 pt.
10 cl	= 1 decilitre (dl)	0.176 pt.	0.211 pt.
10 dl	= 1 litre (1)*	1.76 pt.	2.11 pt.
		(= 0.22 gal.)	(= 0.264 gal.)
10 l	= 1 decalitre (dal)	2.20 gal.	2.64 gal.
10 dal	= 1 hectolitre (hl)	22.0 gal.	26.4 gal.
10 hl	= 1 kilolitre (kl)	220.0 gal.	264.0 gal.

British and U.S.

British and U.S. units		Metric equivalent	
		British	U.S.
	1 minim (min.)	0.059 cm^3	0.062 cm^3
60 min.	= 1 fluid dram (fl. dr.)	3.552 cm^3	2.957 cm^3
8 fl. dr.	= 1 fluid ounce (fl. oz.)	28.413 cm^3	29.573 cm^3
5 fl. oz.	= 1 gill British	142.065 cm^3	
4 fl. oz.	= 1 gill U.S.A.		118.291 cm^3
4 gills	= 1 pint (pt.)	568.261 cm^3	473.163 cm^3
2 pt.	= 1 quart (qt.)	1.136 l	0.946 l
4 qt.	= 1 gallon (gal.)	4.546 l	3.785 l

U.S. and British equivalents

U.S.	British
1 fluid ounce	= 1.0408 fl. oz.
1 pint	= 0.8327 pt.
1 gallon	= 0.8327 gal.

*Note: 1 litre is equal in capacity to 1 cubic decimetre (1 dm^2)

Measurement of mass/weight

Metric

metric units		Avoirdupois equivalent
	1 milligram (mg)	0.015 gr.
10 mg	= 1 centigram (cg)	0.154 gr.
10 cg	= 1 decigram (dg)	1.543 gr.
10 dg	= 1 gram (g)	15.43 gr. = 0.035 oz.
10 g	= 1 decagram (dag)	0.353 oz.
10 dag	= 1 hectogram (hg)	3.527 oz.
10 hg	= 1 kilogram (kg)	2.205 lb.
1000 kg	= 1 tonne (metric ton)	0.984 (long) ton = 2204.62 lb.

Avoirdupois

Avoirdupois units		Metric equivalent
	1 grain (gr.)	64.8 mg
	1 dram (dr.)	1.772 g
16 drams	= 1 ounce (oz.)	28.3495 g
16 oz. (= 7000 gr.)	= 1 pound (lb.)	0.4536 kg
14 lb.	= 1 stone	6.3503 kg
28 lb.	= 1 quarter (qr.)	12.7006 kg
4 qrs. or 112 lb.	= 1 hundredweight (cwt.)	50.8024 kg
20 cwt.	= 1 ton (U.K. or long ton)*	1.01605 tonnes

*Note: in the USA the *short* hundredweight
and *short* ton are more common:

	Metric equivalent
100 lb. = 1 short hundredweight	45.36 kg
2000 lb. = 1 short ton	0.9072 tonnes

Temperature

Equations for conversion

°Fahrenheit $= (\frac{9}{5} \times \chi\ °C) + 32$
°Centigrade $= \frac{5}{9} \times (\chi\ °F - 32)$
°Kelvin $= \chi\ °C + 273.15$

Some equivalents

	Centigrade	Fahrenheit
Normal temperature of the human body	36.9°C	98.4°F
Freezing point	0°C	32°F
Boiling point	100°C	212°F

Table of equivalents

Fahrenheit	Centigrade	Centigrade	Fahrenheit
100°C	212°F	30°C	86°F
90°C	194°F	20°C	68°F
80°C	176°F	10°C	50°F
70°C	158°F	0°C	32°F
60°C	140°F	−10°C	14°F
50°C	122°F	−20°C	4°F
40°C	104°F	−30°C	−22°F

Appendix Two
Selected Irregular Verbs

BASE FORM	PAST FORM	PAST PARTICIPLE
be	was	been
bear	bore	borne
beat	beat	beaten
become	became	become
bet	bet	bet
bid	bid	bid
bring	brought	brought
build	built	built
buy	bought	bought
choose	chose	chosen
cost	cost	cost
creep	crept	crept
cut	cut	cut
deal	dealt	dealt
do	did	done
draw	drew	drawn
drink	drank	drunk
drive	drove	driven
eat	ate	eaten
fall	fell	fallen
feel	felt	felt
fight	fought	fought
find	found	found
fly	flew	flown
forbid	forbade	forbidden
forecast	forecast	forecast
forget	forgot	forgotten
freeze	froze	frozen
get	got	got (AmE: gotten)
go	went	gone
grow	grew	grown
have	had	had
hear	heard	heard
hide	hid	hidden
hit	hit	hit
hold	held	held
hurt	hurt	hurt
keep	kept	kept
know	knew	known
lay	laid	laid
lead	led	led
leave	left	left
lend	lent	lent
let	let	let

BASE FORM	PAST FORM	PAST PARTICIPLE
lose	lost	lost
make	made	made
mean	meant	meant
meet	met	met
pay	paid	paid
put	put	put
quit	quit	quit
read	read	read
ring	rang	rung
rise	rose	risen
run	ran	run
say	said	said
see	saw	seen
sell	sold	sold
send	sent	sent
set	set	set
shake	shook	shaken
show	showed	shown
shut	shut	shut
sink	sank	sunk
sit	sat	sat
slide	slid	slid
speak	spoke	spoken
spend	spent	spent
spread	spread	spread
stand	stood	stood
steal	stole	stolen
stick	stuck	stuck
swing	swung	swung
take	took	taken
teach	taught	taught
tell	told	told
think	thought	thought
throw	threw	thrown
understand	understood	understood
wear	wore	worn
win	won	won
wind	wound	wound
write	wrote	written

Answer Key

1. A vs An

a.
a European
a uniform
a unit
an offer
an undertaking
a one-way street
an $11m dollar loan
an honour
a holding
an eight-digit phone number
a use
a user
a utility
a yield
a hundred
an hourly shuttle
an upturn
an assistant
an inventory

b. 1. Yes, the first 250 miles are free but it costs 5p *per/a* mile thereafter.
2. $50 *per/a* square foot.
3. £1.99 *a* bottle.
4. Over £50,000 *a* year. (In writing £50,000 *per annum*).
5. 55 miles *per* hour (mph). In spoken English we can also say 'miles *an* hour'.
6. £150 *a* night.
7. $25 *a* barrel.

2. A/An vs One

a. 1. one, an, a
2. one
3. a
4. a
5. one
6. one
7. one
8. one

b. 1. a
2. a
3. a
4. an
5. one
6. a
7. one
8. a

3. Abbreviations

a. 1. pp
2. P.T.O
3. c.c.
4. p.a.
5. c/o

b. ATTENTION: JOHN PRICE, STOCK MANAGER
FROM: GIOVANNI BISIGNANI

PLEASE CONFIRM ESTIMATED TIME OF ARRIVAL FOR MILD STEEL ORDER NUMBER 6375B.

THANKS IN ADVANCE

JULY 1 1991   TELEX MESSAGE NUMBER 6745
TO: MARC GIRARD
FROM: MATSUI
        KARAMA MARU

WITH REFERENCE TO YOUR TELEX 855/634

PLEASE OPEN A LETTER OF CREDIT THROUGH OUR BANK:

THE MITSUBISHI BANK LIMITED
1–5 DOJIMAHAMA 1-CHOME
KITA-KU, OSAKA, JAPAN

AWAIT DETAILS OF LETTER OF CREDIT AS SOON AS POSSIBLE.

REGARDS

4. Adjective Formation

a. 1. payable
2. cashless
3. deductible
4. exclusive
5. secretarial
6. unearned
7. supplementary
8. strategic
9. inaccurate

b. satisfy–*dissatisfied* ..... continent–*continental* ..... wealth–*wealthy* ..... optimism–*optimistic* ..... expect–*expected* ..... success–*unsuccessful* ..... disappoint–*disappointing* ..... promotion–*promotional* ..... competition–*competitive* ..... industry–*industrial* ..... dominate–*dominant* ..... lead–*leading* ..... grow–*growing* ..... urge–*urgent* ..... drama–*dramatic*

5. Adjective Position

a. 1. the issues raised
2. the main advantage
3. the shares issued
4. the consumers questioned
5. the articles ordered
6. a major feature
7. involved process

    b. 1. the present members of the committee (*or* the present committee members)
       2. bills outstanding
       3. planning involved
       4. particular case
       5. (an) outstanding contribution
       6. issued from

6. Adjectives + Nouns

    1. common
    2. firm
    3. vested
    4. far-reaching
    5. viable
    6. heated
    7. rough
    8. high
    9. stiff
  10. stumbling
  11. fruitful
  12. last

7. Adjectives + Preposition

    a. Examples only.
       1. answerable to (the Finance Director).
       2. opposed to (racism).
       3. interested in (commercial law).
       4. inclined to (lose my temper).
       5. liable to (forget important dates).
       6. indebted to (my former teachers).

    b. 1. to inform
       2. on
       3. to
       4. to improve
       5. with
       6. in
       7. to

8. Adjectives vs Adverbs

    a. 1. Mrs King works hard.
       2. The plane was delayed / late.
       3. There are hourly trains from Peterborough to London.
       4. It's a direct flight.
       5. The sales results are published quarterly.
       6. You can hardly read the print.
       7. Committee meetings are held fortnightly.

b. 1. + 2. superbly-designed
3. + 4. closely-guarded
5. + 6. highly-sophisticated
7. + 8. fully-guaranteed

9. Adverbs

I am terribly sorry ..... in Dallas on October 5th ..... I have
recently asked ..... the price could possibly rise ..... I have
already seen ..... to work very well ..... together in October

10. Advertising vs Publicity vs Marketing vs Public Relations

a. Marketing   **b.** Advertising   **c.** Public relations

11. Advise vs Warn

1. warn   2. advise   3. advice   4. warning   5. advice

12. Affect vs Effect

1. affect
2. affect
3. effect
4. effected

13. Agent vs Broker vs Distributor vs Retailer vs Dealer vs Representative

These are incorrect:
car retailer   car representative   sole retailer
company dealer   insurance retailer

14. Agree vs Accept

These combinations are correct:
agree   to go ahead / to differ / that quality has suffered / with
             my estimate
accept   your conclusion / her modifications / that quality has
             suffered / a bill

15. All vs Whole

1. all
2. All
3. All (of)
4. On the whole
5. All
6. the whole
7. All
8. the whole
9. the whole

16. Allow vs Permit vs Let vs Enable

a. 1. let
2. enable
3. allow for
4. allow for
5. enable/allow (Enable is preferred to avoid repetition of 'allow').
6. let

b. 1. permit
2. Allow us
3. allow / enable (= make something possible)
4. permit (most closely linked to the idea of permission)

17. Amount

Individual answers

18. Balance of vs Balance of Trade

a) balance of trade   b) balance of payments

19. Bargain vs Bargaining vs Rebate vs Reduction vs Refund vs Discount

1. rebate   2. bargain   3. refund   4. bargain   5. bargaining

20. Barter vs Countertrade

1. countertrade   2. barter   3. buyback arrangement

21. Been vs Gone

1. gone
2. been; been
3. been; gone
4. gone

22. Borrow vs Lend vs Loan vs Overdraft

	FIXED SUM	KNOWN PERIOD	REGULAR REPAYMENTS	DAILY CALCULATION OF INTEREST
loan	YES	YES	YES	NO
overdraft	NO	NO	NO	YES

23. British English vs American English

The changes in the letter are mostly changes in emphasis. However, it is fundamental to change the date.

Gentlemen: 9/11/91

I plan to visit Chicago next fall from Monday, October 12 thru Wednesday, October 21 in order to meet with executives of

American companies who have a strong interest in new technology and are seeking to expand or diversify their operations. Based on the information we have gotten on your company we feel that *Euro Consult* could provide you with a valuable service.

Euro Consult is a service organization whose specialty is to initiate programs which assist businesses in taking advantage of investment opportunities overseas through license, joint venture or acquisition.

Every program *Euro Consult* offers is highly customized to meet individual needs and utilizes specific proven techniques. We can help you analyze your potential position in Europe, inform you of labor legislation and assist you in gaining a foothold in this market.

I am looking forward to the prospect of meeting with you during my visit. A meeting can be set up through your early reply, preferably by telex to 4330986, or FAX 312-491-6274.

Sincerely yours

Arnaud Waechter

24. Bull vs Bear vs Stag

1. stag   2. bull   3. bear

25. Business Operations

1. sole trader
2. partnership
3. private limited company
4. public limited company
5. holding; subsidiary
6. franchise
7. licensing agreement
8. joint venture
9. multinational corporation
10. Export Trading Company

26. Can vs Could vs May vs Might

a. 1. He may not be given a contract.
2. You could have a nervous breakdown if you continue like this.
3. You might not develop so many new products and you may lose market share.
4. The Minister may have to subsidise domestic agriculture.

(There are other possible answers)

   b. She might have mis-typed the name. However, someone might have used her disk and destroyed her file by accident. She can try re-typing the filename but if she has no backup copy nothing can be done.

   c. The two engineers might not have had the business expertise required. The company may have grown too fast and diversified into too many areas. The staff they took on might not have been as competent as they hoped. (You no doubt have other ideas.)

27. Cancel vs Postpone vs Delay vs Extend

  a. 1. delayed
     2. cancel
     3. postponed
     4. cancellation
     5. delay
     6. extension

28. Capital

paid-up capital = issued capital
risk capital = venture capital
current capital = working capital
fixed assets = capital equipment
registered capital = authorised capital

29. Catalogue vs Leaflet vs Booklet vs Brochure vs Insert

  1. booklet
  2. catalogue/catalog
  3. leaflets
  4. insert
  5. brochures

31. Check vs Control vs Monitor

  1. checked
  2. control
  3. monitor
  4. controlling (AmE: controling)
  5. control
  6. check

33. Comparison

  a. 1. Robots are faster, cheaper and more reliable than human beings.
     2. Life in Lisbon is cheaper and more relaxing than life in New York.
     3. The USA has more telephones per inhabitant than Mexico.

4. My company has a wider product range and is more competitive than its nearest rival.

5. We work fewer hours now than we did 30 years ago.

6. It takes less time to make a decision in the USA than in Mexico.

7. Typewriters are slower, more complicated and less versatile than word processors.

8. Road transport is more flexible, less expensive but more time-consuming than rail transport.

b. 1. Sweden
   2. Portugal
   3. False
   4. True
   5. False
   6. False

c. 1. The cheapest is the TD 9.
   2. The most expensive is the SF 250.
   3. The bulkiest is the SF 250.
   4. The fastest is the SF 250.
   5. The heaviest is the SF 250.
   6. The ADM 300 holds the most numbers in its memory.
   7. The SF 250 takes the largest number of sheets.
   8. Possibly the CFT 20.

d. Individual answers.

e. 1. the most
   2. the cheapest
   3. the largest / the biggest
   4. the smallest
   5. bigger / larger
   6. less
   7. than
   8. the most
   9. less than
   10. the longest / the most
   11. better than
   12. The worst
   13. the best / the most
   14. the best
   15. more
   16. than
   17. The least
   18. the least

f. 1. True.
   2. True.
   3. True.

      4. False.
      5. False.
      6. False.

g. Individual answers.

h. 1. The greater
     2. the more
     3. The higher
     4. the smaller
     5. the greater
     6. higher
     7. lower

34. Cost vs Costing vs Costly

a. 1. costing
     2. costs; cost
     3. costed
     4. costly
     5. costs
     6. costs

b. 1. to our cost
     2. counted the cost
     3. cut costs
     4. at cost price
     5. cost of living
     6. at all costs
     7. cost-effective

c. 1. Cost, insurance, freight
     2. Cost-benefit analysis
     3. Fixed costs
     4. Opportunity cost
     5. Cost accounting
     6. Variable costs

35. Countable vs Uncountable Nouns

a. 1. progress
     2. an executive
     3. very little
     4. an arrangement
     5. advice
     6. a review
     7. research
     8. work

b. 1. advice
     2. job
     3. damages

4. step forward
5. course
6. recommendation
7. damage
8. work
9. accommodation
10. training
11. apartment
12. trip
13. Travel
14. progress

36. Currencies

a.

schilling	Austria
pound	Britain
peso	Mexico
yuan	China
markka	Finland
mark	Germany
escudo	Portugal
rupee	India
guilder	Netherlands
dollar	the USA, Australia, etc.
baht	Thailand
peseta	Spain
yen	Japan
zloty	Poland
rouble	the USSR
krone	Denmark
lira	Italy
riyal	Saudi Arabia
franc	France, etc.
leu	Romania

b. schilling
guilder
escudo
krone
Deutschmark
pesetas
dinar
franc
rouble

c. 130,000 divided by 190 = £684.21

d. If the exchange rate had not changed the price would have been $40,000. Now, the fall means that the price is 100 000 divided by 2.25 which is $44,444.44.

37. **Curriculum Vitae**

Individual answer.

38. **Damage vs Damages**

1. damage   2. damages   3. damage

39. **Deal in vs Deal with**

1. deal in
2. deal with
3. clinch the deal
4. deal with

40. **Demand vs Enquiry vs Query vs Request**

a. 1. demand
   2. request
   3. enquiry
   4. query
   5. enquired
   6. demand
   7. demanding
   8. enquire

41 **Director vs Chairperson vs Executive vs Manager**

Individual answers.

42. **Draw vs Withdraw**

1. withdraw
2. draw
3. draw up
4. withdrawn
5. draw on

43. **Earnings vs Income vs Revenue vs Salary vs Wage**

1. income; Revenue
2. earnings; earnings

44. **Economy vs Economics vs Economic vs Economical vs Economise**

1. economics
2. economic
3. economise
4. Economies
5. economical
6. economy
7. economic

45. Effective vs Efficient

a.

	CAMPAIGN	METHODS	SECRETARY	SOLUTION	SPEAKER
effective	✓	✓		✓	✓
efficient		✓	✓		

b. 1. effective
2. efficient
3. effective
4. effective

46. Ensure vs Insure vs Assure

insure, assured, ensures

48. Expect vs Wait

1. expected; wait   2. expect

49. Expense vs Expenses vs Expenditure

1. expenses
2. expense
3. expense
4. expenditure
5. expense
6. expenses
7. expenses
8. expenditure

50 Few vs A few; Little vs A little

a. 1. a little
2. few
3. little
4. a little
5. Few
6. a few
7. a little
8. few
9. little
10. a little

51. Figures

a. Two hundred (and) forty three
a thousand and one
nine thousand two hundred (and) forty seven
two billion

a hundred and twenty five million dollars
nought point nought five
eight million nine hundred (and) eighty thousand
five point eight
two thirds
five ninths
one in three
sixteen times thirty two
sixty six minus thirty four
a hundred (and) forty three plus twenty eight

b. 1. 16 + 18 = 34
2. 25 x 5 = 125
3. 169 ÷ 13 = 13
4. 57 − 39 = 18
5. 1 : 5
6. $\dfrac{\text{cost of stock sold}}{\text{average stock at cost price}}$ = rate of stock turnover

7. $\dfrac{\text{nominal value of a share}}{\text{share's market value}}$ x rate of dividend = yield

52. For vs Since vs During vs While vs Ago

a. 1. since
2. for
3. since
4. since
5. for
6. for
7. since
8. for

b. 1. ago
2. since
3. Since
4. during
5. ago
6. during
7. While
8. for
9. during
10. during
11. for
12. while
13. during

53. Formal vs Informal Language

I am writing with reference to your letter (formal)
Thanks a lot for your letter (informal)

June 12 (formal)
Wednesday (informal)

apologise for the delay in making a reply (formal)
sorry I haven't got back to you sooner (informal)

however, (formal)
anyway, (informal)

the following are my comments (formal)
here are my ideas (informal)

the various points you raise (formal)
the things you wanted clearing up (informal)

UK tax assessment is based on (formal)
You have to fork out about (informal)

It would not be feasible to claim a rebate (formal)
There's no way you can get anything back (informal)

monies (formal)
money (informal)

You would be well-advised (formal)
Your best bet (informal)

claim for tax exemption (formal)
ask not to pay tax (informal)

declare income to the local income tax authorities (formal)
tell the tax people over there how much you earn (informal)

I trust you will find this information useful (formal)
Hope this is OK (informal)

Should you have any further queries (formal)
If there's anything else you want to know (informal)

do not hesitate to contact me (formal)
drop me a line (informal)

Yours sincerely (formal)
All the best (informal)

Robert (formal)
Bob (informal)

a.   1. (I)   +   5. (F)
    2. (F) + 12. (I)
    3. (I)   +   8. (F)
    4. (F) +   7. (I)
    6. (I)   + 10. (F)
    9. (I)   + 14. (F)
  11. (I)   + 13. (F)

b.   1. Dear Mr Price
    2. Thank you

3. pleased
4. However,
5. make any firm decision
6. provide us with
7. concerning
8. we would expect
9. being in a position to
10. We would wish to achieve
11. This said
12. it would be useful
13. discuss
14. further
15. meet
16. convenient
17. satisfactory
18. I look forward to hearing from you in the near future
19. Yours sincerely

c.

Dear Mr MacKenzie

Thank you for your letter of (15 May). I regret that there has been a misunderstanding concerning quantity discounts.

I took over from Mr Grant, our previous Sales Manager, in January of this year and made a decision, during that month, to modify our pricing policy. Our regular customers were mailed a circular letter on 22 January informing them that we had changed the previous policy not to give discounts for bulk orders and that we had slightly increased our unit prices.

I am sure you received a copy of this circular as you have quoted the latest price in force. It would not, therefore, be appropriate for me to make any compensation.

However, I will be in London during the month of May and I suggest we meet at your convenience. In the meantime, I am enclosing a catalogue and price list.

I look forward to meeting you in the near future.

Yours sincerely

Richard Cartwright
Sales Manager

d. I'm writing about our recent conversation about the three possible choices for the US market. I'm sorry but I don't think I can take on a job as big as this at the moment. I've really got so much to do that I wouldn't be able to give it enough time.

But if you do decide to change your policy for the Advertising Specialty Market in the USA I'd like to put forward another idea which we could talk about in Munich at the end of the month.

Best Wishes,

54. The former vs The latter

the former; the latter

55. Frequency

a. Individual answers.

b. 1. I don't usually have to work at the weekend.
2. She rarely finishes her work on time.
3. There is an audit once a year.
4. You should always read the small print.
5. I have often said we should have consulted a lawyer.
6. You must never turn a customer away.

56. The future

a. 1. 3
2. 6
3. 4
4. 2
5. 1
6. 5.2
7. 6
8. 7

b. 1. We'll give you
2. is to inaugurate
3. I'm going to take
4. I'll cancel

c. Individual answers.

d. 1. He will be at home.
2. His plane leaves at 10.30 a.m.
3. He's visiting the new offices in the morning. In the afternoon, he's presenting the new prototype.
4. He'll be meeting the patent attorney.
5. He'll be visiting a night club.
6. He's coming back on Saturday afternoon.

e. The borrower will have paid 8361.52.

58. Have something done vs Have someone do something

a. 1. The production manager had the job done by a sub-contractor.
2. They had the whole campaign organised by an agency.
3. She had a technician clean the machine.
4. We are having the matter investigated by a lawyer.
5. I had the damage assessed by an independent surveyor.
6. She had Mr Messud look at the problem.
7. I have had a number of companies give me a quotation.

b. 1. You can have your shoes cleaned.
2. You can have your clothes washed.
3. ... you can have reception book you a table.
4. If you like you may have the Night Porter bring you drinks to your room.
5. ... you may like to have a telex sent, or a document copied or translated.

c. 1. have   2. typed   3. having   4. built   5. had   6. take
7. having   8. delivered   9. having   10. installed
11. have   12. done   13. have   14. do

59. Hire vs Rent vs Let vs Lease vs Charter

	BUSINESS PREMISES	A VIDEO	A VILLA	OFFICE EQUIPMENT	A CAR	A SHIP	A PLANE	A STAND AT AN EXHIBITION
hire		✓		✓	✓			✓
rent	✓		✓		✓			
let	✓		✓					
lease	✓			✓				
charter						✓	✓	

60. Idioms

a. 1. at a price
2. in the red
3. under par
4. money for old rope
5. foot the bill
6. hard up
7. make ends meet
8. on stream
9. a hard bargain
10. on a shoestring

11. like hot cakes
12. an arm and a leg

b.
1. I don't think Richard is working as hard as he should.
2. ... the quantity of administrative paper-work.
3. ... at the very last moment.
4. ... went bankrupt.
5. ... making absurdly fine distinctions
6. ... very easy.
7. I have quite a lot of experience and I am not easily deceived.
8. trial performance.
9. ... complete unfinished business.
10. ... talking about our work.

61. If

a.
1. will be	11. won't sell
2. will sell	12. will be
3. reduce	13. may/will be
4. won't have	14. says
5. will go down	15. will see/will talk to
6. won't be	
7. make	
8. won't invest	
9. won't have	
10. will price	

b. Suggested reactions
1. I would leave the firm.
2. I would try to find out how they learnt of our existence.
3. I would ring the personnel department immediately.
4. I would refuse (I don't like public speaking).
5. I would ask them to double its value

c. If they had not bought the option they would have had to pay £5,000 more in interest.

d. Individual answers.

62. INCOTERMS

1. Ex Works
2. Delivery Duty Unpaid
3. CIP Carriage and Insurance Paid To
4. Free Alongside Ship
5. Cost and Freight
6. Free Carrier
7. Cost, Insurance and Freight
8. Carriage Paid To
9. Delivered Ex Quay
10. Free On Board

11. Delivered At Frontier
12. Delivery Duty Paid
13. Delivered Ex Ship

63. Inversion

1. Little did we suspect that they had filed a patent.
2. Not until two years ago did we decide to change our image.
3. Under no circumstances will Bywater Inc. be liable for any incidental or consequential damages.
4. Never did I imagine, on joining the firm, that I would one day becomes its president.
5. Seldom have I had the opportunity to speak to such a distinguished audience.
6. On no account should you keep your code number and your credit card together.
7. Only after ten years of extensive testing was the new drug launched.
8. No sooner did we walk (*or* had we walked) into the room than they started complaining.

64. Last vs Latest vs Least

1. the least
2. the latest
3. at last
4. last but not least (*lastly* is also possible but doesn't emphasise the contribution of the workforce)
5. not in the least
6. at the latest
7. at least

65. Legal Language

a. 1. Any dispute between the parties about the contract will go to the International Chamber of Commerce (see Section G).
   2. If I don't collect the articles or allow someone else to collect them within a month I accept that they don't belong to me and you can get rid of them.

b. If any person gives any false indication that goods or services supplied by him are supplied to or approved by the Royal Family, he shall be guilty of an offence.

c. The letter of credit must comply with the terms of the contract. If it does not, then Glanola does not have to perform their obligations under the contract. However, Glanola will have to give written notification. If the L/C is in order or if more than three weeks go by then Glanola has to fulfil the contract.

66. Let vs Leave

1. Leave
2. leave
3. left
4. let
5. let
6. Let's

67. Letter Writing

a.

```
                    Presser UK Limited
                    199 Knightsbridge
                    London SW7 1RJ
                    Tel: 071 586 5733
                      Telex: 22498
                    Fax: 071 586 9474


Our ref: LGM / hp                              Date

Miss Juliette Rocache
84 Ave du General de Gaulle
91160 Longjumeau
France

Dear Miss Rocache,

Thank you for your letter ............
............ please do not hesitate to get in
touch.

Yours sincerely

  Linda Morgan

Linda Morgan (Mrs)

Managing Director - Administration
```

b.

1. I am writing to inform you that
2. I regret (to advise you)
3. I would be grateful if you could
4. I look forward to hearing from you in the near future.

68. Liable to vs Liable for vs Responsible to vs Responsible for

Individual answers.

69. Likely to vs Bound to

There is no key to this exercise as it will depend on your point of view.

70. Linking Words

a. This is a possible paragraph:

There are a number of steps involved in decision-making. First of all, you should decide what the nature of the problem is. Secondly, you should decide exactly what needs to be done. When you have done that, you can implement the decision. Next, you should monitor progress and, in addition, get feedback. Finally, if necessary, the plan of action can be modified before any further decision is taken.

b.

1. THE STAGES OF A CAMPAIGN

First of all, the advertising manager for the client company meets the agency's account executive for a preliminary discussion. They talk about objectives, possible media, and the approximate budget.

Secondly, senior representatives of both the agency and the client meet for a more detailed briefing, a definition of the image and thoughts on the target public.

Thirdly, the creative teams are briefed, the media are chosen and an initial concept is selected.

When they have finished working on a campaign outline they submit the overall campaign strategy to the client firm's Board of Directors.

After approval by the Board the exact budget is agreed on and the finishing touches are put to the campaign.

Finally, the campaign is released on TV, radio, billboards and selected magazines.

Background

reason/result: thus
contrast: although
example: i.e.

The Problem

reason/result: owing to, because of, since, on account of, due to, consequently, as a result of
contrast: despite
example: (none)

An alternative solution

reason/result: therefore
contrast: however
example: for instance

c. 1. as a result   2. due to   3. However   4. despite
d. 1. because of   2. however   3. As a result   4. Furthermore

e. *Conclusion*
   1. Because
   2. However
   3. consequently
   4. Although
   5. Therefore

f. 1. First
   2. since
   3. In addition
   4. Secondly
   5. Although
   6. Consequently
   7. Thirdly
   8. owing to
   9. On the other hand

71. Make vs Brand vs Trademark vs Logo vs Patent vs Copyright

Digital™ is a trademark – it is the trademark of the Digital Equipment Corporation.
Kelloggs is a well-known brand of breakfast cereal. It is also a trademark and logo.

72. Make vs Do

Make	*Do*
a suggestion	the typing
an enquiry	damage
an appointment	business
a profit	research
a decision	
a speech	
an investment	
a bid	

73. Meetings

a. 1. convenes
   2. agenda
   3. minutes
   4. item
   5. agenda
   6. consensus

7. power of attorney
8. proxy
9. casting vote

b. 1. Taking the floor
2. Starting a meeting
3. Disagreeing
4. Coming to the end of a meeting
5. Making your point
6. Agreeing
7. Correcting misunderstandings
8. Avoiding responsibility/Postponing
9. Asking for more information

74. Money

1. one dollar forty five, a dollar forty five
2. eight pounds fifty, eight pounds fifty p/pence
3. a hundred and ninety-nine thousand dollars
4. three hundred and fifty-two pounds, twenty-nine (p)
5. Seventy-five fifty, seventy five dollars fifty
6. two hundred and twenty-five million pounds
7. eighty nine p/pence
8. three hundred (and) fifty-four dollars fifty

75. Money Movements

a. 1. R   7. S
2. N   8. N
3. R   9. S
4. S   10. S
5. S   11. R
6. R

b. 1. fell / went down / decreased
2. all-time low
3. bottom out
4. edged up / crept up / firmed
5. plummeted / collapsed / slumped / plunged
6. rise
7. plummeted / collapsed / slumped / plunged
8. record low
9. rallied / rose / increased / went up steadily
10. plunging / collapsing

76. Must vs Have to vs Need vs Should

a. Non-EC and non-EFTA countries must observe the rules in the official guide.
Duty must be paid on tobacco, hydrocarbon oils, liquor, beer and wine.
Importers must state the tariff classification or duty.

Importers must state the tariff classification or duty liability on the customs entry form.
Exporters must obtain an import licence for certain goods.
Importers must not import firearms, ammunition, endangered species ... drugs into the UK.
Duty does not have to be paid on goods within the EC or from EFTA. You do not have to pay duty on commercial samples ... tourist publicity material.

b. Individual answers.

c. 1. You don't need to / you needn't get a consular invoice.
   2. The procedure needs simplifying / needs to be simplified.
   3. Do these forms need to be filled in / need filling in in quadruplicate?
   4. We didn't need to take a taxi because we had arranged for him to pick us up at the airport.
   5. We didn't need to send a technician ...
   6. We needn't have taken on extra personnel.
   7. I needn't have redesigned the company magazine.

d. 1. Every employee must give his/her services uniquely to the firm.
   2. Employees must live within 50miles of the workplace.
   3. They must contribute at least 6 per cent of salary to the pension scheme.
   4. Staff should take their main holiday during the summer.
   5. They may be away sick for up to 90 days and still receive pay.
   6. A medical certificate must be sent after 48 hours' absence.
   7. Staff may retire before the age of 60. you must retire on reaching 65.
   8. Staff may terminate the appointment after one month's notice has been given.
   9. Employees should keep the firm informed if they are applying for another post.
   10. Employees may appeal against dismissal.

77. Naming and Greeting

1. c 2. e 3. f 4. a 5. b 6. d

78. Nationality Words

a. e.g. Syria, Jordan, Saudi Arabia, Qatar, Bahrain, Oman.
   Argentina, Brazil, Chile, Colombia, Peru, Venezuela.
   Czechoslovakia, Estonia, Hungary, Latvia, Poland, Russia.
   Burma, China, Indonesia, Japan, Malaysia, Thailand.
   Algeria, Angola, Ethiopia, Kenya, Libya, Sudan.

b. The UK, France, Ireland, Spain, Portugal, Belgium,
   The Netherlands, Greece, Italy, Germany, Denmark,

Luxembourg

c. Switzerland – German, Italian, French
Mexico – Spanish
The Netherlands – Dutch
Singapore – Mandarin Chinese, Malay, Tamil and English
Algeria – Arabic
Ivory Coast – French, Abe, Adyukuru, Akye, Anyi, Bakue, Bambara, Bete and many other indigenous languages.

d. *Olivetti* is an Italian company. Its headquarters are in Italy.

ICL is a	British	Britain.
Philips	Dutch	Holland.
Nestlé	Swiss	Switzerland.
Perrier	French	France.
Saab	Swedish	Sweden.
Nokia	Finnish	Finland.
Daimler	German	Germany

79. Noun Formation

a. 1. remittance 2. applications 3. leakage 4. debtor
   5. consignee 6. rotation 7. confusion
   8. correspondence 9. significance 10. investment
   11. Sponsorship 12. mastery

b. 1. consultant 2. officer 3. negotiator 4. surveyor
   5. distributor 6. director 7. engineers; programmers

c. 1. decisions
   2. promotion
   3. competition
   4. manufacturers
   5. advertising
   6. exhibition
   7. record
   8. enquiries
   9. deliveries
   10. complaints
   11. distribution
   12. agreement
   13. expiry
   14. performance
   15. sales

80 Noun Combinations

a. press release, television commercial, venture capital, quality circle, takeover bid, application form, exchange rate, profit margin, balance sheet, retail outlet, pie chart, cash flow.

b. banknote, bank holiday, bank loan

workforce, workplace, workman
pay rise, pay claim, pay award
trade fair, trade union, trademark

c. 1. a four-lane motorway
   2. a fifty-million franc (bank) loan
   3. a six-man team
   4. a thirty-nine-hour week
   5. a six-month project

d. 1. an expense account (c)
   2. a gift voucher (c)
   3. a Bill of Lading (b)
   4. last month's figures (a)
   5. Mr Young's assistant (a)
   6. career opportunities (c)
   7. a shoe store (c)
   8. a letter of resignation (b)
   9. a five year plan (c)
  10. a pay settlement (c)
  11. the company's future (a)
  12. a breach of contract (a)
  13. our sales policy (b)
  14. last year's AGM (c)

e. 1. a deposit account
   2. a price list
   3. a two week visit
   4. an organisation chart
   5. a sales team
   6. a customs officer
   7. a business trip
   8. a training needs analysis
   9. a consumer behaviour research survey
  10. raw materials storage forecasts

f. 1. a fair in which people meet to trade with each other
   2. a guest at a hotel
   3. figures for sales which have been made in an export market
   4. machinery used for construction
   5. tax on income
   6. a loan which is made by a bank for a period of 10 years
   7. a report on the creditworthiness of a potential buyer
   8. a protector for the screen of a computer
   9. a bank guarantee for credit which is made for an export transaction
  10. the results of a poll which is designed to find out the opinions of consumers.

g. 1. Footwear Trade Fair
2. Exhibition Centre
3. Industry Training Board
4. design specialists
5. leather industry
6. export opportunities
7. conference timetable
8. conference date
9. enrolment form
10. Conference Organiser

81. Packaging

a. 1. box 2. carton 3. crate 4. drum 5. barrel 6. sack
7. container

b. 1. drum – sulphuric acid
2. sack – grain
3. refrigerated container – beef
4. crate – diesel engines
5. barrel – wine

c. 1. use no hooks
2. radiation
3. this way up
4. keep dry
5. dangerous chemicals
6. fragile

82. Passive vs Active

a. Sample sentences:
Beer is brewed in China.
Cocoa is grown in Ghana.
Gold is produced in South Africa.
Perfume is produced in France.
Rice is grown in China.
Ships are built in Japan.
Tobacco is grown in the USA.
Wheat is grown in the USA.
Wine is produced in France.
Whisky is produced in Scotland.

b. 1. An attractive price reduction is being offered.
2. The survey was completed last month.
3. Free medical insurance is provided by the company for all employees.
4. A copy of the report was sent yesterday.
5. The contract has been translated into Arabic.
6. The problem is being investigated by a team of consultants.

7. An attractive salary will be offered to the person appointed.
8. In normal circumstances, the goods for export should be cleared by the exporter.
9. The 14.45 flight to Rome has been cancelled.
10. Talks were being held last night at the Union's headquarters.

c. 1. is paid
   2. credited
   3. are drawn
   4. are sorted
   5. sent
   6. are put
   7. sent on
   8. are exchanged
   9. is deducted

d. Mr Chambers and Mrs Shaw have been transferred to the London agency.
   Mrs Patel has been promoted to Head of Creative Services.
   Mr Hunt has been appointed to the post of TV/radio buyer.
   A new position of Assistant Account planner has been created.
   Miss Jay has been appointed to the post of Art Director.
   The posts of market researcher and creative researcher have been combined.

e. 1. I wasn't told a decision had been taken.
   2. He was given a week by the committee to reach a decision.
   3. She was asked by Mr Weston to send a telex.
   4. You will be sent an official reply by the board by the end of next week.
   5. They were shown how to pack the goods.
   6. My expenses were paid by the firm.

h. 1. It was thought the expenditure on entertainment was excessive.
   2. It was felt that more should be spent on training.
   3. It was hoped more could be done to attract suitably qualified staff.
   4. It was thought that it would be a good idea to extend the probationary period.
   5. It was agreed that schedules needed to be respected.
   6. It was felt that low prices did not always attract customers.
   7. It was suggested that our corporate image should be improved.

i. 1. it was felt
2. marketing approach was needed
3. was considered to be out of date
4. it was decided
5. should be launched
6. It was recommended
7. should be attractively packaged
8. advertised heavily
9. It was agreed
10. would be done
11. would be produced
12. would be presented to the MD

83. Past Perfect vs Past Perfect Continuous

a. 1. had dealt with   2. went   3. hadn't prepared   4. was
5. saw   6. had been asking   7. spent   8. had seen
9. (had) told   10. had been having   11. saw   12. said
13. hadn't received   14. had to   15. found out   16. had not
sent   17. went   18. were   19. had forecast   20. had
launched   21. left   22. got   23. realised   24. hadn't eaten

b. 1. closed   2. was   3. had been disappearing   4. was
5. had lost   6. was   7. was   8. had spent   9. had had
10. listened   11. had been   12. encouraged   13. became
14. had grabbed   15. launched   16. (had) joined

84. Past Simple vs Present Perfect

a. 1. never   2. During the past 12 months   3. last month
4. at the end of December   5. a year ago   6. since 1988
7. So far this year   8. over the past month

b. 1. has fallen   2. has led to   3. has increased   4. have risen
5. were   6. announced   7. has reacted   8. underlined

c. 1. was   2. was   3. met   4. explained   5. told   6. have
sent   7. have asked

d. 1. have   2. written   3. said   4. was   5. have been   6. has
been   7. have kept   8. has prevented   9. appeared
10. praised   11. have had

85. Past Simple vs Past Continuous

1. were going down   2. were losing   3. were not investing
4. were not training   5. were becoming   6. were putting
7. (were) dictating   8. became   9. decided   10. had to
11. made   12. expanded   13. committed

86. Pay vs Pay for vs Pay off

1. pay for; paid
2. pay

3. pay back/pay off
4. pay for
5. was paid

87. Payment

a.

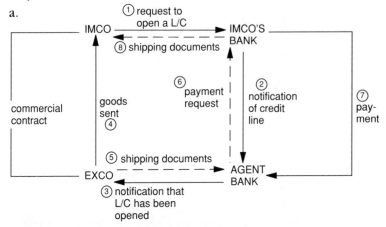

b. The correct order is: 3. 4. 2. 5. 6. 1

88. Personal vs Personnel

1. personnel   2. personal   3. personal

89. Phrasal Verbs

a. TML TAKES OVER REXON
ANDERSON TURNS DOWN TOP CITY POST
BANK OF ENGLAND PUTS UP TUNNEL FINANCE
TRANSPORT TALKS CALLED OFF
MEXICO PUTS UP COPPER PRICES
TEXTILE WORKERS PUT IN 15% WAGE CLAIM
BUSINESS IS LOOKING UP IN LUXEMBOURG
SISA PUTS OFF CAPITAL INCREASE

b. 1. put in for   2. take on   3. get on   4. turned down
5. get on with   6. take on   7. put forward   8. turned out
9. take over   10. looking into   11. looking forward to
12. get on   13. take on   14. put up with

90. Policy vs Politics

politics, political, policy

91. Prefixes and Suffixes

(a) re (b) mis (c) over (d) de (e) under (f) out

a. 1. redo
2. simplify

3. misinform
4. verify
5. misuse
6. collaborate
7. overcharge
8. legalise
9. denationalise
10. classify / categorise
11. outperform
12. notify

b. 1. setback
2. shake-up
3. turnout
4. output
5. intake
6. breakdown
7. outlay
8. upturn
9. spinoff

c. someone who founded something *with* another person
a *former* President
a cheque with a date on it which is *after* the day it was signed
an *alternative* proposal, probably *opposed* to the first proposal
a law *against* trusts

92. Prepositions

a. 1. by 3 p.m. on Monday 5th.
2. on Tuesday.
3. at 14.57 from Euston Station.
4. at 10.00 on Thursday.
5. from Friday 9th to Tuesday 13th.
6. On Monday ..... through his lunch break.
7. at about 11 on Wednesday.
8. at Easter

b.	
1. in	12. by
2. from	13. to
3. to (AmE: through)	14. in
4. at	15. through
5. at / from	16. beyond
6. at	17. from
7. from	18. at
8. in	19. on
9. by	20. at
10. at	21. around
11. to	

c.

WAREHOUSE

STORES

WAREHOUSE

RECEPTION AREA

ADMINISTRATION BLOCK

CAR PARK

DELIVERY BAY

ASSEMBLY WORKSHOP

STAFF CANTEEN

d. 1. by
2. from, to
3. below / under
4. at
5. above / over
6. by, to, over

e. 1. Further to
2. in touch with
3. with reference to
4. in favour of
5. instead of
6. on account of
7. As for
8. regardless of
9. in line with
10. up to

f. 1. through
2. in
3. under
4. for

5. on
6. at
7. out of
8. at
9. under
10. in
11. for
12. out of; in

93. Present Perfect vs Present Perfect Continuous
Individual answers.

94. Present Simple vs Present Continuous

a. 1. stay
2. manufactures
3. are changing
4. include
5. is expanding
6. hold
7. receives; answers
8. have
9. is interviewing
10. are looking
11. is trying

b. 1. is 2. sells 3. employs 4. has 5. is growing 6. is recruiting

c. 1. are having 2. admit 3. realise 4. are doing
5. agree 6. suggest 7. assure 8. promise

d. 1. have 2. are thinking 3. think 4. are trying
5. doubt 6. confirm 7. am spending 8. am sending
9. need

95. Price vs Rate vs Charge vs Fee vs Commission

a. 1. fees; price
2. fee
3. commission
4. charged
5. price
6. rate
7. charge
8. prices
9. rate
10. charge

96. Principal vs Principle

1. principal
2. principle

97. Questions

a. 1. Is Mr Perez coming?
    2. Are you ready?
    3. Can you help me?
    4. Has she completed the survey?
    5. Why is she angry?
    6. Isn't it possible to get here earlier?
       Is it not possible to get here earlier?
    7. Did they sell the subsidiary?
       Have they sold the subsidiary?
    8. Haven't we met before?
    9. What does 'price/earnings ratio' mean?
   10. Why did they come?
   11. When must it be finished?

b. 1. How much has output increased by?
    2. When did Betamix become a public limited company?
    3. How often is the departmental meeting held?
    4. How soon / When will you be able to get back to us?
    5. How much did it cost?
    6. Why was a consultant called in?
    7. Which solution do you prefer?
    8. How many enquiries were there?
    9. Whose ticket is it? / Whose is this ticket?
   10. How far is the bank?

c. 1. Where do you get most of your groceries from?
    2. How much do you spend on groceries every week?
    3. Which of these dairy products do you buy regularly?
    4. How many pots of yoghurt do you purchase on average each week?
    5. When buying your groceries, why do you choose a particular store rather than another?
    6. How often do you cook pasta?
    7. Who owns / drives a car in your household?

98. Remind vs Remember

1. remember   2. remind   3. remember   4. remember
5. remind; remember

99. Reporting Information

a. 1. he's received   2. hopes   3. interested in placing an order   4. wants

b. Hideki Asano phoned from Kyoto. He said that he had spoken to a business friend in Malaysia and that this person was interested in sports shoes. He said that the man's name was Syarikat Dalia Baru and that he was based in Kuala Lumpur. He also said that a lot of American footwear was now going to Malaysia, more than to Singapore.

c. Mr Todd opened the meeting and underlined the importance of reaching an agreement on the choice of site.

Mr Green outlined the reasons for rejecting two of the sites investigated. He pointed out that the two remaining sites, Burnsley and Whitly were similar in size but that the latter was much cheaper.

Mr Marsh explained that the difference in price was probably due to the lack of access to rail and road.

Mrs Grant claimed that the Burnsley site was not a viable choice given the amount of work that needed to be done before it could be built upon. She also mentioned that there were plans to build a motorway extension to Whitly. Mr Marsh, however, stated that Whitly was much farther north and that transport costs would be correspondingly increased.

Mr Todd closed the meeting and announced that a survey would be commissioned to investigate the sites in detail. Tenders would then be invited from contractors.

100. Reporting Questions

a. 1. He asked me where the nearest cashpoint was.
2. She wanted to know how long it takes / took to go from Heathrow to the City.
3. She asked her if she happened to know what the time difference is/was between Boston and Los Angeles.
4. She enquired whether we offer/offered an introductory discount.
5. She wanted to know if I can/could use a spreadsheet.

b. how long she has worked in your firm
what responsibilities she has had
how many people work under her supervision
how well she gets on with her colleagues
how often she has been on assignments abroad
how many foreign languages she can speak

101. Rise vs Raise vs Arise

a. 1. rise
2. arises
3. raise
4. raise
5. arise
6. raise
7. arises
8. rose
9. raise
10. risen

b. 1. rose
2. raise
3. rise
4. raised
5. rise
6. rising
7. rising

102. Salary vs Wages vs Earnings vs Income vs Perks

remuneration package; salary; perks/fringe benefits

103. Save vs Spare

1. save 2. spare 3. spare 4. spared no expense 5. saved

104. Say vs Tell

1. told
2. say
3. telling
4. said
5. say
6. told

105. Sell vs Sale vs Sales vs Seller vs Selling

1. sell
2. out
3. Sales
4. off
5. sale
6. up
7. for sale; sell
8. after-sales
9. best-seller
10. sale

106. Set up vs Establish vs Settle

	a dispute	a business	an invoice	an overhead projector	contact	in business	an international reputation
set up		✓		✓		✓	
establish					✓		✓
settle	✓		✓				

107. Shall vs Will vs 'll

1. I'll   2. I'll   3. will   4. Will   5. won't   6. will   7. shall
8. I'll

108. Should vs Would

a. 1. should
2. should
3. should
4. Would
5. should

b. 1. You should always have literature professionally translated.
2. Obviously you shouldn't do this if you want your agent to represent you as faithfully as possible.
3. You should come to an arrangement, perhaps on a 50–50 basis.
4. You should quote the terms that suit your client. You should probably quote DDP for a client in Europe.
5. You should discover your customer's preference.
6. You should do this – it's safer.
7. You should do this – it's the safest method of payment.
8. You should not waste time like this. With a word processor you can personalise a letter by changing the name and address.
9. You should do this otherwise you don't know whether you are selling at a loss.

c. Individual answers.

d. 1. You should lease a new one.
2. The cheque should have been signed.
3. The value of the consignment should have been the same as the amount authorised.
4. They should advertise in other media.
5. They should have taken out a patent.

e. I would have conducted a thorough investigation to find out who had first started submitting false reports and how long this had been going on. I would have tried to establish if any of the salesmen were more guilty than others. I would have seriously considered dismissal for the worst offenders.

109. So vs Such

a. 1. Why is your price so high?
2. The service is so poor that I won't stay here again.
3. Why is it taking such a long time for him to understand?
4. I am so sorry.
5. The delivery is so late that I'll probably cancel.

b. 1. Mr Owen said the payment could be made at a later date if we so wished.
   2. We can increase our production capacity but Mrs Cook doesn't think so.
   3. They may demand a more attractive financing package. If so, telex me immediately.

110.   Some vs Any; Much vs Many; No vs None

   1. many
   2. any
   3. some
   4. many
   5. no
   6. any
   7. any
   8. much
   9. None
   10. any
   11. no

111.   So that vs To vs In order to vs So as to

   1. They give subsidies to national firms so as to make them more competitive on international markets.
   2. There is a World Bank so that developing countries can benefit from loans at low rates of interest.
   3. Governments impose import quotas in order to protect home industries from foreign competition.
   4. In order to keep stocks to a minimum.
   5. They use a factor to recover debts more easily.
   6. So that they can arrive more quickly.

112.   Spot vs Forward

spot, forward

113.   Still vs Yet vs Always vs Already vs No longer

a. 1. still
   2. yet; still
   3. always
   4. already
   5. no longer

b. 1. still   2. already   3. not yet

c. 1. no longer   2. always

114.   Stocks and Shares

There are many potential answers to this exercise. Here are some of them.

There is the *Hang Seng index* and the *Dow Jones index* of *share* prices.

A *unit trust* is a portfolio of shares spread over different types of *shares* and *debentures*.

Insider trading is against the law. People with inside knowledge of a company's financial health are not allowed to use that knowledge to influence *share* prices.

An *acquisition* of another company can be *friendly* (if desired) or *hostile* (if the firm is taken over by a predator).

A *management buyout* occurs when the management raises the capital needed to acquire the firm they work for.

115. Subject to

1. Any cash bonus will be subject to income tax.
2. Our offer is subject to the approval of the Board of Directors.
3. All textile imports are subject to a 15% tariff.
4. British citizens in France are subject to French law.
5. Our improved pay offer is subject to the workers' return to work/returning to work.
6. This distribution agreement is subject to the rules and regulations of the United Arab Emirates.
7. Whether we go ahead with the plan or not is subject to his confirmation.
8. Promotion is not automatic and is subject to (your) demonstrating initiative and commitment.
9. You will receive 2% commission subject to (your) selling more than 5,000 articles a year.
10. You will be transferred to the permanent staff subject to your satisfactory completion of the probationary period/ subject to (your) completing the probationary period satisfactorily.

116. Subsidy vs Grant vs Allocation vs Allowance

1. grant   2. allowance   3. allocate   4. subsidise

117. Take place vs Happen

1. happen   2. take place

118. Telephone Language

a. The correct order is: 3. 11. 5. 12. 1. 8. 9. 6. 2. 7. 10. 14. 4. 13.
b. There are many possible combinations. Here are some of them.

You can *reverse* the *charges* if you want the person receiving the *call* to pay for it. (In the US this is a collect call.)

If there are three or more people taking part in a telephone conversation then it is a *conference call.*

If you dial a *freefone* number you don't have to pay the cost of the call. (In the US this is a toll-free number.)

When you *ring up* a firm, the first person you speak to may be the *switchboard operator.*

119. Tender vs Bid

1. bid   2. bid   3. tender   4. legal tender

120. The

a. 1. –
   2. the
   3. –; the
   4. The
   5. The; the
   6. The
   7. –, –, –;
   8. The; –
   9. –; –; –
   10. –; –; –; –; –; –; The; –

b. 1. The commission
   2. the application form
   3. The order
   4. the statement

c. *The* undersigned, duly authorised by *the* company, swears that *the* above-mentioned goods have been inspected and certified by *the* Osaka Chamber of Commerce.

d. the IMF, the OECD, the NYSE, the EMS, the UN, the EEC

e. 1. Beijing is in China.
   2. Rotterdam is in the Netherlands
   3. Chernobyl is in the Ukraine.
   4. Jamaica is in the West Indies / the Caribbean.
      Oman is in the Middle East.
      Tahiti is in the Pacific.
   5. Lima is the capital of Peru.
   6. The Hague is the capital of Holland.
   7. Budapest is the capital of Hungary.
   8. They make up the United Kingdom.
   9. China and the USA grow rice.
      Coffee is produced in Brazil.
      Iron and steel are produced in the USA, Poland and in Japan.
      Perfume is produced in France.
      Computers are made in Europe, the USA and Japan

f. 1. the British   2. The Swedes   3. The Japanese   4. the Italians   5. the Americans   6. the Mexicans

g. 1. –   2. –   3. the   4. –   5. –   6. –   7. –   8. –   9. –   10. –   11. the   12. –   13. –   14. the   15. the   16. the   17. –

h. 1. –   2. the   3. –   4. –   5. –   6. The   7. –   8. The   9. –   10. –   11. –   12. the   13. the   14. the   15. the   16. –   17. the   18. –   19. the   20. –   21. –

121.   Travel vs Trip vs Journey vs Voyage vs Tour

    a. 1. voyage
        2. tour
        3. travel
        4. trip
        5. journey
        6. travel

122.   Used to vs Be used to vs Get used to

    a. 1. get used to getting up
        2. used to start
        3. used to live
        4. used to use
        5. get used to
        6. (I)'m used to working

123.   Verb Combinations

    a. 1. travelling
        2. telling
        3. to send
        4. breaking
        5. to receive
        6. to take
        7. to contact
        8. representing

    b. A spreadsheet is a piece of software which enables the user to calculate quickly the effect a change in one variable (e.g. a profit margin, overheads) will have on others.

    A carphone enables you to make phone calls while you are driving in your car.

    A laptop computer is a small computer that enables you to work on the plane or the train.

    A diplomatic passport entitles the holder to travel over a customs border without being searched and questioned.

    An American Express Card entitles the holder to make cashless payments for goods and services in many countries.

A patent entitles the holder to exploit his/her invention commercially.

c. 1. not replying   2. to purchase   3. waiting   4. to obtain
5. to order   6. to sell   7. to order

d. 1. to improve   2. spending   3. making   4. to spend
5. to contact   6. producing   7. placing   8. getting
9. to think   10. giving

124. Verb + Noun Combinations

1. You can raise an objection, funds, a matter.
2. You can reach an agreement, a decision, an understanding, a conclusion, a customer.
3. You can allocate funds, resources.
4. You can make a decision, an objection, a concession, a loss, a requirement, headway, a deal.
5. You can clinch a deal.
6. You can suffer a loss, a setback.
7. You can draw funds, a conclusion.
8. You can meet an objection, a requirement, a customer.

125. Very vs Too vs Enough vs Quite vs Rather vs Fairly

We looked at five hotels from the very big (The Empire) to the very small (Lee Ho Fook). The Empire gives *quite* good service but the facilities are *rather* poor. It is also *too* far from the city centre. The Chang, on the other hand, is *very* convenient, has excellent facilities but is *rather* expensive. We also found that the quality of service was not good *enough* to justify such a high price. The Central is a *fairly* pleasant small hotel with quite good service but is perhaps not comfortable *enough* for more than a very short stay. If you would like to stay near the port then go to the Hing Ming which is *quite* comfortable and not *too* expensive.

Our choice, however, would be the Lee Ho Fook which, despite being *rather* expensive at $HK 1,950, gives excellent service in a very pleasant atmosphere.

126. What vs Which

1. What   2. Which   3. What   4. What

127. Which vs That vs Who vs Whose

a. REFERS TO PEOPLE   REFERS TO THINGS
who, that, whose   which, that, whose

b. 1. which/that
2. which/that
3. whose

4. who
5. which
6. which/that
7. whose
8. who
9. which

c. 1. An attorney is a lawyer who pleads on behalf of a client in a court of law.
2. A balance sheet is a document which shows the financial position of a firm at a certain date.
3. A penalty clause is a clause in a contract which states how much money must be paid by the party who is guilty of breaking the contract.
4. Counterfeit goods are goods which are imitations of famous brands. They are made and sold illegally.
5. A certificate of origin is a document which states the name of the country in which goods destined for export have been made.
6. A CEO (Chief Executive Officer) is the person who is responsible for seeing that a firm is properly and profitably managed.
7. A buyback agreement is a barter arrangement by which a company supplying a plant to a foreign country accepts the product of that plant as payment.
8. A merchant bank is a commercial organisation which specialises in the financing of international trade by accepting bills of exchange and arranging home and overseas loans.
9. A holding company is one that holds more than half the share capital of one or more other companies called subsidiaries.

128. Wish

a. would like; wish

b. 1. He probably wishes he hadn't sold his shares.
2. Peter wishes Christopher didn't/wouldn't smoke.
3. She no doubt wishes she had known earlier that such loans were available.
4. He probably says 'I wish I had my own photocopier' and If only there was a lift'.

129. Within vs By vs Until

Individual answers.

130. Would rather vs Had better

a. Individual answers.

b. 1. I think you'd better take the train.

2. I think we'd better move on to item 4 or we won't have time.

3. I'd better not drink any more, thank you.

4. You'd better buy a copy of *Longman Business English Usage!*

Index